Ancient Civilizations Almanac

VOLUME **1** Egypt–India

Ancient
Civilizations
Almanac

Judson Knight

Stacy A. McConnell and
Lawrence W. Baker, Editors

AN IMPRINT OF THE GALE GROUP

DETROIT · SAN FRANCISCO · LONDON
BOSTON · WOODBRIDGE, CT

Ancient Civilizations: Almanac

Judson Knight

Staff

Stacy A. McConnell, Lawrence W. Baker, *U•X•L Editors*
Carol DeKane Nagel, *U•X•L Managing Editor*
Tom Romig, *U•X•L Publisher*

Rita Wimberley, *Senior Buyer*
Evi Seoud, *Assistant Production Manager*
Mary Beth Trimper, *Composition Manager*

Margaret A. Chamberlain, *Permissions Specialist (pictures)*

Martha Schiebold and Michelle DiMercurio, *Senior Cover Art Directors*
Pamela A.E. Galbreath, *Senior Page Art Director*
Cynthia Baldwin, *Product Design Manager*
Barbara J. Yarrow, *Graphic Services Supervisor*

Linda Mahoney, LM Design, *Typesetting*

Front cover: (top photo) The Parthenon. Reproduced by permission of Susan D. Rock. (bottom photo) Terra cotta statues from the tomb of Shih-huang-ti. Reproduced by permission of AP/Wide World Photos.

Library of Congress Cataloging-in-Publication Data

Knight, Judson
    Ancient Civilizations: Almanac / Judson Knight; edited by Stacy A. McConnell and Lawrence W. Baker
      p. cm.
    Includes biographical references and index.
    Summary: Provides historical information and interpretation on ancient civilizations in Egypt, Mesopotamia, Asia Minor, China, Africa, Israel, and elsewhere.
    ISBN 0-7876-3982-6 (set), — ISBN 0-7876-3983-4 (v. 1). — ISBN 0-7876-3894-2 (v. 2);
    Civilization, Ancient-Juvenile literature. 2. Civilization, Ancient-Miscellanea-Juvenile literature. [1. Civilization, Ancient.] I. McConnell, Stacy A. II. Title
    CB311 .K594 1999

930-dc21   99-046791
[B]-DC21   CIP

To Tyler, from her ancient daddy;
and to Deidre, from her modern husband.

Contents

Egyptian workers depicted on a frieze. *(Archive Photos. Reproduced by permission.)*

Volume 1

Volume 2

Advisory Board

Special thanks are due to U•X•L's Ancient Civilizations Reference Library advisors for their invaluable comments and suggestions:

- Jonathan Betz-Zall, Children's Librarian, Sno-Isle Regional Library, Edmonds, Washington

- Nancy Guidry, Young Adult Librarian, Santa Monica Public Library, Santa Monica, California

- Karen Shugrue, Junior High Media Specialist, Agawam Junior High School, Feeding Hills, Massachusetts.

Reader's Guide

Reader's Guide

Civilization in its purest form is universal, something available to all people. The wisdom that went into the building of the Egyptian pyramids, the creation of Greek democracy, or the construction of the Mesoamerican metropolis Teotihuacán does not belong to any race or nation: it is a part of the human legacy, something all people can appreciate regardless of their heritage. *Ancient Civilizations: Almanac* focuses on twelve civilizations and cultures, beginning with the ancient Egyptians and covering the Sumerians of Mesopotamia, the Shang of China, the Olmec of the Americas, and the Minoan of ancient Greece, among others, and concludes with the rise and fall in A.D. 476 of the Roman Empire. While concentrating on each culture's unique history and customs, *Ancient Civilizations: Almanac* also highlights the similarities between cultures that existed thousands of years—and sometimes thousands of miles—apart from each other.

Arranged into chapters by geographic region, *Ancient Civilizations: Almanac* features more than 110 black-and-white photographs that help bring the civilizations to life. Maps in each chapter place the civilization in a geographic context as well as highlight landmarks relating to that civilization. Numerous sidebar boxes provide lists of words to know or in-depth coverage of topics of high interest, such as the legacy of Saharan rock art. Cross references point the user to related information, while a "For More Information" section concludes each chapter. *Ancient Civilizations: Almanac* also features a glossary of terms used throughout the volumes, a timeline containing significant milestones from each civilization, and an index covering the people, places, and events discussed throughout *Ancient Civilizations: Almanac*.

Comments and Suggestions

We welcome your comments on *Ancient Civilizations: Almanac,* as well as your suggestions for persons to be featured in future editions. Please write, Editors, *Ancient Civilizations: Almanac,* U•X•L, 27500 Drake Rd., Farmington Hills, Michigan, 48331-3535; call toll-free: 1-800-877-4253; fax to 248-414-5043; or send e-mail via http://www.galegroup.com.

Words to Know

A

Acropolis: An elevated fortress in Greek cities.

Ancestor: An earlier person in one's line of parentage, usually more distant in time than a grandparent.

Anoint: To pour oil over someone's head as a symbol that God has chosen that person to fill a position of leadership.

Apostle: A religious figure who is sent out to teach, preach, and perform miracles.

Archaeology: The scientific study of past civilizations.

Architect: Someone who designs a building or other structure.

Aristocrat: A very wealthy and/or powerful person.

Assassination: Killing, usually of an important leader, for political reasons.

B

Baptism: To be lowered into water as a symbol of death and rebirth.

Bureaucracy: A network of officials who run a government.

Bust: A sculpture of a human head, neck, and shoulders.

C

Caravan: A company of travelers, usually with pack animals, traveling through a desert or other forbidding region.

Caste system: A system of ranking people into very social groups, which prevailed in India from ancient times to the modern day.

Census: A count of the people living in any defined area.

Civil servant: Someone who works for the government.

Civil war: A military conflict that occurs when a group of citizens within a nation attempts to break away from the rule of the government.

Commoner: Someone who is not a member of a royal or noble class.

Concubine: A woman whose role toward a man is like that of a wife, but without the social and legal status of a wife.

Constitution: A set of written laws governing a nation.

Contemporary (n.): Someone who lives at the same time as another person.

Cremation: The burning, as opposed to burial, of a dead body.

Crucifixion: A Roman punishment in which the victim was nailed or tied up to a cross until he died.

Cult: A small religious group, most often with specialized beliefs.

D

Deify: To turn someone or something into a god.

Deity: A god.

Democracy: A form of government in which the people, usually through elected representatives, rule.

Descendant: Someone who is related to an earlier person, or *ancestor*.

Disciple: A close follower of a religious teacher.

E

Edict: A command.

Epic: A long poem that recounts the adventures of a legendary hero.

Epistle: A letter.

Eunuch: A man who has been castrated, thus making him incapable of sex or sexual desire.

F

Famine: A period when there is not enough food in a region to feed all its people.

Fasting: Deliberately going without food, often but not always for religious reasons.

G

Gentile: Someone who is not a Jew.

H

Hellenic: Greek.

Hellenistic: Influenced by Greece.

Heresy: Something that goes against established religious doctrine.

Hoplite: A heavily armed foot soldier.

I

Islam: A faith that arose in Arabia in the A.D. 600s, led by the prophet Muhammad (A.D. 570?-632.)

L

Legacy: Something that is left to a later generation.

Legitimacy: The right of a ruler to hold power.

M

Martyr: Someone who dies for their faith.

Medieval: Relating to the Middle Ages.

Mercenary: A professional soldier who will fight for whoever pays him.

Middle Ages: The period from the fall of the Roman Empire to the beginning of the Renaissance, roughly A.D. 500 to 1500.

Middle Class: A group in between the rich and the poor, or the rich and the working class.

Millennium: A period of a thousand years.

Mint (v.): To produce currency.

Missionary: Someone who goes to other lands to convert others to their religion.

Moat: A trench, filled with water, which surrounds a castle or city.

Monarch: A king.

Monotheism: Belief in one god.

Muslim: A believer in Islam.

N

Noble: A ruler within a kingdom who has an inherited title and lands, but who is less powerful than the king or queen.

O

Obelisk: A tall, free-standing column of stone.

Oligarchy: A government ruled by a few people.

P

Pagan: Someone who worships many gods; also used as an adjective.

Papyrus: A type of reed from which the Egyptians made the first type of "paper."

Peasant: A farmer who works a small plot of land.

Phalanx: A column of *hoplites* designed for offensive warfare.

Pharisee: A member of a group of Jewish religious scholars who demanded strict adherence to religious law.

Philosophy: A discipline which seeks to reach a general understanding of values and of reality.

Plague: A disease or other disaster that spreads among a group of people.

Proportion: The size of one thing in relation to something else, and the proper representation of their relationship.

R

Rabbi: A Jewish teacher or priest.

Radical (adj.): Thorough or sweeping changes in society; used as an noun for a person who advocates such changes.

Regent: Someone who governs a country when the monarch is too young, too old, or too sick to lead.

Reincarnation: The idea that people are reborn on Earth, and live and die, again and again.

Relief: In sculpture, a carved picture, distinguished from regular sculpture because it is two-dimensional.

Renaissance: A period of renewed interest in learning and the arts which began in Europe in the 1300s and continued to the 1700s.

Revolution: In politics, an armed uprising against the rulers of a nation or area.

S

Sack (v.): To destroy a city.

Satrap: A governor in the Persian Empire.

Scribes: A small and very powerful group in ancient society who knew how to read and write.

Siege: A sustained military attack against a city.

Stele (or stela): A large stone pillar, usually inscribed with a message commemorating a specific event.

Stupa: A dome-shaped Buddhist temple.

T

Theorem: A statement of fact in logic or mathematics, derived from other formulas or propositions.

Totalitarianism: A political system in which the government exerts total, or near-total, control.

U

Usurp: To seize power.

Utopia: A perfect society.

V

Vassal: A ruler who is subject to another ruler.

Vineyard: A place where grapes are grown for making wine.

Vizier: A chief minister.

W

Western: The cultures and civilizations influenced by ancient Greece and Rome.

Z

Ziggurat: A Mesopotamian temple tower.

Pronunciation Guide

a = h*a*t

ah = t*o*p, f*a*ther

ai or *ay* = h*a*ze, w*ay*s, d*ai*sy

ee = p*ea*ce, fl*ee*ce, an*y*

eh = h*e*lp, s*ai*d, h*ea*d, s*ay*s

g = *g*ood (compare *j*)

hw = *wh*at

ie or *i[consonant]e* or *igh* or *y* = h*i*de, sp*y*

i = l*i*p

j = *j*ust, ad*j*ust, *g*ym (compare *g*)

ks = ta*x*, ta*ck*s

oh = h*o*pe, r*oa*m

oo = z*oo*m, pl*u*me

s = *s*ay, pea*c*e (compare *z*)

ts = dan*c*e, pan*ts*

ü = g**oo**d, c**ou**ld

uh = h**u**sh, d**o**ne

z = thing**s**, **z**one (compare *s*)

zh= occa**s**ion, lei**s**ure, a**z**ure, unu**s**ual

Timeline

c. **2,000,000-c. 10,000 B.C.:** Paleolithic Age.

c. **10,000 B.C.:** Last ice age ends.

c. **10,000-c. 4000 B.C.:** Neolithic Age.

c. **3500 B.C.:** Beginnings of Sumerian civilization.

c. **3100 B.C.:** Pharaoh Menes unites the kingdoms of Upper and Lower Egypt.

c. **3000 B.C.:** Babylon established.

c. **2950 B.C.:** First examples of hieroglyphs in Egypt.

c. **2920 B.C.:** First Dynasty begins in Egypt.

c. **2800 B.C.:** Mycenaeans leave the Black Sea area, moving toward Greece.

c. **2650 B.C.:** Beginning of Old Kingdom in Egypt.

c. **2650 B.C.:** Step Pyramid of Saqqara, designed by Imhotep, built under reign of pharaoh Zoser.

c. **2550 B.C.:** Great Pyramid of Cheops built in Egypt.

c. **2500 B.C.:** Indus Valley civilization begins in India.

c. 2300 B.C.: Early Dynastic Period ends in Sumer; Sargon of Akkad, first great Mesopotamian ruler, establishes Akkadian Empire.

c. 2200 B.C.: Hsia, semi-legendary first dynasty of China, begins.

2150 B.C.: End of Old Kingdom in Egypt; beginning of First Intermediate Period.

c. 2150 B.C.: Akkadian Empire ends with Gutian invasion of Mesopotamia; rise of Ur.

c. 2000 B.C.: Origins of Gilgamesh Epic in Sumer.

c. 2000 B.C.: Phoenician civilization established.

c. 2000 B.C.: Beginnings of Mayan civilization in Mesoamerica.

c. 2000 B.C.: Establishment of Kushite civilization in Africa.

c. 2000 B.C.: Beginnings of Minoan civilization in Crete.

1986 B.C.: Pharaoh Mentuhotep II unites all of Egypt; end of First Intermediate Period and beginning of Middle Kingdom.

c. 1900 B.C.: Indus Valley civilization begins to decline.

1813 B.C.: Shamshi-Adad, first important Assyrian ruler, takes throne.

1792 B.C.: End of Old Babylonia in Mesopotamia; Hammurabi, who later establishes first legal code in history, takes throne.

1766 B.C.: Shang Dynasty, first historic line of Chinese kings, begins.

c. 1760 B.C.: Hammurabi of Babylonia takes control of Assyria.

1759 B.C.: Middle Kingdom ends in Egypt; beginning of Second Intermediate Period.

c. 1750 B.C.: Beginning of Hittite civilization, establishment of capital at Hattush in Asia Minor.

c. 1700 B.C.: Crete experiences earthquake; later the Minoans rebuild their palaces at Knossos and other sites.

c. 1700-1500 B.C.: Phoenicians develop the world's first alphabet.

c. 1670 B.C.: Hyksos invade Egypt.

c. 1650 B.C.: Beginnings of Mycenaean civilization in Greece.

1539 B.C.: Second Intermediate Period ends in Egypt; beginning of New Kingdom.

c. 1500 B.C.: Indo-Europeans invade India; beginning of Vedic Age.

c. 1500 B.C.: Thebes founded on Greek mainland.

c. 1500-c. 1300 B.C.: Kingdom of Mitanni flourishes in Mesopotamia.

1473 B.C.: Pharaoh Hatshepsut assumes sole power in Egypt; becomes first significant female ruler in history.

c. 1450 B.C.: Minoan civilization in Crete comes to an end, probably as a result of volcanic eruption on Thera.

1363 B.C.: Ashur-uballit, who establishes the first Assyrian empire, begins reign.

c. 1347: Pharaoh Amenhotep IV changes his name to Akhenaton and introduces sweeping religious reforms.

1323 B.C.: Death of Tutankhamen in Egypt; power struggle follows, along with effort to erase memory of Akhenaton.

c. 1300 B.C.: City of San Lorenzo established in Mesoamerica.

1200s B.C.: Moses dies.

1279 B.C.: Beginning of Pharaoh Ramses II's reign in Egypt.

1285 B.C.: Battle of Kadesh between Egyptians and Hittites.

c. 1200 B.C.: Sea Peoples bring an end to Hittite civilization in Asia Minor.

c. 1200 B.C.: Aramaeans, after briefly controlling Babylonia, conquer Syria.

c. 1200 B.C.: Olmec civilization established in what is now Mexico.

c. 1200 B.C.: Bantu peoples migrate southward from what is now Nigeria.

c. 1200 B.C.: Trojan War.

c. 1200 B.C.: Etruscans settle on Italian peninsula.

c. 1200-900 B.C.: Carving of giant heads by Olmec in Mesoamerica.

c. 1140 B.C.: Macedonians move southward, displacing the Dorians from northern Greece.

1125 B.C.: King Nebuchadnezzar I begins reign in Babylon.

c. 1100 B.C.: Dorians bring an end to Mycenaean civilization; beginning of Dark Ages in Greece, which last for four centuries.

1070 B.C.: End of New Kingdom in Egypt; Third Intermediate Period Begins.

1027 B.C.: Revolt led by Prince Wu Wang brings an end to Shang Dynasty, and the establishment of Chou Dynasty, in China.

c. 1000 B.C.: Saul killed; David becomes ruler of Israel.

c. 1000 B.C.: End of Vedic Age, beginning of Epic Age, in India.

c. 1000 B.C.: Beginnings of Chavín civilization in South America.

c. 1000 B.C.: Celts begin to spread from Gaul throughout Europe.

900s B.C.: Phoenicians begin establishing trade routes and overseas colonies.

c. 960 B.C.: David dies; Solomon becomes ruler of Israel.

934 B.C.: Beginning of Assyrian conquests which will lead to establishment of Neo-Assyrian Empire.

922 B.C.: End of Solomon's reign, and of unified kingdom of Israel.

800s B.C.: Dorians establish Sparta.

883 B.C.: Ashurnasirpal II assumes throne in Assyria, establishes Neo-Assyrian Empire.

879 B.C.: Beginning of King Ben-Hadad II's reign in Syria.

c. 850 B.C.: Greeks start trading with other peoples; beginning of the end of the Dark Ages.

c. 850-750 B.C.: Rise of city-states in Greece.

c. 800 B.C.: Carthage established by Phoenicians.

c. 800 B.C.: Poets Homer and Hesiod flourish in Greece.

776 B.C.: First Olympic Games held.

771 B.C.: Invasion by nomads from the north forces Chou Dynasty of China to move capital eastward; end of Western Chou period.

753 B.C.: Traditional date of Rome's founding; Romulus first of seven legendary kings.

c. 751 B.C.: Piankhi takes throne in Kush.

722 B.C.: Spring and Autumn Period, a time of widespread unrest, begins in China.

c. 732 B.C.: Assyrians gain control of Syria.

c. 725 B.C.: King Mita, probably the source of the Midas legend, unites the Phrygians.

721 B.C.: Sargon II of Assyria conquers Israel and carries off its people, who become known as the Ten Lost Tribes of Israel.

715 B.C.: End of war with Messenia brings a rise to Spartan militarism.

712 B.C.: Kushites under Shabaka invade Egypt, establish Twenty-Fifth Dynasty; end of Third Intermediate Period, and beginning of Late Period.

c. 700 B.C.: End of Dark Ages, beginning of two-century Archaic Age, in Greece.

c. 700 B.C.: City-state of Athens, established centuries before, dominates Attica region in Greece.

600s B.C.: State of Magadha develops in eastern India.

600s B.C.: Important developments in Greek architecture: establishment of Doric order, first structures of stone rather than wood.

695 B.C.: Cimmerians invade Phrygia, ending Phrygian civilization.

689 B.C.: Assyrians sack Babylon.

c. 685 B.C.: Gyges founds Mermnad dynasty in Lydia.

681 B.C.: Sennacherib dies; Esarhaddon takes Assyrian throne.

672 B.C.: Assyrians first drive Kushites out of Egypt, install Necho I as pharaoh.

669 B.C.: Beginning of Ashurbanipal's reign; last great Assyrian king.

667 B.C.: Assyrian troops under Ashurbanipal complete conquest of Egypt from Kushites.

Mid-600s B.C.: Meröe Period begins when Kushites, removed from power in Egypt, move their capital southward.

Mid-600s B.C.: Establishment of Ionian Greek trading colony at Naucratis in Egypt.

Mid-600s B.C.: Age of tyrants begins in Greece.

c. 650 B.C.: Scribes in Egypt develop demotic script.

648 B.C.: Ashurbanipal of Assyria subdues Babylonian revolt; his brother Shamash-shum-ukin reportedly commits suicide.

625 B.C.: Nabopolassar establishes Chaldean (Neo-Babylonian) Empire.

621 B.C.: Draco appointed by Athenian oligarchs; creates a set of extremely harsh laws.

616 B.C.: Power-sharing of Sabines and Latins in Rome ends with Etruscan takeover under legendary king Tarquinius Priscus.

613 B.C.: First recorded sighting of Halley's Comet by Chinese astronomers.

612 B.C.: Babylonians and Medes destroy Nineveh; end of Neo-Assyrian Empire.

605 B.C.: Nabopolassar dies; his son Nebuchadnezzar II, the greatest Babylonian ruler, takes throne.

c. 600 B.C.: Pharaoh Necho II of Egypt sends a group of Carthaginian mariners on voyage around African continent.

c. 600 B.C.: Nebuchadnezzar builds Hanging Gardens in Babylon, one of the Seven Wonders of the Ancient World.

Late 600s, early 500s B.C.: Romans wage series of wars against Sabines, Latins, and Etruscans.

500s B.C.: Careers of Lao-tzu and Confucius, Chinese philosophers.

500s B.C.: High point of Etruscan civilization in Italy.

594 B.C.: Solon appointed archon of Athens.

586 B.C.: Nebuchadnezzar II destroys Israelites' capital at Jerusalem; beginning of Babylonian Captivity for Israelites.

585 B.C.: Thales, first Western philosopher, comes to fame in Greece for correctly predicting a solar eclipse on May 28.

c. 560 B.C.: Beginning of Croesus's reign in Lydia.

Mid-500s: Israelite prophet Daniel, a captive in Babylon, flourishes.

559 B.C.: Cyrus the Great of Persia takes the throne.

550 B.C.: Cyrus the Great of Persia defeats the Medes, establishes Persian Empire.

c. 550 B.C.: King Croesus of Lydia conquers Greek city-states of Ionia.

c. 550 B.C.: Temple of Artemis at Ephesus, one of the Seven Wonders of the Ancient World, is built.

546 B.C.: Persian armies under Cyrus the Great depose King Croesus and take over Lydia.

546 B.C.: Cyrus the Great of Persia conquers Ionian city-states of Greece.

538 B.C.: Persians conquer Babylonia; end of Chaldean (Neo-Babylonian) Empire, and of Israelites' Babylonian Captivity.

529 B.C.: Cyrus the Great of Persia dies, succeeded by his son, Cambyses II.

c. 528 B.C.: In India, Gautama Siddartha experiences his enlightenment; becomes known as the Buddha.

527 B.C.: Peisistratus, tyrant of Athens, dies; he is replaced by his sons, Hippias and Hipparchus, who prove unpopular.

522 B.C.: Returning to Persia to deal with rebellious forces, Cambyses II dies, and is succeeded by Darius the Great.

521 B.C.: Darius the Great of Persia conquers Punjab region of western India.

510 B.C.: Four years after the assassination of his brother Hipparchus, Athenians remove Hippias from power.

509 B.C.: Traditional date of Roman overthrow of Etruscan rule.

507 B.C.: Founding of Roman Republic.

502 B.C.: Athenians adopt a new constitution based on reforms of Cleisthenes, ending the age of tyrants; birth of democracy.

c. 500 B.C.: End of Epic Age in India.

c. 500 B.C.: Kingdom of Aksum established in Africa.

c. 500 B.C.: End of Archaic Age, beginning of Classical Age, in Greece.

c. 500 B.C.: Celts (Gauls) enter northern Italy, while other Celtic tribes settle in Britain.

499 B.C.: Persian Wars in Greece begin with revolt of Ionian city-states against Persians.

490 B.C.: Persian troops under Darius the Great burn Ionian Greek city-state of Eretria.

490 B.C.: Battle of Marathon: Greeks defeat Persians.

486 B.C.: Darius the Great of Persia dies and is succeeded by his son Xerxes, the last powerful emperor of Persia.

481 B.C.: End of Spring and Autumn Period of Chou Dynasty in China.

480 B.C.: King Xerxes of Persia launches massive attack against Greece.

480 B.C.: Battle of Thermopylae in Greece; Persians victorious despite heroic Spartan defense.

480 B.C.: Xerxes burns Athens.

480 B.C.: Battle of Salamis: Athenian-led Greek naval force defeats Persians under Xerxes.

479 B.C.: Battle of Plataea: Spartan-led force overwhelms Persians under Mardonius.

479 B.C.: Battle of Mycale: naval victory by Greeks expels Persians from mainland Greece for good.

479 B.C.: Golden Age of Greece begins.

478 B.C.: Delian League founded in Greece, with Athens as its leading city-state.

474 B.C.: Carthaginians end Etruscan dreams of empire with defeat at Cumae; Etruscan civilization begins to decline.

468 B.C.: Delian League of Greece defeats Persian fleet off Ionian coast.

462 B.C.: Pericles and Ephialtes institute a series of democratic reforms in Athens.

460 B.C.: Pericles becomes sole archon of Athens, beginning the Age of Pericles.

450s B.C.: Athenian Empire subdues various Greek city-states, wages wars throughout Mediterranean and Aegean seas.

459 B.C.: Spartans and Athenians clash over control of Megara; first of conflicts leading to Peloponnesian War in 431 B.C.

453 B.C.: Warring States Period begins in China, only ending when Ch'in Dynasty replaces the Chou dynasty in 221 B.C.

453 B.C.: Pericles of Athens becomes first leader to establish pay for jurors.

451 B.C.: The "Twelve Tables," the first Roman legal code, established.

449 B.C.: Persian Wars officially come to an end.

c. 440 B.C.: Parthenon built in Athens.

c. 440 B.C.: Phidias sculpts Statue of Zeus at Olympia, one of the Seven Wonders of the Ancient World.

431 B.C.: Peloponnesian War between Athens and Sparta begins in Greece.

430 B.C.: Herodotus begins publishing *The History.*

429 B.C.: Plague breaks out in war-torn Athens.

425 B.C.: Athens defeats Sparta in battle, bringing temporary end to Peloponnesian War.

420 B.C.: Because it broke Olympic truce by attacking Athens, Sparta keeps it athletes out of the Olympic Games.

412 B.C.: Ionian revolt effectively ends power of Delian League.

404 B.C.: Athens surrenders to Sparta, ending Peloponnesian War.

404 B.C.: Golden Age of Classical Greece comes to an end.

c. 400 B.C.: Decline of Chavín civilization in South America.

300s B.C.: Ch'in state emerges in western China.

300s-200s B.C.: Romans conquer most Etruscan cities.

396 B.C.: Rome breaks a century-long peace treaty by conquering Etruscan city of Veii.

395 B.C.: Athens, Corinth, and Thebes revolt against Sparta, beginning Corinthian War.

390 B.C.: Celts (Gauls) invade Rome.

390 B.C.: Beginnings of Roman military buildup after expulsion of Gauls.

386 B.C.: Spartans put down revolt of Athens and other city-states, ending Corinthian War.

Mid-380s B.C.: Plato establishes Academy in Athens.

371 B.C.: Theban commander Epaminondas defeats Spartans at Leuctra, bringing an end to Spartan power over Greece.

Mid-300s B.C.: Mausoleum at Halicarnassus, one of the Seven Wonders of the Ancient World, is built.

359 B.C.: Philip II takes throne in Macedon, and five years later begins conquest of Balkan peninsula.

346 B.C.: Philip II of Macedon brings an end to war between Greek leagues over control of Delphi, calls for Hellenic unity.

339 B.C.: Philip II of Macedon completes conquest of Balkan peninsula.

338 B.C.: Macedonian forces under Philip II defeat Greek city-states at Charonea; Macedonia now controls Greece.

336 B.C.: Philip II assassinated; 20-year-old Alexander III (Alexander the Great) becomes king of Macedon.

335 B.C.: Alexander consolidates his power, dealing with rebellions in Macedon and Greek city-states.

335 B.C.: Aristotle establishes the Lyceum, a school in Athens.

334 B.C.: Alexander begins his conquests by entering Asia Minor.

334 B.C.: Beginning now and for the last twelve years of his life, Aristotle writes most of his works.

333 B.C.: In April, Alexander's forces defeat Persian armies under Darius III in Cilicia; Darius flees.

332 B.C.: Alexander conquers Syria, Phoenicia, and Palestine.

332 B.C.: Alexander invades Egypt.

332 B.C.: End of Late Period in Egypt; country will not be ruled by Egyptians again for some 1,500 years.

331 B.C.: Alexander establishes city of Alexandria in Egypt.

331 B.C.: Alexander's army completes defeat of Persians under Darius III at Gaugamela in Assyria; Darius is later assassinated.

331 B.C.: Alexander conquers Mesopotamia.

330 B.C.: Persepolis, capital of the Persian Empire, falls to Alexander the Great.

330 B.C.: Alexander embarks on four-year conquest of Iran, Bactria, and the Punjab.

324 B.C.: Chandragupta Maurya, the founder of Mauryan dynasty, takes the throne of Magadha in eastern India.

323 B.C.: Beginning of Hellenistic Age, as Greek culture takes root over the next two centuries in lands conquered by Alexander.

323 B.C.: Ptolemy, one of Alexander's generals, establishes dynasty in Egypt that lasts for three centuries.

312 B.C.: Seleucid empire established over Persia, Mesopotamia, and much of the southwestern Asia.

c. 310 B.C.: Greek explorer Pytheas sets off on voyage that takes him to Britain and Scandinavia.

c. 300 B.C.: Composition of *Mahabharata,* an Indian epic, begins; writing will continue for the next six centuries.

c. 300 B.C.: Hinduism develops from the Vedic religion brought to India by the Aryans.

290 B.C.: Romans defeat Samnites, establish control over much of southern Italy.

287 B.C.: Plebeians establish power over Roman Senate.

282 B.C.: Colossus of Rhodes, one of the Seven Wonders of the Ancient World, completed; destroyed in earthquake fifty-four years later.

c. 280 B.C.: Lighthouse of Alexandria, last of the Seven Wonders of the Ancient World, built.

279 B.C.: Celts invade Greece, but are driven out by Antigonus Gonatas.

275 B.C.: Romans defeat Greek colonists in southern Italy, establishing control over region.

272 B.C.: Bindusara, ruler of Mauryan dynasty of India, dies; his son Asoka, the greatest Mauryan ruler, later takes throne.

264 B.C.: First Punic War between Rome and Carthage begins.

262 B.C.: Mauryan king Asoka, disgusted by his killings in battle with the Kalinga people, renounces violence.

260 B.C.: Asoka begins placement of rock and pillar edicts throughout India.

c. 250 B.C.: Kushite civilization reaches its height. It will remain strong for the next four centuries.

247 B.C.: Beginning of Parthian dynasty in Iran.

246 B.C.: End of Shang Dynasty in China.

241 B.C.: First Punic War ends with Roman defeat of Carthage; Rome controls Sicily, Corsica, and Sardinia.

230s B.C.: Asoka loses power over Indian court as rebellious advisors gain influence over his grandson Samprati.

229 B.C.: Rome establishes military base in Illyria; first step in conquest of Greece.

223 B.C.: Antiochus the Great, most powerful Seleucid ruler, begins reign in Syria.

221 B.C.: Ch'in Shih Huang Ti unites China, establishes Ch'in Dynasty as first Chinese emperor.

221 B.C.: Chinese under Ch'in Shih Huang Ti begin building Great Wall.

221 B.C.: Unification of China under Ch'in Shih Huang Ti begins driving the nomadic Hsiung-Nu and Yüeh-Chih tribes westward.

218 B.C.: Hannibal of Carthage launches Second Punic War against Romans, marching from Spain, over Alps, and into Italy.

216 B.C.: Carthaginians under Hannibal deal Romans a stunning defeat at Cumae.

213 B.C.: Emperor Ch'in Shih Huang Ti calls for burning of most books in China.

207 B.C.: End of shortlived Ch'in Dynasty in China; power struggle follows.

206 B.C.: Rebel forces under Hsiang Yü take capital of China.

202 B.C.: Having defeated Hsiang Yü, Liu Pang (Kao Tzu) becomes emperor, establishes Han Dynasty in China.

202 B.C.: Roman forces under Scipio defeat Hannibal and the Carthaginians at Zama.

c. 200 B.C.: Eratosthenes, librarian of Alexandria, makes remarkable accurate measurement of Earth's size.

198 B.C.: Seleucids gain control of Palestine.

197 B.C.: Romans defeat Macedonian forces under Philip V at Cynocephalae; beginning of end of Macedonian rule in Greece.

195 B.C.: Antiochus the Great, at height of his power, arranges marriage of his daughter Cleopatra I to Ptolemy IV of Egypt.

195 B.C.: Hannibal flees Carthage, takes refuge with Antiochus the Great.

191 B.C.: Roman forces defeat Antiochus the Great at Thermopylae.

190 B.C.: Romans under Scipio defeat Seleucid king Antiochus the Great at Magnesia, and add Asia Minor to their territories.

186 B.C.: Mauryan Empire of India collapses.

170s B.C.: Parthians begin half-century of conquests, ultimately replacing Seleucids as dominant power in Iran and southwest Asia.

165 B.C.: Nomadic Yüeh-Chih tribes, driven out of China, arrive in Bactria; later, Kushans emerge as dominant tribe.

c. 150 B.C.: Greco-Bactrians under Menander invade India.

149 B.C.: Romans launch Third Punic War against Carthage.

146 B.C.: Romans complete their conquest of Greece.

146 B.C.: Romans completely destroy Carthage, ending Third Punic War.

133 B.C.: Chinese emperor Han Wu-ti launches four decades of war which greatly expand Chinese territory.

130 B.C.: Wu Ti establishes first civil-service exams in China.

c. 130 B.C.: Kushans begin a century-long series of conquests, ultimately absorbing Greco-Bactrian kingdom.

128 B.C.: Emperor WuTi effectively destroys the power of feudal lords in China.

121 B.C.: Roman reformer Gaius Gracchus commits suicide after some 3,000 of his followers are murdered.

c. 120 B.C.: Chang Chi'en, on a mission for Emperor Wu Ti, makes first Chinese contact with Greek-influenced areas.

108 B.C.: China, under Wu Ti, conquers Korea.

101 B.C.: Marius defeats Cimbri, a northern European tribe.

c. 100 B.C.: End of Olmec civilization in Mesoamerica.

95 B.C.: Tigranes II, who later makes Armenia a great power, assumes throne.

88 B.C.: Social War ends; Rome extends citizenship to non-Roman Italians.

88 B.C.: Sulla, rival of Roman consul Marius, becomes commander of forces against Mithradates the Great of Pontus in Asia Minor.

77 B.C.: Roman general Pompey sent to crush uprising in Spain.

c. 75 B.C.: Julius Caesar distinguishes himself with successful attacks against Cilician pirates, as well as Mithradates of Pontus.

73 B.C.: Slaves under Spartacus revolt in Capua, beginning Gladiatorial War; soon they have an army of 100,000.

71 B.C.: Gladiatorial War ends with defeat of slave army by Crassus.

69 B.C.: Rome begins taking over lands conquered by Tigranes of Armenia; conquest largely complete within three years.

60 B.C.: Julius Caesar, Pompey, and Crassus form First Triumvirate.

55 B.C.: Roman troops under Julius Caesar invade, but do not conquer, Britain; another invasion follows the next year.

51 B.C.: After death of her father, Ptolemy XII, Cleopatra becomes coruler of Egypt with her brother and husband.

49 B.C.: Pompey orders Julius Caesar to return from Rome; Caesar crosses the River Rubicon with his army.

48 B.C.: Cleopatra forced out of power in Egypt by a group loyal to her brother.

48 B.C.: Julius Caesar's forces defeat Pompey at Pharsalus in Greece; Pompey flees to Egypt, where he is assassinated.

48 B.C.: Julius Caesar arrives in Egypt, meets and begins affair with Cleopatra.

47 B.C.: Julius Caesar helps Cleopatra defeat her brother, Ptolemy XIII.

46 B.C.: Cleopatra goes to Rome with Julius Caesar.

44 B.C.: On March 15, a group of conspirators assassinates Julius Caesar in the chambers of the Roman senate.

44 B.C.: Octavian, Mark Antony, and Lepidus form Second Triumvirate.

41 B.C.: Cleopatra and Mark Antony begin political and personal alliance.

37 B.C.: Mark Antony leaves his wife, Octavian's sister, and joins Cleopatra; launches military campaigns in southwest Asia.

37 B.C.: Herod the Great becomes vassal king in Roman-controlled Judea.

36 B.C.: Octavian removes Lepidus from power, begins dealing with Mark Antony.

32 B.C.: Roman senate, at the urging of Octavian, declares war on Cleopatra.

31 B.C.: Roman forces destroy Mark Antony and Cleopatra's fleet at Actium in Greece on September 2; Antony commits suicide.

31 B.C.: Beginning of Octavian's sole control of Rome, end of a century of unrest.

31 B.C.: Beginning of *Pax Romana*, or "Roman Peace," which prevails throughout Roman world for two centuries.

30 B.C.: Suicide of Cleopatra VII; Romans establish control of Egypt.

27 B.C.: Octavian declared Emperor Augustus Caesar by Roman senate; Roman Empire effectively established.

24 B.C.: Romans attempt unsuccessfully to conquer southwestern Arabia.

17 B.C.: Vergil's *Aeneid* published.

c. 6 B.C.: Jesus Christ born.

****

9 A.D.: Wang Mang usurps throne of Han Dynasty in China, establishing Hsin Dynasty.

9 A.D.: Forces of Augustus Caesar defeated by Germans, ending Roman expansion to the north.

14 A.D.: Augustus Caesar dies; his stepson Tiberius becomes emperor, marking official establishment of Roman Empire.

23 A.D.: Han Dynasty regains control of China; beginning of the Later Han Period.

c. 30 A.D.: Jesus Christ dies.

c. 36 A.D.: Saul has vision on road to Damascus which leads him to embrace Christianity; becomes most important apostle.

41 A.D.: Caligula killed by Roman military; Claudius becomes emperor.

43 A.D.: Rome launches last major conquest, in Britain.

47 A.D.: Victorious in Britain, Romans demand that all Britons surrender their weapons.

49 A.D.: Council of Jerusalem, early meeting of Christians attended by the apostle Paul, is held.

c. 50 A.D.: Josephus, Jewish historian whose work is one of the few non-biblical sources regarding Jesus, flourishes.

60 A.D.: After the Romans attack her family, Boadicea, queen of the Iceni people in Britain, leads revolt.

64 A.D.: Rebuilding of Temple in Jerusalem, begun by Herod the Great in 20 B.C., completed.

64 A.D.: Fire sweeps Rome; Nero accused of starting it.

64 A.D.: Nero blames Christians for fire in Rome, beginning first major wave of persecutions.

65 A.D.: After suicide of his advisor, the philosopher Seneca, Nero becomes increasingly uncontrollable.

69 A.D.: Vespasian becomes Roman emperor, begins establishing order throughout empire.

70 A.D.: Future Roman emperor Titus, son of Vespasian, destroys Jerusalem and its temple.

c. 78 A.D.: Kaniska, greatest Kushan ruler, takes throne; later extends Buddhism to China.

79 A.D.: Mount Vesuvius erupts, destroying the city of Pompeii in Italy.

81 A.D.: Death of Titus; his brother, the tyrannical Domitian, becomes Roman emperor.

c. 90 A.D.: John writes Revelation, last book in the Bible.

98 A.D.: Roman historian Tacitus publishes *Germania,* one of the few contemporary accounts of German tribes and Britons.

100 A.D.: The Sakas, a Scythian tribe, take over Kushan lands in what is now Afghanistan.

c. 100 A.D.: Taoism, based on the ideas of Lao-tzu six centuries before, becomes a formal religion in China.

c. 100 A.D.: Establishment of Teotihuacán, greatest city of ancient America.

c. 100 A.D.: Old Silk Road, trade route between East and West, established.

135 A.D.: Roman emperor Hadrian banishes Jews from Jerusalem.

c. 150 A.D.: Nomadic Hsien-Pei tribe of China briefly conquers a large empire.

161 A.D.: Tiber River floods, causing famine in Rome.

161 A.D.: Greek physician Galen goes to Rome; later becomes physician to Marcus Aurelius and other emperors.

165 A.D.: Romans destroy Parthian capital at Ctesiphon, bringing an end to Parthian control over Persia.

175 A.D.: Roman general Avidius Cassius revolts against Marcus Aurelius in Syria, but is assassinated by one of his soldiers.

180 A.D.: Marcus Aurelius, last of the four "good" Roman emperors, dies; he is replaced by his wild son Commodus.

184 A.D.: Yellow Turbans lead revolt against Han Dynasty emperor of China; revolt is crushed five years later by Ts'ao Ts'ao.

192 A.D.: Roman emperor Commodus assassinated; Septimus Severus (r. 192-211), tries unsuccessfully to restore order.

200s A.D.: Diogenes Laertius writes *Lives of the Eminent Philosophers,* primary information source on Greek philosophers.

c. 200 A.D.: Zapotec people establish Monte Albán, first true city in Mesoamerica.

c. 200 A.D.: Anasazi tribe appears in what is now the southwestern United States.

220 A.D.: Later Han Dynasty of China ends.

221 A.D.: Three Kingdoms period in China begins.

c. 226 A.D.: Sassanian dynasty begins in Persia.

235 A.D.: Rome enters period of unrest in which 20 emperors hold the throne in just 49 years.

mid-200s A.D.: Shapur I, Sassanian ruler, takes Syria from Romans.

253 A.D.: Roman recovery begins with the emperor Gallienus, who later brings persecution of Christians to temporary end.

265 A.D.: Three Kingdoms period in China ends.

270 A.D.: Aurelian begins reign as Roman emperor.

270 A.D.: Queen Zenobia of Palmyra launches revolt against Roman Empire, conquers most of Syria and Egypt.

284 A.D.: Aurelian assassinated, Roman army chooses Diocletian as emperor; Diocletian ends period of unrest with series of reforms.

300s A.D.: Buddhism enters China.

300s A.D.: Books of the Bible compiled; some—the so-called Apocryphal Books—are rejected by early Christian bishops.

301 A.D.: Armenia becomes first nation to officially adopt Christianity.

302 A.D.: Diocletian resumes persecution of Christians.

307 A.D.: Constantine, last powerful Roman emperor, begins reign.

313 A.D.: Constantine declares an end to persecution of Christians in Roman Empire.

317 A.D.: Eastern Chin Dynasty established in China.

c. 320 A.D.: Candra Gupta establishes Gupta Empire in India.

325 A.D.: King Ezana of Aksum goes to war against Kush and destroys Meröe.

325 A.D.: Council of Nicaea adopts Nicene Creed, Christian statement of faith; declares Arianism a heresy.

330 A.D.: Constantine renames Greek city of Byzantium; as Constantinople, it becomes eastern capital of Roman Empire.

c. 335 A.D.: Candra Gupta dies; his son Samudra Gupta takes throne, and later conquers most of Indian subcontinent.

c. 335 A.D.: King Ezana converts to Christianity; nation of Aksum embraces the religion.

c. 355 A.D.: Huns appear in eastern Europe.

361 A.D.: Roman emperor Julian begins reign; later tries to reestablish pagan religion.

376 A.D.: Samudra Gupta, ruler of Gupta Empire in India, dies; Candra Gupta II, greatest Gupta ruler, takes throne.

379 A.D.: Theodosius becomes Roman emperor; last to rule a united Roman Empire.

383 A.D.: At Fei Shui, an Eastern Chin force prevents nomads from overrunning all of China.

386 A.D.: Toba nomads invade northern China and establish Toba Wei Dynasty.

394 A.D.: Roman emperor Theodosius I brings an end to ancient Olympic Games.

c. 400 A.D.: End of Kushite kingdom in Africa.

401 A.D.: Visigoth chieftain Alaric, driven out of Eastern Roman Empire, moves westward.

410 A.D.: Visigoths under Alaric sack Rome on August 24, hastening fall of western empire.

420 A.D.: End of Eastern Chin Dynasty in China.

434 A.D.: Huns arrive in what is now Austria; around this time, Attila emerges as their leader.

448 A.D.: Huns, under Attila, move into western Europe.

c. 450 A.D.: Hunas (Huns or Hsiung-Nu) invade Gupta Empire in India.

451 A.D.: Huns under Attila invade Gaul; defeated at Châlons-sur-Marne.

500s A.D.: African kingdom of Aksum establishes control over "incense states" of southern Arabia.

c. 500 A.D.: Japanese adopt Chinese system of writing; beginnings of Japanese history.

c. 500 A.D.: Bantu peoples control most of southern Africa.

c. 540 A.D.: End of Gupta Empire in India.

554 A.D.: End of Toba Wei Dynasty in northern China.

575 A.D.: Sassanid Persians gain control over Arabian peninsula.

581 A.D.: Establishment of Sui Dynasty, and reunification of China.

600s A.D.: Rise of Islam and Arab power.

600s A.D.: Three kingdoms emerge as Korea establishes independence from China.

c. 600 A.D.: Civil-service examinations, pioneered by Emperor Han Wu-ti seven centuries before, formally established in China.

c. 600 A.D.: African kingdom of Aksum declines.

618 A.D.: End of Sui Dynasty, beginning of T'ang Dynasty, in China.

622 A.D.: Mohammed and his followers escape from Mecca (the *Hegira*); beginning of Muslim calendar.

642 A.D.: Founding of Cairo, Egypt.

672 A.D.: Muslims conquer Egypt.

c. 750 A.D.: Decline of Teotihuacán in Mesoamerica.

1300s A.D.: Lighthouse of Alexandria destroyed in earthquake.

1687 A.D.: Parthenon damaged by explosion during war.

1776-88 A.D.: British historian Edward Gibbon publishes *The History of the Decline and Fall of the Roman Empire.*

1798 A.D.: French forces under Napoleon invade Egypt; later French scholars develop modern Egyptology.

1799 A.D.: Rosetta Stone discovered by French troops in Egypt.

1800s A.D.: Gilgamesh Epic of Mesopotamia recovered by scholars.

1800s A.D.: Linguists discover link between Indo-European languages of India, Iran, and Europe.

1813 A.D.: French publication of *Description of Egypt,* first significant modern work about Egyptian civilization.

1821 A.D.: Jean-François Champollion deciphers Rosetta Stone, enabling first translation of Egyptian hieroglyphs.

1860 A.D.: First discovery of colossal stone heads carved by Olmec in Mexico.

1871 A.D.: Heinrich Schliemann begins excavations at Hissarlik in Turkey, leading to discovery of ancient Troy.

1876-78 A.D.: Heinrich Schliemann discovers ruins of Mycenae in Greece.

1894 A.D.: Pierre de Coubertin establishes modern Olympic Games; first Games held in Athens two years later.

Late 1800s A.D.: Archaeologists discover first evidence, outside of the Bible, of Hittite civilization in Asia Minor.

1922 A.D.: British archaeologist Howard Carter discovers tomb of Egyptian pharaoh Tutankhamen.

1947-50s A.D.: Dead Sea scrolls discovered in Palestine.

1952 A.D.: Mycenaean Linear B script deciphered.

1960s A.D.: Archaeologists discover evidence of volcanic eruption on Greek island of Thera c. 1500 B.C.

Research and Activity Ideas

- Pretend you are a pharaoh who has ordered the building of a pyramid, or a Chinese emperor preparing his tomb. What people and items would you want to have with you in the next life? Write a list of these, and explain why each is important.

- Like Hammurabi, Moses, or the Romans who wrote the "Twelve Tables," your job is to create a set of laws to govern a nation. Make a list of things identified as crimes, and the punishment you think would be fair; also make a list of activities you would want to encourage, and how the government could do so. Conduct the group like a Greek democracy: all members of the group have an equal vote, though it is advisable that you first elect a leader to direct the discussion. After creating an initial set of proposed laws, conduct a vote to decide which should become official. Voting should be by secret ballot.

- Just as the ancient peoples had their myths and legends to explain the world, there are myths and legends in modern life. Who are the great heroes and villains of today, and of recent years—for example, political leaders and entertainment figures—and why do you think they are perceived as heroes or villains? How do you think they will be remembered, and what legends have developed or will develop around them? Modern legends often develop from rumors accepted as fact: what rumors have you heard, about things or events of local or national interest, which turned out not to be true? Discuss as a class.

- Choose a civilization covered in this book, and find pictures showing how people dressed in that place and time. Make simple costumes, using materials easily available at home, that resemble the clothing of that ancient civilization. On a given day, all members of the class should come to school in their costumes (or change clothes at school for the event) and conduct class as though it were a gathering of people from different civilizations. Talk to each other "in character," as though you were an Egyptian, for instance, or a Roman. Discuss your beliefs and your world, how you are different and similar—-thus, for instance, if you are a Hindu from India, you believe in reincarnation; or if you are an Israelite, you worship Yahweh.

- Find a map of the Persian "Royal Road," the Old Silk Route in Asia, or the Roman roads (for example in Roy Burrell's *Oxford First Ancient History,* listed in the Bibliography). Compare the length of these roads to interstate highways that run through your area. What problems would travelers on those ancient highways face that people on modern interstates do not?

- Divide into seven groups, each of which will report on one of the Seven Wonders of the World. This may include creating a model, if possible, though models do not need to be detailed. For the Hanging Gardens of Babylon, for instance, one could use houseplants and stacked cardboard boxes. (The Colossus of Rhodes may be depicted with clothing.)

- Look up examples of ancient Sahara rock art in Basil Davidson's *Ancient African Kingdoms,* pp. 43—57 (see bibliography of AFRICA chapter); in the June 1999 *National Geographic* ("Ancient Art of the Sahara" by David Coulson, pp. 98—119); or some other source. Pick out a piece of artwork that interests you, read the caption to learn more about it, and draw your own version.

- Interview a doctor about the Hippocratic Oath. What does it mean to him or her? What are some situations in which he or she has applied the Oath? How do doctors sometimes fail to apply it? Present the results of your interview in class, and discuss as a group.

- Pick a five-page section of text in this series or another appropriate volume. Copy the pages, then read them and highlight all words of more than two syllables. Look these words up in a dictionary and make a list of all those derived from Latin, as well as those derived from Greek. Also include the original Latin or Greek word and its meaning. For example, *section* comes from the Latin *secare,* to cut; *appropriate* from *proprius,* to own; and *volume* from *volumen,* a roll or scroll.

- Conduct an athletic event similar either to a *tlatchli* match, substituting handball, tennis, or volleyball for the Mesoamerican game; or a Greek footrace in the Olympics. Class members should choose whether to be participants or spectators, since both are necessary, but unlike ancient games, girls should be encouraged to take part in competition. If participating in a *tlatchli* game, remember that in Mesoamerican culture, those who lost were sacrificed; therefore players on both sides should later report to the class how they felt while playing. If simulating an Olympic event, class members should be appointed to write an ode to the winner, and to prepare a laurel crown (using small leafy tree branches, for example) for him or her.

- Many ancient peoples were concerned with what happened to a person after they died: the Egyptians and Chinese believed that, with proper preparation, a person would live on the earth; the Hindus believed in reincarnation; the Greeks and Romans believed that most people went to Hades, and a very few good or bad ones went either to the Elysian Fields or Tartarus; and the Christians, of course, accepted the idea of Heaven and Hell. Divide into groups, each of which pretends to hold a certain belief. Explain why your group believes in its explanation of the afterlife.

- Imagine that you are a young person in China, Greece, or Rome, or that you are a member of one of the "barbarian" tribes that threatened those societies. Depending on which group you belong to—-civilized or "barbarian"—-write two pages concerning how you feel about the other group.

Ancient
Civilizations
Almanac

Arabic

Egypt

The world's first major civilization developed in Egypt more than five thousand years ago. It flourished longer than almost any society in human history. The Egyptians, who were very concerned about what happens in the afterlife—that is, in a life after death—built vast tombs called pyramids for their kings, the pharaohs. Many of the pyramids are still standing. They represent some of the greatest architectural achievements of human history. Closer to home, a legacy (a gift from the past) of ancient Egypt can be found in many a modern household, thanks to the Egyptians'domestication, or taming, of the house cat. The Egyptians were also one of the first peoples to develop a system of writing, which they called *hieroglyphics*; and a basic type of "paper," derived from the papyrus (pronounced puh-PIE-russ) plant. (The word *paper* comes from *papyrus*.) Though Egyptian society declined after 332 B.C., it exerted a huge influence over Greece and Rome. Out of Greek and Roman civilizations ultimately came the cultures of Europe and the nations influenced by those cultures—including the United States.

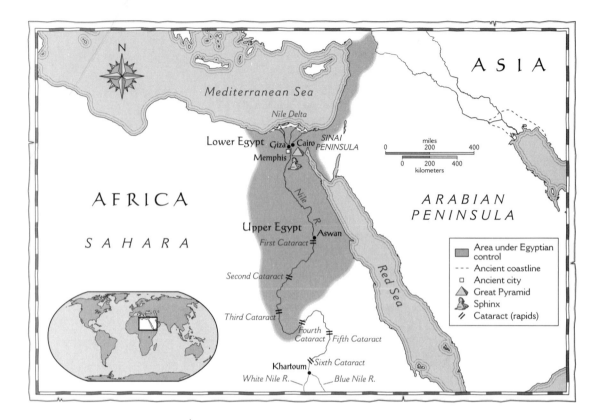

Map of Egypt.
XNR Productions.
The Gale Group.

Where to find Egypt

Egypt lies in the northeastern corner of the African continent, along the Nile River. The Nile flows through a vast desert, including the Sahara, which separates Egypt from most of Africa. To the northeast of Egypt is the Sinai (SIGH-nye) Peninsula, which links Africa with the Asian land mass. To the east is the Red Sea, which separates Africa from the Arabian Peninsula. North of Egypt is the Mediterranean Sea, on the shores of which many ancient civilizations developed. Today, the region around Egypt is called the Middle East. To historians studying the ancient world, this area is known as the Fertile Crescent.

Facts of life (and death) in Ancient Egypt

It is impossible to talk about ancient Egypt without talking about the Nile River, the center of Egyptian life. Just as a person's body is built around their spine, the Nile was the spine of Egypt; without it, there would have been no pharaohs or pyramids or any Egyptian civilization of any kind—only desert.

Not only is the Nile the world's longest river, at 4,160 miles (6,695 kilometers), it is also the only major river on Earth that flows northward. From its source deep in the African continent, in the present-day nation of Burundi, the Nile flows into Lake Victoria, crosses the Equator, and spans half the length of Africa, running through the countries of Uganda and Sudan before entering Egypt.

More than halfway along its course, near the Sudanese capital of Khartoum, the Nile changes in two important ways. The first of these changes is the beginning of the *cataracts,* or rapids, which interrupt the smooth flow of the river. Just above Khartoum is the Sixth Cataract. As the Nile snakes gradually northward, it passes through several more of these rapids, each numbered in descending order. The First Cataract lies near the modern city of Aswan; above this point, Egyptian civilization developed.

Even more important than the cataracts, however, is the second change. At Khartoum two rivers come together to form the Nile as the ancient Egyptians knew it. These two bodies of water are the White Nile, which flows up from the south; and the Blue Nile, which originates to the southeast, in Ethiopia. The White Nile has a relatively stable flow, whereas the Blue Nile experiences a dramatic rise and fall during the course of the year because it comes from an area prone to heavy summer rains.

In ancient times, the Blue Nile caused flooding from July to September. These floods, rather than being disasters, were essential to the life of Egypt. As the floodwaters receded each year, they left a deposit of *silt,* a type of soil rich in minerals. Silt has a consistency somewhere between that of sand and clay. The enriched earth was perfect for growing wheat and barley. Most years the farmers of Egypt had bountiful harvests.

Thanks to the Nile, Egypt was known as the Black Land—that is, a place of black earth good for crops. Beyond the Nile Valley, however, lay the Red Land. This was the desert, which covered more than ninety percent of Egypt. With the exception of a few scattered oases (green areas), this area was

Words to Know: Egypt

Afterlife: Life after death, in which peoples' spirits go on living in an afterworld, or future world.

Architect: Someone who designs a building or other structure.

Assassination: Killing, usually of an important leader, for political reasons.

Astronomy: The scientific study of the stars and other heavenly bodies, and their movement in the sky.

Barge: A type of boat used for transporting cargo.

Bureaucracy: A network of officials who run a government, and sometimes make it difficult to achieve progress.

Cartouche: A vertical oval with hieroglyphs inside it, spelling out the name of a king.

Cataracts: Rapids along the Nile.

Census: A count of the people living in a country.

Chariot: A small and highly mobile open-air wagon drawn by horses.

Class: Social rank or group.

Colonize: To turn a place into a territory of another country.

Commoner: Someone who is not a member of a royal or noble class.

Concubine: A woman whose role toward her husband is like that of a wife's, but without the social and legal status of a wife.

Decipher: To translate a code.

Decomposition: The decaying of a dead body.

Deity: A god.

Delta: A triangle-shaped area where a river's waters empty into the sea.

Diplomacy: The use of skillful negotiations with leaders of other nations in order to influence events.

Disillusionment: Loss of faith in old beliefs, without the adoption of new beliefs to replace the old.

Divine: God-like.

Dynasty: A group of people, often but not always a family, who continue to hold a position of power over a period of time.

Embalming: The process of preparing a dead body so that it will not rapidly decompose.

Engineer: A person who oversees the building of large structures.

Famine: A period when there is not enough food in a region to feed all its people.

Hieroglyphics: A system of symbols, called hieroglyphs, which made up the Egyptians' written language.

Intermediate: In between.

Ironic: When something is intended to be one way, but turns out to be quite different from what was intended.

Islam: A faith that arose in Arabia in the A.D. 600s, led by the prophet Muhammad (A.D. 570?–632.)

Legitimacy: The right of a ruler to hold power.

Mason or stonemason: A type of craftsman who builds with stone.

Mastaba (MAHS-tah-buh): Rectangular mud-brick tombs that preceded the pyramids in Egyptian history.

Metallurgy: The science of metals.

Monotheism: Belief in one god.

Mortuary: A place where bodies are prepared for burial by *morticians*.

Mummification: The Egyptian art of embalming, which included wrapping a body in linen bandages.

Muslim: A believer in Islam.

Nomarch: A governor of a province in ancient Egypt.

Outcropping: A large piece of rock sticking up from the earth.

Pagan: Worshiping many gods.

Papyrus: A type of reed from which the Egyptians made the first type of "paper."

Perspective: An artistic technique of representing faraway objects so that they appear smaller than objects close by.

Pharaoh: The title for the king of ancient Egypt.

Pictograms, phonograms: Two types of written symbol, the first of which looks like the thing it represents, the second of which represents a specific syllable.

Plateau: A large flat area.

Polytheism: Worship of many gods.

Propaganda: A type of writing or other art that a government uses to influence peoples' opinions about the government and its opponents.

Proportion: The size of one thing in relation to something else, and the proper representation of their relationship.

Pyramidon: A small pyramid.

Quarry: A place from which stone or rock is removed from the earth.

Radical: (adj.) thorough or sweeping changes in society; (noun) a person who advocates such changes.

Reclamation: The raising of land formerly covered by water.

Sarcophagus: A brightly decorated coffin of ancient times, which often bore the face of the person buried within.

Scribes: A small and very powerful group in ancient society who knew how to read and write.

Silt: A type of soil rich in minerals, deposited by a flooding river.

Sophistication: Development, complication, or refinement.

Spatial relationship: The space between and within objects, a concept closely related to the idea of *proportion*.

Standing army: A full-time, professional army.

Successor: Someone who comes after someone else, as for instance a king who follows another. Its opposite is *predecessor.*

Theocracy: A government controlled by religious leaders.

Usurper: Someone who seizes power.

Vizier: A chief minister.

and is a hellish place where no living creature could long survive. No wonder, then, that the Egyptians' religion depicted the red god of the desert, Set, as an evil *deity* (DEE-ih-tee).

Even with the Nile, Egypt is a hot, dry, country; without it, the climate would be almost unbearable. Although the modern nation of Egypt is more than 700 miles wide at its widest point, virtually all of Egyptian civilization—both now and in ancient times—focuses on a narrow strip of land that spreads out for a few miles on either side of the Nile. This land is the Nile Valley, which forms the rim of the river as it flows for some 500 miles through Egypt.

Cairo, the modern capital, is close to the site of Memphis, one of ancient Egypt's capitals. Near Cairo the Nile begins its final stage before flowing into the Mediterranean Sea. This region is the Nile Delta, an area perhaps 100 miles long and about as wide. Most major rivers have a *delta,* a triangle-shaped region where the river slows down before emptying into the sea. In a delta, the river's waters fan out, depositing great loads of silt and creating particularly rich soil for farming.

Not only was the Nile the source of all life in ancient Egypt, it was also the principal highway for commerce and other transportation. If people wanted to go from southern Egypt (Upper Egypt) to the north, the currents would carry their boat. If they wanted to travel from the north (Lower Egypt) to the south, they had only to rely on the Mediterranean winds to push a sailboat. Thus the river formed the framework of Egyptian civilization. A later historian would describe Egypt as "the gift of The Nile." The Egyptians in turn believed that the Nile came from the source of all life and the source of all things both good and bad: the gods.

Gods, pharaohs, and the afterlife

Most ancient cultures placed a strong emphasis on gods or deities, which they used as a means of explaining things in the natural world such as the ocean and the thunder. With the exception of the Hebrews, virtually all ancient cultures had a pagan belief system—that is, they worshiped many gods. These beliefs were certainly held by the Egyptians, who usually represented their gods as beings with bodies of men or women but the heads of other creatures.

Principal among the Egyptian deities were Ra, the sun god, who later came to be called Amon-Ra; Osiris (oh-SIGH-riss), the god of the underworld; Isis (EYE-siss), the goddess of the home; the evil Set; and the falcon-headed Horus (HORE-us). There were hundreds of gods, each with its own priests, temples, and rituals. And then there were the men who the Egyptians believed were close to gods: the pharaohs.

In modern America, people are used to following the lives of celebrities, stars they read about in magazines and see on television shows. In ancient Egypt, by contrast, there was only one "star," and he was the pharaoh. The word *pharaoh* (FAIR-oh) means "great house" or "one who lives in the palace." This was the title for the king of Egypt, but the pharaoh was much more than a mere king. He was seen as a link between the gods and humankind, and the people viewed him more as a divine being than as a human. They addressed him as "son of Ra" or by other godlike names, and they considered him an earthly embodiment of Horus. Thus Egyptian illustrations often portrayed the pharaoh as a falcon, like Horus, whose wings covered the world.

When a pharaoh died, the Egyptians believed, he became one with the god Osiris and ruled over the dead. This role might seem unpleasant, but to the Egyptians, the afterlife was more important than life on earth. They believed that a person did not really die: the person's spirit would continue to live for eternity—*if* the people who prepared the body for burial followed certain procedures. Therefore the Egyptians built enormous tombs, the pyramids, for the pharaohs.

Pyramids were not simply graves. They were houses in which the pharaoh's spirit would live until it came time to emerge and begin life again in the afterworld. Along with dolls

Osiris, god of the underworld. *Archive Photos. Reproduced by permission.*

symbolizing their wives and servants, pharaohs were buried with various treasures, including jewelry as well as models of furniture, chariots, and boats. So that they would not go hungry, their tombs contained great quantities of food and drink, which would often be supplemented by offerings of more food and drink at a temple attached to the pyramid.

The pyramids housed the pharaoh's body, but that body first had to be preserved. Therefore the Egyptians developed the art of mummification. Eventually not only pharaohs, but Egyptian nobles and ultimately even rich commoners (nonroyalty) began having themselves mummified and buried in their own elaborate tombs. Indeed everyone, not just the pharaohs and the upper classes, believed that they would continue living in the afterworld. Only the select few, however, could afford to make what Egyptians considered the proper preparations.

Everything about the pharaoh distinguished him from other people—even the items he wore. One of these items was a rectangular-shaped ceremonial beard (i.e., it was not his real hair), that hung straight down from the chin about six inches. Often pharaohs were shown with arms crossed over their chests, each hand holding objects that symbolized their power: usually a whip and a crook. A pharaoh's crook is a long, hooked, striped object that looks a bit like a candy cane.

As it is today in the desert, headgear was extremely important in the hot, dry climate of Egypt. The pharaoh's head cloth, called a *nemes,* served to distinguish him from his subjects. From the front, the nemes (pronounced NEM-ease) had a shape like thick hair that hung down over both of his shoulders, to about the center of his rib cage. Like the crook, it was striped; across the top, over his eyebrows, it had a band of gold. At the center of this band were one or two golden cobras, the fearsome poisonous snakes that lived in the deserts around Egypt. This stood for the cobra goddess that protected the kings and queens of Egypt.

As impressive as the nemes looked, it was not the pharaonic crown. (The word "pharaonic" is simply *pharaoh* transformed from a noun to an adjective.) To describe his crown and its symbolism, however, it is necessary to appreciate what happened when a pharaoh named Menes united the kingdoms of Upper and Lower Egypt in about 3100 B.C.

Egypt before the Old Kingdom (5500–2650 B.C.)

Before the time of ancient Egypt, there were two lands called Upper Egypt and Lower Egypt. One might assume that Upper Egypt would be north of Lower Egypt, but this was not so: the terms upper and lower refer to the two regions' relative elevation or height along the Nile. Because northern Egypt was downstream from southern Egypt, it was "lower."

Based on what historians know, Lower Egypt was *not* "lower" than Upper Egypt in terms of culture. In fact, it was more developed, as symbolized by the establishment of the first Egyptian capital in the northern city of Memphis. Yet it appears that in the unification of the country that occurred in about 3100 B.C., Upper Egypt conquered Lower Egypt and then adopted much of its northern neighbor's culture.

According to tradition, the king who brought together the two Egypts—in effect, the first pharaoh—was named Menes (MEN-ease), though he may have been named Narmer or Aha. Because of uncertainty about his identity, he is usually considered a semi-legendary figure. In other words, he may have lived, but most likely much of what historians "know" about him is mere legend.

What is certain is that Egypt was unified and that this unification created the world's first national government. For almost 3,000 years, Egypt would be ruled by a series of *dynasties,* or royal houses, who would each in turn claim the title of pharaoh for themselves. A dynasty is a group of people, often but not always a family, who continue to hold a position of power over a period of time. The ruling dynasty might change (in all, Egypt had thirty-one dynasties), but the unified kingdom of Egypt continued to exist. It provided a single government that made trade and travel possible throughout the Nile Valley and Delta. The pharaoh's crown became a symbol of the unified kingdom: it combined the tall white crown of Upper Egypt with the squat red crown of Lower Egypt.

Early dynasties

Apart from the shadowy figure of Menes, history has preserved little concerning the identities of pharaohs in the almost five centuries between the unification of Egypt and the

Egyptian hieroglyphics, photograph. *Archive Photos. Reproduced by permission.*

beginning of what historians call the Old Kingdom of Egypt. The First Dynasty followed Menes by some 200 years, appearing in about 2920 B.C. The end of the Second Dynasty nearly thee hundred years later ushered in the Old Kingdom.

Historians do know that these early dynasties already featured many of the characteristics commonly associated with ancient Egypt. For instance, these early Egyptians had a type of burial mound called a *mastaba* (MAHS-tah-buh), which would later develop into pyramids during the Old Kingdom. Rectangular in shape and with sloping sides, mastabas were tombs made of mud bricks. They looked very much like the houses in which the common people of Egypt lived, but these were houses for royalty, and they were meant to last for eternity.

Even more important than these early pyramids, however, was another element of Egyptian life that dates back to the early dynasties. This was the development of writing through use of a system of symbols called hieroglyphs.

Hieroglyphics

The Egyptian system of writing was called *hieroglyphics,* and the symbols it used were called *hieroglyphs.* Whereas the English alphabet uses only twenty-six letters, hieroglyphics made use of some *700* different symbols. There were two types of hieroglyphs, *pictograms,* which looked like the things they represented—for example, a picture of flowing water to stand for the word "water"—and *phonograms,* which stood for an entire syllable. For an English speaker, the concept of a phonogram is difficult to understand: It would be as though the "syl" in *syllable,* for instance, could be represented with just one letter instead of three. Chinese and Japanese are modern examples of languages that make use of phonograms.

Whereas most people in America can read and write, the vast majority of Egyptians were illiterate. Even pharaohs were not likely to be literate. Because written communication is essential to any civilization, the people who *could* read and write were bound to be very powerful. This literate group was known as *scribes,* and indeed they were enormously influential. Their equivalent in modern society would be people who can write computer programs and develop software.

Egyptians were strong believers in magic, and to them, words were magical. This was particularly true of written words. Indeed the term *hieroglyph* is Greek for "sacred carving." Given the sacred, magical nature of words, the scribes became like priests of a sort. The complicated nature of hieroglyphics, incidentally, was no accident: scribes deliberately made the system difficult in order to maintain their positions of influence.

The Sphinx sits in front of the Giza pyramid in Cairo, Egypt. Originally, the Sphinx was plastered and brightly painted.
The Library of Congress.

Originally these symbols were also difficult to write down, though this probably had nothing to do with the scribes' efforts to keep themselves in a job. *Hieroglyph* comes from a root word meaning "to carve," and the first hieroglyphs—the oldest known example dates from about 2950 B.C.—were carved into stone. Likewise *scribe,* a word coined much later by the Greeks, means "to scratch an outline." During the Middle Kingdom, the development of hieratic script, along with the use of papyrus, would make writing much easier The scribes' influence, however, would remain strong. Next to the royalty, high government officials, and priests, they were the most powerful figures in Egyptian society.

The Old Kingdom (2650–2150 B.C.)

Historians have difficulty placing exact dates on ancient Egyptian history before the period of the New King-

Egyptians pulling building materials. *Archive Photos. Reproduced by permission.*

dom, which began in the 1500s B.C. Generally, however, the half-millennium (500 years) from the beginning of the Third Dynasty in about 2650 B.C. to the end of the Sixth Dynasty in 2150 B.C. is considered the Old Kingdom of Egypt. This is a period noted for the building of the greatest and most impressive pyramids, which occurred during the Fourth Dynasty. But the pyramids would not have been possible without the establishment of a strong central government that commanded the willing submission of its subjects.

One misconception many people have about the building of the pyramids was that it was done by slave labor; in fact the vast majority of workers on these enormous projects participated of their own free will. A large portion of them were farmers who worked during the Nile's summer floods, and they received food and shelter (the Egyptians did not use money as such) in return for their labor.

Indeed, there were few slaves in ancient Egypt, though this is not to say that all people were equal in that society. On the contrary, the pharaoh occupied the highest class, followed by a group that included priests, scribes, and soldiers. Below this was a larger class of merchants, overseers, and other professionals, and at the bottom was the bulk of the population, mostly farmers and servants.

The people built the king's tomb by the sweat of their brows. History would remember the pharaohs as the "builders" of the pyramids, even though few of them had anything to do with the design, much less the labor. Yet few Egyptians saw anything unfair about the humble state of the people compared with the wealth and splendor of the pharaoh. By helping the king build his eternal house, the common people believed, they were ensuring their own protection in the afterworld.

Because the Egyptian king was like a god, the allegiance of the people to their ruler was absolute; otherwise, it would have been impossible for the pharaohs to demand the vast sacrifices of sweat and toil (not to mention resources such as food for the workers) required to build the pyramids. The people's belief that they needed the pharaoh's protection, both in the present world and the next, was the "glue" that held the Old Kingdom together.

As for the need to protect Egypt from outside invaders, there was little to fear—thanks to nature, not the pharaohs. An invading army could only come into Egypt by one of two routes: across the desert, which was impossible, or up the Nile, which the Egyptians controlled. Egypt at this time had no need for a standing army (that is, for a full-time military prepared for warfare at any time). There were minor campaigns far beyond Egypt's borders, as they fought the Nubians to the south and the people of the Sinai Peninsula to the northeast for control of valuable mines. For the most part, however, the pharaohs were free to devote themselves to what they considered the most important aspect of life: preparing for death.

Limestone figure of Pharoah Zoser.
Roger Wood/Corbis.
Reproduced by permission.

From the Step Pyramids to the Bent Pyramid

As noted earlier, the first royal tombs were boxlike structures called mastabas. However, by the time of the pharaoh Zoser (or Djoser), who reigned from about 2630 to 2611 B.C., the mastabas had begun to seem too plain for a king's eternal dwelling. Zoser's need for a structure that would properly glorify him in the afterlife led to the creation, by his brilliant architect Imhotep, of the first pyramid.

Imhotep, who held the rank of *vizier*, or chief minister, was among the most learned men, not only of his time, but of any time. Trained as a scribe, he was also an engineer, a math-

The gods of Egypt

Given the importance of the Nile, one might think that the principal Egyptian deity would be the god of the river, but that honor went to a god who represented the other great natural force in the life of Egypt: the sun. Ra, the sun god and king of the gods, had come from Nun, a state of disorder that preceded the creation of the world. The light Ra brought to the Earth gave life. But Ra disappeared each night. Some worshipers believed he was born each day, then got older as he traveled across the sky, until he died when he went below the horizon. Ra was usually depicted with a sun-like disk, much like a halo but flat, over his head. In southern Egypt, there was a similar god named Amon, and eventually his identity was joined with Ra's to make Amon-Ra, the supreme god.

Ra's children were twins, a boy named Shu (pronounced like "shoe") and a girl named Tefnut (TEFF-noot). Shu ruled over the air, holding up the sky, and Tefnut helped him. The strain of this task caused her to shed tears, which provided the morning dew. Just as the royalty of Egypt tended to marry their relatives, the same was true of the gods: Shu and Tefnut produced two children, Geb and Nut (like Tefnut, rhymes with "loot"). The two were born holding one another, so Ra commanded Shu to separate them; Geb became the sky, and Nut the earth.

Geb and Nut had two sons and two daughters. The most notable of these was the son Osiris, who educated the Egyptians in agriculture and city-building. He married his sister Isis, goddess of the home, and was murdered by their brother Set, who threw Osiris's body into the Nile. Later Isis rescued Osiris with the help of Nephthys (NEFF-thiss), Set's twin sister. Yet Osiris decided to stay in the land of the dead, or the underworld, and became the god of that region. The Egyptians believed that like Ra, he remained in a constant

ematician, a master builder, and a renowned wise man. Ironically it was he, and not Zoser, who would come to be glorified by successive generations, who worshiped him as a god because of his great genius.

Imhotep built a structure composed of six mastabas on top of one another, each smaller than the one below. This became the Step Pyramid of King Zoser, built in the town of Saqqara (suh-CAR-uh) near Memphis. The Step Pyramid stood some 200 feet, or twenty stories high. Around it was an elabo-

state of death and rebirth, symbolized by the yearly rise and fall of the Nile.

Osiris was usually depicted as a pharaoh (or king), with an Egyptian crown and the other emblems carried by the pharaoh. Isis usually had angel-like wings. Above her head a moon disk like Ra's sun disk, surrounded by cow's horns. The evil god Set was usually seen with the head of a crocodile or that of a monster.

As the god of the relatively more barren southern half of Egypt, Set desired the fertile lands ruled by Osiris, and this led to the murder of his brother. With Osiris dead, Set began to mistreat his sisters Isis and Nephthys. Nephthys was also Set's wife and became the goddess of mourning.

While Osiris was alive, Nephthys had disguised herself as Isis and had a child with him, and though Isis later found out, she was not angry with her sister. This child was Anubis (uh-NEW-biss), god of the dead, who helped prepare bodies for the afterlife. He was typically shown with the body of a man and the head of a jackal or dog.

Osiris also had a son by Isis, Horus, who was born weak and became more vulnerable still when he lost his father and had to be raised by his mother. He was often tormented by his wicked uncle Set. But Osiris came back to life periodically to teach Horus how to fight, and eventually Horus—depicted as a man with the head of a falcon, and the sun and moon for eyes—became a powerful warrior. Later he defeated Set in battle. Ra forced Set into the desert, where he ruled over a kingdom of sand, rocks, and scorpions.

These were some of the principal gods and goddesses, but there were many, many more. Each geographical area had its own deities. There were hundreds of gods, each of which had its own temple and priests.

rate walled complex that included a temple as well as buildings that looked like temples but were not. They had false doors and could not be entered, a tactic to fool grave robbers. There was also a long court on which King Zoser, watched by crowds from all over Egypt, once ran a course to prove to his subjects that he was physically fit. This was perhaps the world's first recorded spectator sporting event.

The pharaohs that followed Zoser built step pyramids modeled on Imhotep's, and from these later structures it is clear

Bent pyramid at Dashur.
Corbis/Marilyn Bridges.
Reproduced by permission.

that building techniques developed and improved over time. Not until Sneferu (SNEFF-eh-roo), who built four pyramids between 2575 and 2551 B.C., did the smooth-sided pyramid make its first appearance. The most well-known of these is the "Bent Pyramid," which was originally intended to be very steep; but halfway up, the builders changed the angle. Various reasons have been given for this: Either the pyramid had to be completed in a hurry or (more likely) the builders began to find cracks in it caused by the extremely steep angle. Whatever the reason, the Bent Pyramid is an unusual-looking structure.

The Great Pyramids

Sneferu's son Cheops (KEY-ops), or Khufu (COO-foo), would build the greatest of all the pyramids. Often referred to simply as "the Great Pyramid," this one and the two beside it in Giza, on the west side of the Nile near modern-day Cairo, are what most people think of when they hear the word "pyramid."

The Great Pyramid, completed in about 2550 B.C., originally stood 481 feet (147 meters) tall, and though it is now 33 feet (10 meters) shorter, it remains a structure of staggering proportions. Its height makes it equivalent to that of a fifty-story building, which would not seem all that tall in a modern American city—but the Great Pyramid was built more than 4,500 years ago. Furthermore, its sheer size would make it an impressive addition to any city: it is 755 feet (230 meters), along a side, meaning that its base would cover ten football fields. Though it is possible a few structures of the ancient Middle East and Europe were taller, the Great Pyramid is by far the tallest that has survived. It would be almost 4,000 years before there would be a taller structure, the cathedral in Cologne, Germany. Built in the 1200s, the cathedral is slightly taller.

As for Cheops himself, little is known, but based on his ability to mobilize the men and resources necessary for such an enormous project, he must have been one of the most powerful rulers in the history of the world. Khafre (CAH-frah), who

Stepped Pyramid near Cairo. *Archive Photos. Reproduced by permission.*

was either Cheops's son or brother, ruled from 2520 to 2494 B.C., and built the second of the Great Pyramids. Last came Menkaure (min-KAW-ray), who was probably Khafre's son. His pyramid was by far the smallest of the three Great Pyramids, standing only 218 feet (66 meters). The Pyramid of Khafre, by contrast, was only nine feet, or three meters, shorter than that of Cheops, and in many photographs it appears taller because it sits on higher ground.

Indeed, today it actually *is* taller because the limestone facing has been removed from the earlier and taller Pyramid of Cheops. Originally all three pyramids were covered in a smooth limestone finish, so that they gleamed in the desert sun. However, later conquerors of Egypt stripped away these coverings. All that remains is a small portion of limestone on Khafre's pyramid—near the top, where it would have been hardest to reach. Because it still has its covering, the Pyramid of Khafre is actually taller than its neighbor.

Excavation of Cheops.
AP/Wide World. Reproduced by permission.

From Imhotep's Step Pyramid onward, few pyramids were solitary structures: Most had a number of buildings around them. The Great Pyramids were no exception. By far the most notable of its surrounding structures was a statue called the Sphinx. The Sphinx has the body of a cat and the face of a man—probably Khafre's. It sits crouched very much the way a house cat does, facing toward the sun in the east. The Sphinx seems to guard the Great Pyramids.

Presumably the Sphinx was carved from a large piece, or outcropping, of limestone that lay next to the Great Pyramids. The Giza pyramids stand on a flat spot, or plateau, where enormous quantities of rock form a solid foundation. Like most pyramids from Zoser's onward, they were built on top of large stone outcroppings. The outcropping not only served as a strong base for the structure but also gave the builders material with which to start.

The building of the Great Pyramids was a triumph of engineering seldom equaled in human history. For that reason, some observers have developed fanciful explanations, including the idea that beings from another planet built them. Such speculation is outside the realm of history, which deals in facts that can be demonstrated through archaeological research. That does not mean that historians cannot be intrigued by the mysteries of the pyramids. Indeed, it is hard not to be. The air of mystery surrounding the pyramids only increases as soon as one goes *inside* these great structures.

The rituals of death

It is easy to get so caught up in the majesty and spectacle of the pyramids that one forgets their original purpose: They were tombs, or rather houses in which the dead would "live" during the next life. For this reason, all the pyramids (the Egyptians constructed more than eighty) were built on the west side of the Nile, toward the place where the sun went down, or "died," each night.

Deep inside each pyramid was a burial chamber for the pharaoh. Because they buried their kings with great stores of treasure, the Egyptians were aware that robbers might try to get in and steal the valuables, so they designed the pyramids with confusing networks of passages, including blind alleys and doors that led nowhere. Before a pyramid was closed up for good, the builders sealed its chambers shut with granite blocks or huge quantities of sand.

These "tricks" were another feature pioneered by Imhotep in the Step Pyramid, which contained a complex of underground chambers. The Great Pyramid, too, has a number of passageways, including a vast hallway called the Grand Gallery. Originally its entrance was concealed under polished blocks that looked exactly the same as the rest of its exterior.

Beyond these barriers and passageways, deep inside the pyramid, was a burial chamber that would serve as the home of the pharaoh's body in the next life. A dead body, however, will rapidly decompose if simply left to decay; therefore the Egyptians developed a means to preserve the bodies, a process called *mummification*. Mummification involves embalming, a chemical process meant to preserve a corpse, or dead body. Embalming is still practiced in modern funeral homes.

The Egyptians, because they intended for corpses to last for centuries, made an art of the embalming process. Modern

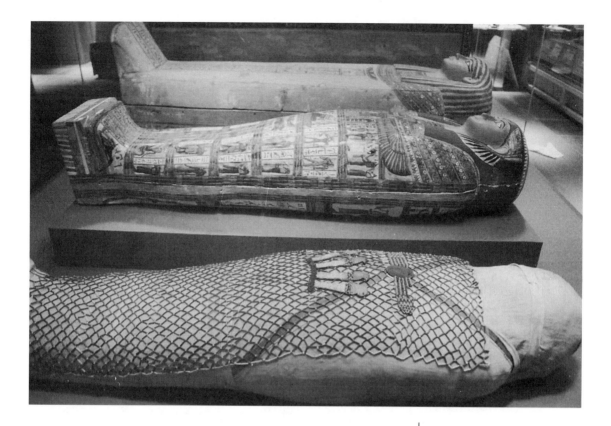

Three mummies laying side-by-side, displayed for a museum exhibit in Boston, Massachusetts.
AP/Wide World Photos. Reproduced by permission.

Americans tend to approach this subject with a little fear and disgust, but it was perfectly natural to the Egyptians, who called the *mortuary* (a place where bodies are prepared for burial) the "Beautiful House." Morticians, or mortuary workers, believed they were guided by the god Anubis. Indeed, their work ranks among the great achievements of ancient Egypt. From their experiments in the preservation of bodies comes some of the world's earliest anatomical and medical knowledge.

The morticians first removed most of the corpse's internal organs. Then they dried the body using a variety of chemicals, most notably *natron*, a compound much like baking soda that came from the surrounding desert. Usually they would let the body sit in natron crystals for forty days. Next they stuffed the areas of the body from which organs had been removed, using natron, spices, sawdust, or a mixture of these ingredients. Then they sewed up the cuts they had made in the corpse when removing its insides, and rubbed the body with oil.

How the Pyramids Were Built

The building of the pyramids was one of the greatest achievements in human history. The pyramids are a monument not only to the pharaohs' power but also to the genius of the architects, engineers, and government officials who planned and built them.

First a site had to be selected. It had to be on the west side of the Nile, above flood level. It had to be near the water, because boats would be bringing in the blocks needed for building. The stone came from various places, but the hard granite that surrounded the interior chambers of the pyramid came from 500 miles up the river in Aswan. There, workers in a quarry, a place where stone is "mined" from the earth, spent most of the year cutting giant blocks of granite. Once the Nile flooded in the summer, they loaded the blocks onto boats, or barges, and floated them downriver to the building sites.

When the barge arrived, the blocks had to be unloaded. Most of these blocks weighed about 2.5 tons, or 5,000 pounds

(2.27 metric tons, or 2,270 kilograms), so it was not easy to get them from the shore to the top of a pyramid. Workers, usually in team of thirty men, pulled the blocks out onto giant sleds atop rows of logs. With ropes attached to the sleds, they would pull the blocks up long temporary ramps made of mud and brick, which were built on a gentle slope to make it easier to drag stones up them. The ramps were also wide, not only so that there would be plenty of room for the sleds, but also so that there would always be a part of the ramp that could be closed off while it was being raised. The ramp, of course, had to rise with the pyramid.

Among the pyramid builders, the workers who dragged the stones up the ramps were at the lowest social level, but they were not slaves. Some of them left behind graffiti (pronounced grah-FEE-tee) or wall writings, that showed how much they felt like an essential part of the project—as indeed they were. Blocks used in Sneferu's Medium Pyramid include inscriptions celebrating the various work

After this, they wrapped the body with linen, using resins to seal up the wrapping. The wrapped corpse was called a mummy. At the funeral, priests performed a ceremony in which they "opened the mouth" of the dead person so that he or she could eat, speak, and breathe in the afterlife. The mummy was then placed in a brightly decorated coffin, called a *sarcophagus* (sar-KAHF-uh-gus), which often bore the face of

gangs: "Enduring Gang," says one inscription, and another celebrates the "Vigorous Gang."

In a class above these common laborers were the skilled workers, especially masons (a type of craftsman who builds with stone). Above the masons were the planners and their assistants, the scribes. The scribes recorded figures for the amount of stone used in a given period of time and helped keep track of the tools and the teams to which they were assigned. Among the scribes' writings that have survived is a written excuse for a worker who "called in sick."

The scribes also took note of the intricate calculations taken by the builders. It was not enough to plan the pyramid at the beginning, and go from there: the builders had to constantly measure angles and lengths to make sure that they were correct. Their calculations were amazingly sophisticated. One can see how careful they were by measuring the Great Pyramid, the longest side of which is only about eight inches longer than the shortest side. Plenty of *houses* in America do not have measurements as nearly perfect as these!

The precision of the measurements is particularly impressive in light of the Egyptians' lack of technological sophistication in other areas. For instance, at the time of the Old Kingdom, they had not yet entered the Bronze Age. They may not have even known about the wheel. Furthermore, Egyptian art of the time suggests that they did not have a very well-developed sense of space.

Given these circumstances as well as the suitability of the pyramids' placement for astronomical observations (that is, observation of the stars), some people have speculated that beings from another planet built the pyramids of Egypt, along with those of Mexico. Such claims are hard to prove or disprove, given the archaeological evidence; less questionable is the opinion that the Great Pyramids are some of the most amazing structures on earth.

the person buried within. And so the dead body would sit, entombed in its quiet chamber within the pyramid, for the rest of eternity.

By almost any measure, the pyramids were and are spooky places. First of all, their very purpose as tombs is a little chilling in most people's view. Second, they have stood for so long: hence an old saying, "Time laughs at all things, but the pyramids laugh at time." Even within ancient Egypt, which would continue to exist for almost 2,000 years after the end of the Old Kingdom, people thought of the pyramids as ancient. They would remain a testament to the first, and in some ways, greatest phase of ancient Egyptian history.

The First Intermediate Period (2150–1986 B.C.)

All civilizations, no matter how great they are, eventually fall. Historians, with the benefit of hindsight, can sometimes see evidence of a civilization's impending (that is, upcoming) decline even at a time when that civilization appears to be strong and healthy. Thus although the Old Kingdom still flourished in the Fifth Dynasty of the 2400s B.C., there were already signs that its best years lay in the past. Like their predecessors in the Fourth Dynasty, the kings of the Fifth Dynasty built pyramids, but theirs were neither as impressive nor as lasting. The pharaoh Nyuserra, for instance, built a pyramid whose name means "the places of Nyuserra are enduring." This proved ironic, because that pyramid today is little more than a heap of stones

The rule of the Memphis pharaohs still seemed strong during the Sixth Dynasty, one of whose kings was Pepi II. Pepi held power longer than any leader in history: he ruled from 2246, when he was just six years old, to 2152 B.C.—ninety-four years. The end of Pepi's reign marked the end of the Old Kingdom. With the beginning of the Seventh Dynasty, Egypt entered what is called the First Intermediate Period. (The word *intermediate* refers to something that divides.) This period of about 125 years divided the Old Kingdom from the Middle Kingdom.

Why did the Old Kingdom decline? There were several reasons. One was the rise of *nomarchs,* or governors of provinces, who challenged the authority of the pharaohs. There was also an increase in government *bureaucracy,* which put further strain on the system. A bureaucracy is a web of offices and officials who create conflicting, often unnecessary, and sometimes senseless rules and regulations, thus making it hard for anyone to get anything done. Furthermore, there was a widespread sense of *disillusionment,* an emotional state that occurs when people lose their old beliefs without finding something new to believe in.

Writings from the era, particularly those of the scribe and wise man Ipuwer (IP-oo-weer) suggest that society was in a state of upheaval. The old faith in the pharaohs no longer motivated the people; indeed, the rulers of the Ninth and Tenth dynasties were former nomarchs who had seized power. Ipuwer wrote of increasing suicides, and of a social order that had been turned upside-down: "Look! The poor of the land have become rich; the possessor of things [has become] the one who has nothing." Another scribe wrote about an increasing attitude of dishonesty among people: "To whom do I speak today? / Brothers are evil, / Friends of today are not of love."

To top it off, it appears that during this time there was also a *famine,* or a period when there was not enough food for everyone. Stability only began to return with the Eleventh Dynasty, which established its capital at Thebes (pronounced like "thieves," but with a *b* instead of a *v.*) Finally, a king named Mentuhotep II (min-too-HOE-tep) united all of Egypt under his rule in about 1986 B.C. This effectively ended the First Intermediate Period and ushered in the second great age of ancient Egypt, the Middle Kingdom.

The Middle Kingdom (1986–1759 B.C.)

The Eleventh and Twelfth dynasties made up the period known as the Middle Kingdom in Egypt. Though there would again be great building projects, nothing would ever equal the scale of the Old Kingdom's pyramids. What was missing was the system that had made the pyramids possible. The pharaohs were still powerful, but now nomarchs and scribes enjoyed an increasing share of power, a fact symbolized by the much larger number of people who had themselves mummified after death. Also, the disillusionment brought on by the First Intermediate Period had left the Egyptian people less committed to the old ways of doing things.

Although his power was not as great as it had been, the pharaoh was still, as people might say in modern times, "running the show." The kings who followed Mentuhotep II carried on trade, and sometimes waged war, with other parts of North Africa and the Middle East. In particular, they sought to open trade with the eastern and southeastern regions, along the Red Sea and in what is now Ethiopia. Also, as in the Old Kingdom, they waged war with the people of the Sinai, and with the Libyans, a desert nation to the west.

One of the most powerful kings of this era was Amenemhet I (ah-min-NIM-het), who established the Twelfth Dynasty in 1937 B.C. Amenemhet had been a vizier, and it appears that he was a *usurper* (you-SUR-purr)—that is, someone who seizes power. Around the time he ascended to the throne, a book called *The Prophecy of Neferti* began to circulate. It depicted a scene at the court of Sneferu in which the pharaoh receives a prophecy concerning a future king who will save Egypt. Clearly this predicted savior is Amenemhet.

Several elements of *The Prophecy of Neferti* are interesting. It is perhaps the first example of *propaganda,* a type of writing or other art (for instance, posters) that a government uses in order to convince people that the government is good and everything opposed to it is bad. Propaganda would be widely used during the twentieth century, both by free and peaceful governments such as that of the United States and by clearly evil regimes such as those of Nazi Germany and Soviet Russia. Also, *The Prophecy of Neferti* highlights the concept of *legitimacy,* which is closely tied to propaganda. Legitimacy simply means that the ruler has a right to rule. In America, the votes of the people give their leaders legitimacy. In ancient Egypt, a leader gained legitimacy by being identified with the gods and the great pharaohs. Because Amenemhet had more or less stolen the throne, it was important for him to gain legitimacy.

No doubt for the same reason, Amenemhet wanted to ensure that there would be a smooth transition to the next ruler, his son Senusret (sin-OOS-ret), or Sesostris I. He shared power with Senusret for about nine years; but in spite of his efforts, Amenemhet was assassinated by a group within his royal court. This group was also hostile to Senusret, who was away at battle when the killing occurred. He did, however, manage to hold on to power.

Many of these events were recorded in another book from the same era, *The Story of Sinuhe.* The tale was similar to what modern people would call a novel. It portrayed fictional (that is, invented) characters against a historical backdrop. A modern example of this technique would be the book *Gone with the Wind* (1936), which made use both of invented characters and real events—specifically, the American Civil War (1861–1865). Another important text from the end of Amenemhet's reign and the beginning of his son's was *The Testament of Amenemhet,* sometimes called *The Lesson of Amenemhet.* Unlike *The Story of Sinuhe,* this book was not a story, but consisted of the dying king's advice to his son. The book's content could be summed up by the modern expression,"It's lonely at the top." In the *Testament,* Amenemhet warns Senusret that a king has few friends and many enemies who are eager to take his power and his life from him.

It might seem ironic that Amenemhet was giving this advice, but in fact he probably had nothing to do with the *Testament,* which was undoubtedly written after his death. As with *The Prophecy of Neferti* and *The Story of Sinuhe,* its author is unknown. These texts, however, point up a key aspect of the Middle Kingdom: the growing significance of the written word.

Developments in writing

The pharaohs were certainly powerful rulers, but they could not have controlled their kingdoms without the help of scribes; nor would historians know the names of the pharaohs if there had been no one to write them down.

Though the scribes remained an exclusive and powerful class in the Middle Kingdom, writing itself became much easier owing to two developments. The first of these was *papyrus* (puh-PIE-russ). Papyrus is the name for a kind of reed, which the Egyptians cut into strips. They crisscrossed these strips and soaked them in water, then flattened them with a smooth shell or a piece of ivory. When it had dried, the papyrus became like paper, and indeed the English word "paper" comes from *papyrus.*

No longer did the scribes have to carve hieroglyphs into stone; nor did they have to painstakingly draw out each hieroglyph, thanks to the development of *hieratic* (high-RAT-ick) script. Hieratic was a simplified form of hieroglyphics that could be written much faster, just as it is easier to write in cursive lettering than it is to print. As is true of many modern languages such as Arabic and Chinese, hieratic was written from right to left. For the next 1,300 years, hieratic would remain the system for everyday writing, including legal documents, letters, and stories; then, around 650B.C., the scribes would develop an even simpler form, called *demotic* (deh-MOTT-ick). During this time, however, hieroglyphics remained in use for types of writing intended to be more lasting—for example, on tombs—and were still often carved into stone.

Several other varieties of written communication developed around the time of the Middle Kingdom. There were seals, which like their modern equivalents carried something stamped on the bottom that could be transferred by rubbing the seal in ink, then placing an impression on a document. Scribes used labels, which may have assisted them in creating an early type of filing system: A label attached to a papyrus scroll identified its contents and the name of the pharaoh at the time of its writing.

On the doors of kings and other important figures were doorplates, which contained not only the name of the person who lived there but a message as well—for instance, "There shall always exist the son of Re [Ra] whom he loves, Amenhotep the god, ruler of Thebes." The name of the pharaoh, either on a doorplate or elsewhere, would be contained within a *cartouche* (car-TOOSH), a vertical oval with hieroglyphs inside it.

The rise and fall of the Middle Kingdom

Senusret I and the kings that followed him continued a tradition established by Amenemhet: In the latter part of a pharaoh's reign, he would allow his successor (usually his first-born son) to share power with him. The rulers also carried on Amenemhet's efforts to expand Egyptian influence through trade and warfare.

Senusret sent mining expeditions to Nubia and the eastern desert, which yielded gold and high-grade building stone, respectively. His grandson, Senusret II, had floodgates built along part of the Nile Valley in order to reclaim valuable farmland. Later, Senusret III ordered the First Cataract cleared, which made it possible for boats to pass through. This removed one of Egypt's natural barriers, and for that reason he had fortresses built to protect the country from invasion by Nubians or Kushites to the south.

Amenemhet III, who reigned from 1817 to 1772 B.C., would prove one of the greatest of the Middle Kingdom's pharaohs. Under his leadership, the Egyptians reclaimed some 153,600 acres, or 240 square miles (621.6 square kilometers), of fertile farmland from the Nile and developed an irrigation system to keep it watered. He also led a number of building projects, including construction of Egypt's last major pyramids. The pyramid at Hawara, though not nearly as large as its predecessors from the Fourth Dynasty, was an impressive achievement in its own right, containing an intricate set of trapdoors, blind hallways, and other "tricks" designed to keep robbers out.

Soon after Amenemhet III, however, the Middle Kingdom fell into decline. Already at the time of Senusret II, nearly seventy years before, it had seemed that the world was growing old. Thus one of the scribes in Senusret's court complained that everything had already been done: "Would that I had words that are unknown," he wrote, "utterances and sayings in new language ... without that which hath been said repeatedly." Similar views have been expressed in different words by people in modern life, proving that some things never change. One of those unchangeable facts of human history is that civilizations rise and fall: thus the Middle Kingdom ended, to be followed by a period of unrest.

The Second Intermediate Period (1759–1539 B.C.)

As would later be the case in Rome, ancient empires in decline tended to have huge numbers of kings in a row. Some early historians estimated that during the five dynasties that followed the Twelfth, a span of some 220 years known as the Second Intermediate Period, Egypt had 217 kings—almost one per year. In truth it probably was not *that* bad, but it does appear that the country had quite a number of pharaohs (many of whom ruled at the same time) during this time.

The First Intermediate Period had been characterized by a general decline in the society, which was not the case in the Second Intermediate Period. However, Egypt during this

How the Egyptians *Saw* the World

Usually, but not always, one can learn a great deal about a civilization's level of sophistication by observing its visual arts. For most of human history, until the development of the camera in the mid-1800s, drawing and other forms of visual art, such as painting and sculpture, were the primary means for recording the appearances of people and things. As societies developed, likewise their artists' ability to"see" the world developed, much as a child goes from drawing scribbles to stick figures to more detailed representations of human figures.

It is surprising, then, that the Old Kingdom society that produced the pyramids could also have produced the visual arts it did. The pyramids were built to a degree of exactness that still baffles scientists. Their design indicates that the people who created them had a great understanding of spatial relationships. The phrase *spatial relationships* refers to the space between and within objects, concepts that are also closely related to the idea of *proportion*. Proportion describes the size of one thing in relation to something else: if someone drew a picture of a man whose head was twice as big as his body, one would say the picture was "out of proportion."

Egyptian visual art of the Old Kingdom, however, shows little sense of spatial relationships, proportion, or *perspective,* which helps artists to represent faraway objects as being smaller than objects close by. The Egyptians did not know how to do this, so if they wanted to show that something was farther away, they simply put it on top of the thing that was closer. In a crowd scene, for instance, they would show the first row of men standing side by side, then the next row above them, and so on.

Along with this lack of perspective, there was a lack of depth in early Egyptian

second phase of unrest confronted something it had not had to face before: invasion.

The conquerors were called Hyksos (HICK-sose), and they entered Egypt in about 1670 B.C. They seem to have come from the region of Palestine, later occupied by the Hebrews; in fact, it is possible that the Hyksos and the Hebrews were one and the same. Egyptian texts from the time refer to one of the Hyksos chieftains as *Ya'kob,* which may be a reference to the biblical name Jacob.

artwork. Everything seemed to be flat, as though the people in the pictures were crammed up against a sheet of glass. Their bodies were turned away from the viewer in strange, unnatural ways, with their arms and legs stretched sideways, while their eyes (which always looked more or less the same) faced outward. (The title of a hit song from the 1980s, "Walk Like an Egyptian" by the Bangles, played on the weird stance of figures in Egyptian artwork.)

Egyptian artists also showed the pharaoh much larger than other men, as though he were twelve feet tall. This was not a problem with proportion: the artists simply wanted to point out that he was more important than others. By the time of the New Kingdom, however, much had changed in both society and art. Thanks to the influence of other cultures, Egyptian art had become considerably more realistic. Also, the pharaoh's status had become more human; for example, artists during the reign of Akhenaton depicted their king with a fat stomach and skinny legs.

Still, sculpture continued to be more advanced than drawing or painting. Sculptors work in three dimensions—length, width, and depth—whereas painting or drawing involves only length and width. Though two-dimensional art improved greatly, the Egyptians still had a hard time figuring out how to translate three-dimensional figures to a flat surface. By contrast, the bust (a sculpture of a head) of Akhenaton's wife Queen Nefertiti represents some of the most advanced and realistic artwork of the ancient world.

With the end of Akhenaton's reign in 1336 B.C. came a widespread reaction to the reforms he had brought. Part of the reaction was manifested in a return to more traditional styles of artwork, including a less realistic representation of the human figure.

Whatever the case, the Egyptians hated the Hyksos, but they were unable to resist them due to their enemies' superior military technology. Whereas the Egyptians went to war in donkey-carts, the Hyksos rode into battle in horse-drawn chariots, which made them a much more powerful fighting force. Rather than repel the Hyksos, Lower Egypt came under their domination; these were the Fifteenth and Sixteenth dynasties, composed of Hyksos kings. Other Egyptians gathered around their own pharaoh at Thebes in Upper Egypt.

Sarcophagus lid depicting Ahmose I. *Corbis/Gianni Degli Orti. Reproduced by permission.*

The Theban pharaohs of the Seventeenth Dynasty found themselves caught between the Hyksos in the north and the kingdom of Kush in the south. At one point the Hyksos tried to become allied with the Kushites against the Egyptians, but they failed to do so. The Egyptians, meanwhile, had learned from their enemies and began to make use of chariot warfare. Led by Ahmose (AH-moze) I, they expelled the Hyksos in about 1550 B.C., a victory that opened the way for another great period in Egyptian history.

The New Kingdom (1539–1070 B.C.)

Not since the Fourth Dynasty a thousand years before was there an Egyptian dynasty as memorable as the Eighteenth. And whereas the Fourth Dynasty is remembered chiefly for its great building projects, most notably the Great Pyramids of Giza, the Eighteenth Dynasty is most famous for its colorful leaders: Hatshepsut (hah-CHEP-sut), the woman who ruled as king; Thutmose (TUT-moze) III, the great conqueror; and Akhenaton (ock-NAH-ton), who tried and failed to change the entire Egyptian religion. As with the Fourth Kingdom, there were great building projects, most notably in the Valley of the Kings. There were also developments in the visual arts that indicated a revolution in Egyptian thought.

Ahmose, after he drove out the Hyksos, led a number of other military expeditions and *colonized* Kush—that is, he made it a part of Egypt. His son Amenhotep I (ah-min-HOE-tep) continued with this colonial expansion. Amenhotep also became the first king to have himself buried in a hidden tomb. Like many a pharaoh before him, his memorial included a temple with a small pyramid called a *pyramidon;* Amenhotep, however, was buried somewhere else in hopes of protecting his tomb from grave robbers. Thutmose I, his successor, selected a burial site near Thebes in what came to be known as the Valley of Kings. Over the succeeding centuries, some sixty-two pharaohs, mostly from the Eighteenth and Nineteenth dynasties, would be buried there.

Thutmose's son, Thutmose II, married a princess named Hatshepsut. When Thutmose II died, Thutmose III, his son by another wife, was supposed to take the throne. But Hatshepsut claimed that she had been personally selected by the supreme god Amon to take the Egyptian throne. She managed to bring legitimacy on herself by claiming a connection with the gods.

But Hatshepsut had to fight more of an uphill battle than others who tried to take power in Egypt, because she was a woman. Therefore she was often portrayed as a man,

Hatshepsut claimed the throne after her husband's death, claiming that she had been personally selected for the role by the god Amon. *Archive Photos. Reproduced by permission.*

complete with a ceremonial beard, and sculpture showed her leading troops into battle although no evidence exists that this actually happened. She did, however, initiate foreign trade with the nation of Punt, in the area of modern-day Somalia, and had a number of structures built in her honor. Among the latter was an obelisk (OBB-uh-lisk; a tall, pointed column) in the city of Karnak (CAR-nack) near Thebes, which became the site of many Eighteenth and Nineteenth dynasty monuments.

Hatshepsut ruled from about 1473 to 1458 B.C., and after she died, Thutmose III paid her back for keeping him out of power for so long: he removed her pictures and nameplates from any of her monuments. Then he went off to war. Thutmose has been called "the Napoleon of Egypt," a reference to the French emperor Napoleon Bonaparte (1769–1821), who conquered most of Europe during his reign. Under the leadership of Thutmose, Egypt fought a major battle against rebel forces in Palestine. It extended its reach throughout most of the Sinai Peninsula and the region of what would become Israel. To the south, its borders went farther up the Nile than ever, taking in most of the Nubians' kingdom. Ancient Egypt under Thutmose was as large as it would ever be. Thutmose would be remembered as the first of many great conquerors in world history. Others would include Cyrus the Great and Alexander the Great.

But Thutmose did not only use war as a means of influencing foreign countries: he also made use of *diplomacy*—that is, skillful negotiations with leaders of other nations. His successors likewise conducted diplomatic activities, an important development because Egypt was fast becoming one of several powers (including the Assyrians and the Hittites) competing for control of the region. A valuable record of ancient Egyptian diplomacy exists in the form of the Amarna Letters, some 400 exchanges between the court of Amenhotep III (reigned 1382–1344 B.C.) and leaders of Mesopotamia and surrounding regions. Egyptian kings also used marriage as a form of diplomacy: they had many wives, but could always afford to take on more. An easy way to develop ties with another country was to marry one of its princesses. Several pharaohs did this, thus establishing links, for instance, with the Mitanni people of southwest Asia.

Akhenaton turns the world upside down

After Amenhotep III came a pharaoh who very nearly turned the ancient Egyptians' world upside down. This was Amenhotep IV (reigned 1352–1336 B.C.), who adopted the name Akhenaton, which means "Servant of Aton." Aton was the name of the deity whom he declared was the *only* god. Up to then, of course, the Egyptian religion had included numerous deities. Akhenaton proposed to sweep away all those old gods. Just as there was only one god, so there was only one prophet of Aton, and that was Akhenaton.

To break all ties with the past, Akhenaton established a new capital. He ordered that the new capital be built at a location along the Nile almost exactly midway between the old capital at Thebes and the even older capital at Memphis. Akhenaton called his new capital city Akhetaton (ock-TAH-ton), or "The Horizon of Aton." He and his wife Nefertiti (neff-ur-TEE-tee) moved the royal court there in the 1340s B.C. Akhenaton took with him very few of the people who had attended him in Thebes. Instead, he established an entirely new court and avoided contact with the priests of the old Egyptian religion. To ensure that no one worshiped the old deities, he ordered that their statutes and other images be removed from temples.

The old religion was *polytheistic,* meaning that it had many gods; what Akhenaton proposed was *monotheism,* the worship of one god. Egyptian paganism represented its gods as having bodies (though usually not faces) like those of humans; Aton, by contrast, was symbolized only by a golden, sun-like circle.

From the perspective of history, Akhenaton was a man ahead of his time. Most of the ancient cultures (except the Hebrews) had polytheistic religions, but most of these pagan belief systems would fade away. Judaism, which was influenced by the monotheistic ideas of the Zoroastrian faith in Persia, would survive and influence Christianity and Islam, two of the world's biggest religions in terms of their followers. By contrast, the only remaining polytheistic religion of any importance is Hinduism, the religion of India. As for Akhenaton's idea of Aton as having no physical form, this too was a forward-looking concept. One of the Ten Commandments later adopted by the Hebrews forbids any attempt to represent Jehovah with any "graven image." Islam would later establish even stricter rules against trying to depict Allah.

Ancient Egypt, however, was not ready for the radical changes proposed by Akhenaton, and much of the blame for this can be placed on the pharaoh himself. Instead of trying to bring about gradual change, he was impatient and acted hastily. He won few friends by upsetting the old traditions as he did.

After Akhenaton died, the Egyptians departed Akhetaton as quickly as they had moved there. In their hurry they left behind the Amarna Letters, which would give historians an extremely valuable record of the time. The next pharaoh claimed his own reign had begun after Amenhotep III, in effect removing Akhenaton from history.

After that pharaoh came a king who was only nine years old when he took the throne—yet he already had a wife, who was Akhenaton's daughter. He had adopted a name given to him by his father-in-law, but once he assumed power, he

Whatever Happened to the Treasures of Egypt?

One of the saddest aspects of Egypt's legacy is that because of greed, ignorance, or simple neglect, the world has lost a great deal of the archaeological riches from that great civilization.

Architects of the earliest pyramids were aware that robbers would try to steal the gold and other treasures stored with the pharaoh's tombs. For that reason, they built in elaborate devices, including blind passageways, trap doors, and air shafts filled with sand, to stop robbers from breaking in.

In spite of these efforts, every known pyramid had been looted by 1000 B.C. In many cases the theft was an "inside job" by the very priests whose responsibility it was to protect the tombs. These corrupt priests moved a number of the treasures to another location, supposedly for safekeeping but in fact to loot the gold. Perhaps if the gold items had been preserved intact, they might

have later resurfaced, but in order to avoid detection, the robbers usually melted down the treasures they stole. Therefore the world will probably never know what gorgeous objects were buried with pharaohs such as Cheops and Khafre.

Ancient Egyptian law set extremely harsh penalties for grave-robbing. There were tales of a curse over those who disturbed the eternal sleep of the pharaohs. Thus when Howard Carter discovered the tomb of Tutankhamen, it was said that he brought a curse on himself. Several strange things did happen, including the sudden death of Lord Carnarvon, who financed Carter's expedition. But Carter himself lived to be 65 years old, so it would be hard to prove that he had suffered a "curse."

Curse or not, great damage has been done by people who did not know how to value the historical treasures of Egypt. In the A.D. 600s, the Arab

officially ended the religion of Aton and went back to the old faith and his old name. That name would become more familiar to the modern world than it ever was to the ancients: Dead at the age of eighteen, Tutankhamen was destined to become one of the most famous pharaohs of all time.

Ramses and the end of the New Kingdom

After Tutankhamen died in 1323 B.C., there was a struggle for power as the aged vizier Aya and a general named

Funerary mask of Tutankhamen. The gold mask was inlaid with enamels and semi-precious stones. *The Library of Congress.*

conquerors ordered the Great Pyramids stripped of their elegant limestone facing so that they could build new structures in and around Cairo. The only part left untouched was the top of Khafre's pyramid.

Even in ancient times, many treasures of Egypt had fallen into disrepair. By the 1400s B.C., for instance, the Egyptians had allowed the sands of the desert to cover the Sphinx up to its neck. Once a young prince fell asleep in the shadow of the great statue, and had a dream in which the Sphinx itself told him he would become pharaoh if he had the sand removed. So he ordered the Sphinx uncovered and placed between its paws a stone tablet telling the story of what had happened. By then the Sphinx's prediction had come true, and the young prince reigned as Thutmose IV.

In the A.D.1400s Muslim soldiers broke off the nose of the Sphinx. They did this because Islam prohibits making statues or images of a god. More recently, the Sphinx and the Great Pyramids have suffered the damages of pollution, which is gradually eroding their surfaces.

Horemhab (hoe-REEM-hob) competed for the hand of his widow. She in turn tried to initiate a marriage with the son of a Hittite king, but the Hittite prince was apparently assassinated by Aya. Aya married her, then sent Horemhab to make war on the Hittites. Soon the old man died, however, and Horemhab took the throne.

As leadership of Egypt passed from the Eighteenth and Nineteenth dynasties, Horemhab was followed by a minor pharaoh named Ramses (RAM-sees) I, whose son was Seti (SETee) I. Seti conducted important military campaigns in Palestine and Syria and began building a giant temple at Karnak, which his own son, Ramses II, would complete. Seti's tomb, carved some 300 feet into the cliffs, was the largest in the Valley of the Kings.

Ramses II, who reigned from 1279 to 1213 B.C., would become known as Ramses the Great. He fought a number of campaigns against the Syrians and Hittites, including a battle at Kadesh (KAY-desh) in 1285 B.C., but he later made peace with the Hittites. His building projects include the massive temples at Abu Simbel, work on the Karnak temple, and many others. Ramses lived for ninety-six years and reigned for nearly sixty-seven, allegedly fathering ninety-six sons and sixty daughters with his more than two hundred wives and concubines. (A concubine, pronounced "CONG-cue-bine," was like a wife, but had lower social and legal status than a wife.)

The last of the truly great pharaohs, Ramses died in 1213 B.C. His son, Merneptah (mare-NEP-tah), had to face invasion by a mysterious group known as "the Sea Peoples," which may have included the Philistines mentioned in the Bible. That is not Merneptah's only connection with the Old Testament: he may have been the pharaoh from whom Moses secured the freedom of the Israelites, although some scholars suggest that it was Ramses. A succession of lesser pharaohs followed, a list that includes Tworse (TORE-say), one of the only ruling queens other than Hatshepsut.

In 1186 B.C., Setakht (set-OCT) established the Twentieth Dynasty, and was followed by Ramses III, who fought numerous campaigns against the Libyans and the Sea Peoples. Just as Ramses II had been the last of the great pharaohs, Ramses III was the last of the *semi*-great, and the end of his reign in about 1163 marked the beginning of the end of the New Kingdom.

Other forces were on the rise in Egyptian society. The army and the priests, the very elements which had previously upheld the pharaoh's power, now threatened it. Earlier pharaohs had created a standing army, but now that army was like an attack dog whose master could no longer control it. As for the priests and scribes, they had become corrupted by wealth and power. Some of them were so greedy they even participated in robbing the tombs. The pharaohs, once supreme rulers, found that they had become insignificant. When a priest named Herihor in effect declared himself king, the last pharaoh of the New Kingdom, Ramses XI, could do nothing to stop him.

Later periods in Egypt (1070 B.C.–A.D. 640)

There would be eleven more dynasties in Egypt, but its most important years were long past. The Twenty-First through the Twenty-Fourth dynasties made up what was called the Third Intermediate Period (1070–712 B.C.) During this time, the pharaohs took up residence in Tanis, far to the north, while the priests maintained control in Thebes. Eventually the latter became a separate nation, a *theocracy* (thee-OCK-ruh-see; a government controlled by religious leaders) called the Divine State of Amon. In the Twenty-Second Dynasty, Libyans began to take control.

In 712 B.C. the Kushites, who once had been ruled by the Egyptians, invaded and became the new rulers of the nation. This initiated what was called the Late Period (712–332 B.C.) In 672, the Assyrians drove out the Kushites and put in an Egyptian king named Necho (NEE-koh; r. 672–664 B.C.), who they thought would do their bidding. Instead, he ushered in the last phase of Egyptian independence for many centuries to come. It was during this final flowering of Egyptian culture that demotic script developed.

By the beginning of the Twenty-Seventh Dynasty, Egypt had come under the influence of the Persians. Just as the era of Necho was a mere shadow of Egypt's glory days, the dynasties from the Twenty-Eighth to the Thirtieth (404–343 B.C.), when Egyptians ruled one last time, were a mere shadow of Necho's time. In the Thirty-First and last dynasty, Persians once more took control.

Then in 332 B.C., troops under Alexander the Great conquered Egypt. They would set up the dynasty of the Ptolemies, of which Cleopatra would become the most famous. The Romans took Egypt out of her hands in 30 B.C.. It would remain part of the Roman Empire, and later of the Byzantine Empire that evolved from Rome, for nearly 700 years. Egypt came under the influence of the Coptic branch of Christianity, which still exists in parts of the country today.

The land would remain in Byzantine hands until A.D. 640, when it was conquered by Muslim troops from Arabia.

The legacy of Egypt

The Nile Delta adjoins the only part of modern Egypt where there is a significant population that does *not* live on the Nile: the Mediterranean coast. This area came to be populated only after Egypt fell to the Greeks. Its most notable city is Alexandria, named after Alexander the Great. In Alexandria, the Greeks developed one of the biggest and most notable libraries of the ancient world. By that time, Egypt had long been considered a center of learning. The Greeks and later the Romans greatly admired the achievements of the Egyptians, particularly in the areas of art and architecture. The influence of Egypt on their cultures—and through Greece and Rome, on the rest of the world—was wide-ranging. Among the debts civilization owes to the Egyptians are their invention of one of the world's first systems of writing, hieroglyphics. Along with their well-known triumphs in engineering and architecture, the Egyptians made developments in agriculture, in metallurgy (pronounced MEH-tuhl-ur-gee; the science of metals), and in glass-blowing. In fact, they were the first civilization to make and use glass.

The Egyptians gave the world the concept of government administration: bureaucracy, with its good and bad points, as well as the ideas of a census (a count of all the citizens) and a postal system; on the bad side, bureaucracy. Theirs was the first national government of any significance. They became the first to put in place a civil-service system, or a means of testing the qualifications of government workers. Later the Persian postal system would become much more notable, as would the Chinese civil-service system, but the seeds of these ideas were sowed in Egypt long before.

Before the time of the Hebrews, the Egyptians developed a monotheistic religion. Long before the Greeks, they had great poetic tales of national heroes. Long before the philosophical movements of latter-day Rome, the Egyptians had experienced disillusionment and loss of faith in the old ways of doing things. When modern people look at their ancient society, existing as it did on a narrow river valley in a desert thousands of years before Christ, it is hard for them not to be awed by the Egyptians.

Some people have claimed that the Egyptians did not develop their civilization on their own, but that they had help from alien visitors who built the pyramids for them. This sort of thinking goes against serious historical study. Like claims that the Greeks simply stole their whole civilization from Egypt, such thinking insults the achievements of a great ancient culture. Yet when one looks at the majesty of the pyramids, one can understand why people would find it hard to believe the Egyptians built them on their own.

As the old saying goes, "the pyramids laugh at time." For thousands of years they have stood, the most notable but far from the only symbol of Egypt's great achievements. From across the sands and across the years, they seem to call out to those who are curious and brave enough to explore their mysteries. It is a call that has been answered time and again.

Jean-Francois Champollion deciphered and translated the Rosetta Stone.
Library of Congress.

The continuing discovery of Egypt

Many secrets of Thebes disappeared forever when that city was destroyed in an earthquake in 27 B.C. Knowledge of Egypt as a whole began to fade away with the end of the Roman Empire, which brought on a period of decreased learning and scholarship. For many centuries, Europeans tended to think of Egypt merely as a former colony of Greece and Rome. As for the question of who built the pyramids, they had no idea, because they were completely ignorant of Cheops and Khafre.

During that period, Egypt was ruled first by the Arabs, who converted the country to Islam, and later by a group of Egyptian warlords. From the 1500s, the Ottoman (OTT-uh-

The Rosetta Stone. The stone was carved by priests as a thank you note to Ptolemy V. *Corbis-Bettmann. Reproduced by permission.*

mun) Empire of the Turks held the country, but by the late 1700s their power had begun to decline. Great Britain had begun to show an interest in Egypt, so in 1798 a French invasion force arrived with the aim of defeating British ambitions. The leader of this force was an officer named Napoleon Bonaparte, who would one day become his nation's greatest leader. In Africa he proved his ability as a military commander—and changed the world's understanding of Egypt.

Napoleon brought with him men to survey and map the area, and among them were many with an intense interest in learning more about Egypt's history. By that time, the western world was in the midst of a period of accelerated learning called the Enlightenment. People were curious as never before to learn about the past. Out of the French studies of the country came *Description of Egypt* (1813), the first significant modern book about ancient Egyptian civilization.

One of the most important developments that emerged from the French expedition was the discovery of what came to be known as the Rosetta (pronounced roe-ZEH-tah) Stone. A large rock discovered near the town of Rosetta on the Nile, it was covered with writing in what appeared to be three languages, but the only recognizable script was ancient Greek. A French archaeologist named Champollion (shom-POE-lee-ahn) set himself to figuring out what the strange writing said. Since the Greek portion made several mentions of Ptolemy, the Greek ruler of Egypt, Champollion looked for recurring symbols among the other two "languages."

As it would turn out, these were not two languages, but one language in two different forms: hieroglyphics and demotic. Eventually Champollion deciphered, or translated, the entire Rosetta Stone, which turned out to be a long thank-you note from a group of priests to Ptolemy V (r. 203–180 B.C.)

—who, like all the Ptolomies, spoke Greek rather than Egyptian. Through his tireless efforts, Champollion unlocked the secret of hieroglyphics and founded the branch of archaeology called *Egyptology*, the study of ancient Egypt.

After Champollion, by far the most important Egyptologist was Howard Carter, a British archaeologist who in 1922 discovered the tomb of the boy-king Tutankhamen. By that time, Egyptology had progressed to the point that people believed there were no more undiscovered pharaonic tombs. So far, it appeared that the robbers had gotten there long before the archaeologists. It seemed that the treasures of the kings' tombs were lost to history. Then Carter made his discovery.

After six hard years of searching, Carter finally discovered a hidden burial chamber in the Valley of the Kings. It contained all manner of archaeological treasures, including a gorgeous golden mask of "King Tut," as he came to be called. Because he had reigned such a short time, and because he had

Howard Carter examines coffin in Burial Chamber of King Tutankhamen's tomb. *Archive Photos. Reproduced by permission.*

followed the despised Akhenaton, Tut had been forgotten by history; but in the 1920s, he became one of the most famous pharaohs in all of Egyptian history. The King Tut exhibit went on tour, and the 1920s saw a growing interest in Egypt that affected the architecture and even the fashions of the day.

Egypt in modern times

During World War II (1939–1945), American and German forces first fought each other in North Africa. Britain had made a colony of Egypt after the defeat of the Ottoman Empire in World War I (1914–1918), and in October of 1941, British troops defeated the Germans at the Egyptian town of El-Alamein (pronounced el-ahl-uh-MAIN). It was to be one of the war's most important battles. The North African campaign involved an instrument of warfare that, had it existed in the time of the pharaohs, would have changed the future of Egypt: the tank. Only with tanks was it possible to invade Egypt across the great expanses of desert that protected it.

The pharaohs were long gone, but Egyptian leaders remained powerful figures in world history. The nation gained its independence after the war, and Gamal Abdel Nasser (1918–1970) came to power in 1954. Under Nasser, Egypt built the Aswan High Dam in what was once Upper Egypt. Completed in the 1960s, the dam harnessed the flow of the Nile for hydroelectric power, and provided irrigation for farmers in Egypt and Sudan, ending the pattern of seasonal flooding. It also created Lake Nasser, which spans the Egypt-Sudan border and covers the Second Cataract. In 1956, Nasser seized control of the Suez Canal, which had opened the way for a sea route from the Mediterranean to the Red Sea. Egypt closed the canal in 1967, after a war with Israel, and did not open it until 1975.

Nasser became the most important of all Arab leaders during his time, and his funeral in 1970 was the largest in history. It was a fitting tribute to the leader of the land once ruled by the pharaohs. Whereas Nasser built his career by waging war on Israel, his successor, Anwar Sadat (pronounced AHN-wahr suh-DOT, 1918–1981) reversed the trend. In 1978, he signed a historic treaty with Israel, which earned a joint Nobel Peace Prize for Sadat and Israeli leader Menachem Begin (pronounced men-AH-kem BAY-gin, 1913–). But Muslim radicals did not

Ancient Egypt at the Movies

During the 1950s, Hollywood produced a number of movies about the ancient world. Most of these films, called Biblical epics, were extremely expensive to make. Elaborate sets represented the cities of ancient Egypt, Judea, Greece, or Italy. In many cases the stories themselves were not very well written. A typical example was *Cleopatra* (1963), one of the most costly flops of all time, which *Videohound's Golden Movie Retriever* (Detroit: Visible Ink Press, 1999) describes as "a blimp-sized, multicolored sleeping tablet."

Director Cecil B. DeMille, who had made a version of *Cleopatra* in the 1930s, filmed the story of Moses as *The Ten Commandments* in 1923. In 1956 he remade *The Ten Commandments* in a version which proved to be one of the few Biblical epics that succeeded both artistically and commercially. The *Golden Movie Retriever* notes its "exceptional cast," including Charlton Heston as Moses and Yul Brynner as Pharaoh, and commented that the scene showing the parting of the Red Sea "rivals any modern special effects." The costumes, architecture, and other features of the movie make it highly educational as well as entertaining, though it does present the false impression that slave labor built the pyramids. The story of Moses, as well as that of Joseph, has been interpreted for young viewers in movies such as Disney's *The Prince of Egypt* (1998).

Moviemakers have often used ancient Egypt as a backdrop for fantasy. From *The Mummy* in 1932, a film for which actor Boris Karloff modeled his appearance on the actual mummy of Ramses III, to *The Mummy* in 1999, there have been plenty of horror films that make use of the fright inspired by the Egyptians' fascination with death. Less chilling, but plenty suspenseful, is *Raiders of the Lost Ark* (1981), which involves a brilliant plot concerning the whereabouts of the Israelite's Ark of the Covenant—in a tomb deep beneath the surface of the ancient Egyptian city of Tanis. Likewise *Stargate* (1994), a science-fiction movie that has little to do with the reality of ancient Egypt, provides an intriguing scenario regarding the identity of the sun god Ra. In the 1970s, there was even a popular Saturday morning children's show, *Isis,* about an archaeologist who could change into the ancient Egyptian goddess and perform superhero-like feats.

There have been at least seventy films that involve Egypt in some way or another. In addition, ancient Egypt has been celebrated in popular songs such as Steve Martin's comedy hit "King Tut" (1977) and the Bangles' "Walk Like an Egyptian" (1986).

The Washington Monument is an example of an obelisk.
Archive Photos. Reproduced by permission.

want peace with Israel, and one of them assassinated Sadat in 1981. President Hosni Mubarak (HAWS-nee moo-BAR-ek, 1928–) has continued Sadat's policy of better relations with Israel.

Egypt lives on

Meanwhile, through all the years and the changes in Egypt, the impact of its ancient culture lives on. One symbol of Egypt is as common as it is important: the domestic house cat, first tamed by the Egyptians, who worshiped the cat goddess Bastet. Egypt is a part of everyday language; terms such as *pharaoh, mummy, pyramid,* and *paper*—none of which is Egyptian in origin, but all of which describe Egyptian concepts—are household words.

Towns throughout America have their Shriners' organizations, clubs that contribute to the community by organizing charity events. The Shriners are associated with the Masons (also called Freemasons), a worldwide organization that claims a link with the masons who helped build the pyramids, though in fact it originated much later. Both the Shriners and, to a greater extent, the Masons make considerable use of images from ancient Egypt.

The towns of America reflect their Egyptian cultural heritage in their names. There is a Cairo, Illinois and a Cairo, Georgia. (Cairo, Egypt was founded in A.D. 642; that makes it a young city by Egyptian standards.) Much older is the name Alexandria, of which there is a famous town in Virginia, along with Alexandrias in four other states. Still older, of course, is the name Memphis. Memphis, Tennessee is the more famous city in the United States, though there is also a Memphis in Texas.

In the nation's capital, one can find a great example of an obelisk, the Washington Monument. Likewise the back of a dollar bill shows a pyramid with the all-seeing eye of God above it. Far from Washington, in a desert near a great river,

there is a splendid city with its own pyramid. But the river is the Colorado, not the Nile, and the city is Las Vegas, whose Luxor Hotel stands thirty stories tall. Completed in 1993 at a cost of $300 million, it is smaller than the Great Pyramid, but the Sphinx out front is larger than the original. The interior includes an Egyptian theme park complete with a small version of the Nile running through it.

The Luxor Las Vegas Hotel and Casino was built in the shape of a pyramid. Photograph by Neal Lauren. *Reuters/Corbis-Bettmann. Reproduced by permission.*

For More Information

Books

Balkwill, Richard. *Food & Feasts in Ancient Egypt*. South Melbourne, Australia: Macmillan Education, 1994.

David, Rosalee. *Growing Up in Ancient Egypt*. Illustrated by Angus MacBride. Mahwah, NJ: Troll Associates, 1994.

Diamond, Arthur. *Egypt, Gift of the Nile*. New York: Dillon, 1992.

Dijkstra, Henk. *History of the Ancient & Medieval World,* Volume 2: *Egypt and Mesopotamia.* New York: Marshall Cavendish, 1996, pp. 151–92.

Fisher, Leonard Everett. *The Gods and Goddesses of Ancient Egypt.* New York: Holiday House, 1997.

Harris, Nathaniel. *Everyday Life in Ancient Egypt.* New York: Franklin Watts, 1994.

Hart, George. *Ancient Egypt.* New York: Knopf, 1990.

James, T. G. H. *The Archaeology of Ancient Egypt.* Illustrated by Rosemonde Nairac. New York: Walck, 1973.

Krulik, Nancy. *Mysteries of Ancient Egypt.* Illustrated by Alfred Giuliani. New York: Scholastic, 1996.

Payne, Elizabeth Ann. *The Pharaohs of Ancient Egypt.* New York: Random House, 1992.

Perl, Lila. *Mummies, Tombs, and Treasures: Secrets of Ancient Egypt.* Drawings by Erika Weihs. New York: Clarion Books, 1987.

Putnam, James. *Pyramid.* New York: Knopf, 1994.

Steele, Philip. *I Wonder Why Pyramids Were Built: And Other Questions about Ancient Egypt.* London: Kingfisher, 1995.

Web Sites

"Ancient Egypt." *Exploring World Cultures.* http://eawc.evansville.edu/egpage.htm (February 14, 1999).

Ancient Egypt Webquest. http://users.massed.net/~mdurant/AncientEgyptWebquest.htm (February 22, 1999).

Egyptian Ministry of Tourism Presents Tour Egypt: Official Egypt Web Site on Egyptian Travel. http://interoz.com/egypt/index.htm (February 14, 1999).

"Kids Fun Page." *The Curse of the Pharaohs.* http://www.geocities.com/TheTropics/7210/kidsfun.htm (February 14, 1999).

Theban Mapping Project. http://www.kv5.com/html/home.html (February 22, 1999).

Mesopotamia

M esopotamia, often called "the Cradle of Civilization," was the birthplace of the world's first civilization, Sumer. Mesopotamia was home to some of the world's greatest civilizations as well—not only of Sumer and the related culture of Akkad but also of Babylonia and Assyria. From these countries came the world's first legal system, the Code of Hammurabi, and the first great tale in Western civilization, the Gilgamesh Epic. The cuneiform (pronounced cue-NAY-i-form) of Sumer was the first known form of writing and probably influenced Egyptian hieroglyphics. Israel felt the influence of Mesopotamia: Tales from the region provide the source for many of the great stories in the early chapters of the Bible, and later the Israelites would become captives of the Assyrians and Babylonians. From the mud of Sumerian huts to the stars mapped by the astronomers of Babylon, there were few aspects of ancient life not touched by the brilliant cultures of Mesopotamia.

Where to find Mesopotamia

The name *Mesopotamia* is Greek for "between rivers." On the eastern edge of this region, located in southwest Asia, is the

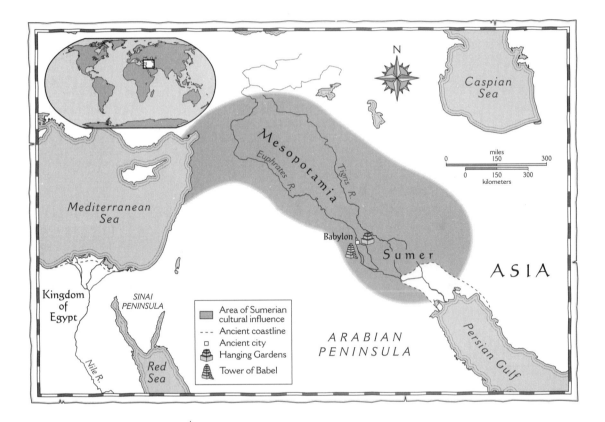

Map of Mesopotamia.

XNR Productions. The Gale Group.

Tigris (TIE-griss) River; to the west is the Euphrates (you-FRAY-tees). The rivers flow out of the mountains in southeastern Turkey and ultimately come together before emptying into the Persian Gulf. Today the whole of Mesopotamia lies inside the nation of Iraq (ear-OCK), which has continued to be a focal point for the world's attention. It is a dry, parched land, but once its soil was so rich that historians refer to Mesopotamia as part of "The Fertile Crescent." The Fertile Crescent describes a strip of land that included the Nile Valley in Egypt as well as Mesopotamia. The region is so named because a line in the shape of a *crescent,* or half-moon, would join the two regions. Today the area surrounding Mesopotamia is called the Middle East.

Sumer (3500–2000 B.C.)

Even though historians tend to treat Egypt as the world's first major civilization, in fact civilization first developed in the region of Sumer (SOO-mur). No one knows quite when this happened: the first settlers could have arrived anywhere between 6000 and 4500 B.C.

This first group was the Ubaid (oo-BYE-ad) culture, which settled in the marshes of southern Mesopotamia—an area that remains marshy today. Historians know little about the Ubaidans, but they seem to have had a fairly sophisticated knowledge of *irrigation,* or methods of keeping crops watered. They also knew how to make pots of baked clay, and built their houses of reeds from the nearby marshes. At some point their area was invaded by *Semitic* (seh-MIT-ick) tribes from the southwest, in modern-day Saudi Arabia, but the two groups eventually became one through marriage.

By about 3500 B.C., the intermarriage between various groups produced the people known as the Sumerians. The Sumerians in turn established virtually all the essentials of civilization over the next 800 years.

An explosion of knowledge (3500–2750 B.C.)

The Sumerians developed the plow, which could be drawn by an animal such as an ox. Before that time, people had planted and tended crops with simple handheld tools such as hoes. The plow made it possible to cultivate (plant crops on) a much larger area of ground in a much shorter period of time. This invention in turn made possible a well-developed agricultural economy, one of the main ingredients of civilization. Beginning from this basis in farming, Sumerian society emerged.

Thanks to the plow, the Sumerians progressed beyond *subsistence agriculture,* or farming just to produce enough food to stay alive. As a result, there came to be a *division of labor,* meaning that not everybody had to do the same work for survival—another key ingredient of civilization. Some people, for instance, became *craftsmen,* or skilled workers who produced items according to their specialty. A craftsman might fashion clay pottery, for instance, or he might be a *brick mason* who built houses. In Egypt, masons built with stone, but Mesopotamia had very little rock. It also lacked other *natural resources* such as metals and timber; therefore, the people of Sumer became involved in trade with people in other parts of the Middle East.

Words to Know: Mesopotamia

Accounting: Maintaining a record of income and expenses. *Accountants* perform this function for businesses.

Assimilate: To be mixed into a larger group of people.

Astrology: The study of the stars and planets in the belief that their movement has an effect on personal events.

Astronomy: The scientific study of the stars and other heavenly bodies, and their movement in the sky.

Barter: Exchange of one item for another.

Cabinet: A group of key advisors to a leader.

Campaign: A military operation conducted with the aim of conquering an area.

Centralized government: Government that is strongly controlled, usually by leaders in a capital city.

Chariot: A small and highly mobile open-air wagon drawn by horses.

City-states: A city that is also a type of self-contained country.

Craftsmen: Skilled workers who produce items according to their specialty.

Crescent: The shape of a partial or half-moon.

Cultivate: To plant and tend crops on an area of ground.

Cuneiform: A type of wedge-shaped writing used in Mesopotamia.

Deity: A god.

Deportation: Forced removal of a person or a group of people.

Divert: To change the course of something.

Division of labor: A situation in which different people in a group do different types of work, which enables the larger group to achieve more.

Drought: A period of time when there is not enough water in a given area.

Dynasty: A group of people, often but not always a family, who continue to hold a position of power over a period of time.

Empire: A large political unit that unites many groups of people, often over a wide territory.

Epic: A long poem that recounts the adventures of a legendary hero.

Excavation: Digging up something that is buried, as for instance, at an archaeological site.

Fortifications: Defensive walls.

Horoscopes: Astrological charts.

Infamous: Having a bad reputation.

Ingenious: Extremely clever.

Innovation: A new and usually better way of doing things.

Ironic: When something is intended to be one way but turns out to be quite different from what was intended; especially refers to the use of words to express the opposite of the words' meaning.

Irrigation: A method of keeping crops watered, often by redirecting water supplies.

Islam: A faith that arose in Arabia in the A.D. 600s, led by the prophet Muhammad (A.D. 570?–632.)

Legitimacy: The right of a ruler to hold power.

Lingua franca: A common language by which people of two different native languages can communicate.

Lunar: Related to the Moon.

Mason or brick mason: A type of craftsman who builds with brick.

Middle class: A group in between the rich and the poor, or between the rich and the working class.

Millennium: A period of a thousand years.

Muslim: A believer in Islam.

Mutual: Shared or common between two people or things.

Natural resources: Materials from nature, such as trees or minerals, that are useful to the operation of business or a society.

Neo-: New or renewed.

Nomadic: Wandering.

Phonograms, pictograms: Two types of written symbols. The first type which looks like the thing it represents; the second represents a specific syllable.

Polytheism: Worship of many gods.

Prevailing: Most common or general.

Procreation: Parenting children.

Prologue: An introduction to a written work.

Relief sculpture: A carved picture, distinguished from regular sculpture because it is two-dimensional.

Scribes: A small and very powerful group in ancient society who knew how to read and write.

Semitic: A term describing a number of groups in the Middle East, including the modern-day Arabs and Israelis.

Siege: A sustained military attack against a city.

Smelting: Refining a metal, such as iron.

Standing army: A full-time, professional army.

Stele (or stela): A large stone pillar, usually inscribed with a message commemorating a specific event.

Subsistence agriculture: Farming in which the farmers produce just enough food to stay alive, without any surplus to sell.

Tell: A small mound of earth heaped over layers of ruins.

Theocracy: A government controlled by religious leaders.

Thwart: To frustrate or stop somebody from doing something.

Trade: The exchange of goods for units of value (money, gold, or other goods) between two individuals or two countries.

Usurp: To seize power.

Vassal: A ruler who is subject to another ruler.

Western: A term referring to the cultures and civilizations influenced by ancient Greece and Rome.

Working class: A group between the middle class and the poor, who typically earn a living with their hands rather than behind a desk.

Zodiac: An imaginary circle in the sky, divided into twelve constellations or astrological "signs" such as Libra.

**Ziggurat at Ur, an example
of ancient Sumerian
architecture.**
The Library of Congress.

The term *trade* refers to the exchange of goods for units of value (money, for instance, or gold) between two individuals or two countries. A *tradesman* is a merchant or shop-owner, another class of people that developed in Sumer as business-people sold various goods. In those days, trade really meant trading, since there was not yet such a thing as money in the form of coins. Instead, people might *barter* (exchange) a bronze tool for grain with which to make bread or another Sumerian specialty, beer.

With such a highly organized society, it is not surprising that the Sumerians established the world's first cities, or rather *city-states,* self-contained political units that were not part of a larger nation. These apparently resulted from people's mutual need to protect themselves from outside invasion. Of the dozen Sumerian city-states, the two most important were Ur and Uruk (OO-rook). By modern standards, these city-states were not large: Uruk, for instance, took up less than half a square mile and contained only a few thousand people.

At the center of the Sumerian city-state of the 3000s B.C. was what one might describe as history's first skyscrapers: a ziggurat (ZIG-uh-raht). These were temple towers as tall as seven stories, each story of which was smaller than the one below. Thus they may have influenced the pyramids of Egypt, which began to appear about nine hundred years after the beginnings of Sumerian civilization: indeed, the first pyramid, the Step Pyramid of Zoser, resembled a ziggurat. The infamous Tower of Babel in the Bible's Book of Genesis was most likely a ziggurat; and in coming centuries, successive Mesopotamian cultures would perfect the ziggurat form.

Ziggurats may have been at the physical center of Sumerian life, but the spiritual center lay with the gods, and with the political system. In most cultures, ancient and modern, the prevailing religious beliefs (or the lack of them) are closely linked with the form of government; and initially in Sumer, there was little distinction between the two. At the highest level in Sumerian society was the *ensi,* a priest who also served as leader and claimed to rule under the direction of the gods. Sumer developed a sophisticated religion whose four primary gods and goddesses supervised various aspects of creation. Second-rung deities such as Inanna (ee-NAH-nuh), the goddess of love and procreation (that is, having children), were typically linked with the notion of sustaining life.

Yet there was something in Sumer more splendid than its religion, its government, its cities, or its ziggurats. It was perhaps their most wonderful contribution to civilization: writing.

Cuneiform

Without writing, the only way to communicate ideas is verbally, which means that a thought can only travel so far. Only through writing can people convey complex thoughts and pass on detailed information, across time and space.

Even before the Egyptians first used hieroglyphics, the Sumerians of the fourth millennium B.C. produced the first form of written language, *cuneiform* (cue-NAY-i-form). The name cuneiform is Latin for "wedge-shaped." Indeed its symbols do look like wedges placed at various angles to one another.

Cuneiform may have influenced the development of hieroglyphics, with which it shared many similarities. As with

A clay tablet covered with cuneiform writing. The tablet was found in Ebla, Syria. *Archive Photos. Reproduced by permission.*

hieroglyphics, the earliest cuneiform symbols were *pictograms,* or pictures of the thing they represented: a picture of a man, for instance, for "man." Some of these pictograms came to stand for other concepts related to the function of the object depicted. Thus a foot could symbolize walking, or symbols could be joined to produce a new idea. Hence the combination of pictograms for *mouth* and *water* meant *drink*. Eventually the Sumerians developed *phonograms,* symbols that stood for sounds or syllables. This made writing much easier. Before the introduction of phonograms, cuneiform had as many as *2,000* symbols. Later, the number was reduced to 600—which is still a large number compared to the twenty-six letters of the English alphabet.

The Sumerians used cuneiform to record the great Gilgamesh Epic (GIL-guh-mesh). They also developed a much more practical use for cuneiform: keeping track of money. In any business situation, it is important to maintain a record of what one spends and what one receives. This is called *account-*

ing. People keep accounts on a personal level today (for example, by balancing a checkbook). Businesses do it on an even bigger scale, often employing full-time accountants for the task.

Using a sharp stick called a *stylus,* a Sumerian accountant would make an impression in a soft clay tablet, recording the details of who paid what to whom. Later the tablet would be baked and would harden, a permanent record of a business transaction. Thousands and thousands of years later, when archaeologists examined the ruins of Sumer, some of the first evidence of Sumerian culture that they found were what people today would call receipts!

The Early Dynastic Period (2750—2300 B.C.)

Eventually the ensi became greedy and began to oppress the people, who looked to powerful landowners for leadership. A man who owned a great deal of property was called a *lugal,* which literally meant "great man," and in time the lugals became like kings. Thus the *theocracy* (thee-OCK-ruh-see; government controlled by religious leaders) was replaced by a *monarchy,* or rule by a king. Whereas the ensi were priests who became political leaders, the lugals were kings who became religious leaders as well. In order for a Sumerian ruler to have *legitimacy,* or the right to rule, he needed to have the approval of the gods: therefore it was necessary to combine political and religious functions.

Historians refer to this period of some four centuries as the Early Dynastic Period, "dynastic" (die-NASS-tick) being a form of *dynasty.* The dynasties of Sumer were different from the dynasties of Egypt, established around the same time: the Sumerian dynasties were much shorter and less powerful, and they spent much of their time at war with one another.

Sumer, at least during this phase, would never become a single country in the way that Egypt was—not until it was invaded by a brilliant conqueror from a neighboring land. Later Greece would have a similar experience, and as in Sumer, the city-states of Greece would not unite until brought together by Alexander the Great from neighboring Macedonia. Sumer's Alexander was named Sargon I. He came from the nation of Akkad (AH-kahd) in the north.

The Akkadian Empire (2300–2150 B.C.)

The Akkadians had come to Mesopotamia with the Semitic tribes who had migrated to the region centuries before. Their culture was similar to that of the Sumerians. When Sargon (SAHR-gahn; c. 2334–2279 B.C.) conquered Sumer, he was not so much destroying a civilization as he was unifying two related peoples.

Sargon was not born to royalty; he came from among the people, the son of a single mother who had been forced to give him away when he was an infant. Raised by a fruit grower, he ultimately rose to power, but he never forgot his roots. He worked hard to promote the interests of the *working class* and the growing *middle class* by keeping taxes low and encouraging trade.

Around 2300 B.C., he conquered the city-states of Sumer and united them under one system, perhaps the first *empire* in history. Under Akkadian rule, cuneiform developed further. The Akkadians began to produce works of literature. Sargon also moved the government of Sumer further away from a theocracy: now the word *ensi* came to mean not a representative of a god but a representative of a king.

Despite Sargon's achievements, his successors had a hard time holding on to power. His grandson Naram-Sin (NAR-ahm SIN) declared himself "The Lord of the Four Quarters," which was another way of saying "king of the world," but in fact he faced rebellions among the Sumerians. Later Akkadian kings also had to deal with an uncivilized group called the Gutians (GOO-tee-uhns), who invaded from the mountains to the north in about 2150 B.C.

Renewal in Ur (2150–2000 B.C.)

After a period of unrest, in about 2150 B.C. a group of lugals in the city-state of Ur reestablished order. Unlike Sargon, they favored a highly *centralized* government, with the other cities under the control of authorities in Ur. The economy, which had been allowed to run free under the Akkadians, was now placed under state control, with priests in charge. Despite the harsh nature of this system, it restored order and allowed for a renewal of Sumerian culture.

The Garden, The Flood, and The Tower

"Now the Lord God had planted a garden in the east, in Eden." So says the Book of Genesis, Chapter 2. The text later goes on to identify the location of that famous Garden, home of Adam and Eve, as a place where four rivers began. The locations of the first two rivers, the Pishon and the Gihon, are unknown; but the other two are much more familiar: the Tigris and the Euphrates.

This is the first of many places in the Bible that make some reference to Mesopotamia. Besides the Garden of Eden, for instance, at least two other links with Mesopotamia appear in the first few chapters of Genesis. In the Great Flood described in Genesis, Chapter 7, God destroyed all living creatures except Noah, his family, and the creatures in the ark (or boat) with them. This story has parallels in Sumerian legend, most notably in the Gilgamesh Epic.

The next major event after Noah and before Abraham is the building of the Tower of Babel. According to Genesis 11:1-9, everyone on Earth spoke a common language up to that time. The people joined together and decided to build a

Tower of Babel, engraving. *Archive Photos. Reproduced by permission.*

tower to Heaven. This was a symbol of defiance to God, who caused everyone to start speaking different languages—which separated them and halted work on the tower. Many scholars believe that the Tower of Babel story describes a ziggurat built by Nebuchadnezzar. However, others argue that the Book of Genesis was written much earlier. In any case, all sides agree that Babel is another name for Babylon.

This period is known as the Third Dynasty. In about 2000 B.C., however, this final chapter of Sumer's history came to an end when Mesopotamia was overrun by a group from the west called the Amorites (AM-uh-rites.) The Amorites would in turn establish the next great Mesopotamian civilization in Babylon.

The Hanging Gardens of Babylon, one of the Seven Wonders of the Ancient World. *Archive Photos. Reproduced by permission.*

Babylonia (3000–539 B.C.)

One of the most brilliant cities of the ancient world was Babylon (BAB-uh-lahn). In its legal codes and its sciences, it stood at the furthest advances of human understanding. Its Hanging Gardens were among the Seven Wonders of the Ancient World.

Founded by the Amorites, a previously *nomadic* (no-MAD-ick; wandering) people from Arabia, it existed as early as 3000 B.C. For nearly a thousand years, it remained under the control of Ur and later the Akkadians. But the invasion of Ur in 2000 B.C. was an indication that the Amorites were on the move, and in 1894 B.C., an Amorite chieftain named Sumu-abu (SOO-moo AH-boo) took over Babylon. A century after Sumu-abu would come the only truly great leader in early Babylonia—and one of the great figures of human history.

Hammurabi's reign (1792–1750 B.C.)

Hammurabi (hah-moo-ROB-ee) began ruling in 1792 B.C. and quickly distinguished himself as a leader of great power. He thwarted, or frustrated, the ambitions of a neighboring king to take over Isin (EE-zin), an important neighboring city, and over the next thirty years defeated the kings of all surrounding regions. Eventually the empire of Hammurabi stretched from Babylon, in the southern part of modern-day Iraq, all the way to the Mediterranean Sea far in the west. He also built many ziggurats and great fortifications (defensive walls) to protect his nation from foreign conquest. But the greatest achievement of Hammurabi was his legal code, or system of laws.

He was probably not the first leader to create laws, but Hammurabi's is certainly the oldest surviving code, and it continues to influence the law of modern times. The law was written on a stele (STEE-lee), a great stone pillar which bore at the top a carved picture (or a *relief sculpture*) of Hammurabi receiving the laws from Shamash (SHAH-mosh), the god of justice.

Stele depicting King Hammurabi dispensing Code of Laws. *Corbis. Reproduced by permission.*

Aspects of Hammurabi's code might not seem very fair to modern people. Its justice is built around the idea of "an eye for an eye," and its punishments relate to a person's social rank. Babylonian society was sharply divided according to classes—rich, middle class, and slaves. The rich, or free people, were by far the smallest (but also the most influential) group in society. Next came the common people or middle class, which were a somewhat larger but much less powerful force in Babylonia. At the bottom rung were the slaves, who were the most plentiful group and the lowest-ranking but who nonetheless enjoyed some rights.

The Code of Hammurabi clearly established more harsh penalties for a wrong done to a rich person than for one done to a slave, but it was a remarkable legal code because it offered *some* protection for the more unfortunate members of society [see sidebar "The Code of Hammurabi"]. Nor was Hammurabi's code the only great achievement of Babylonia, which made many advances in mathematics and science as well as law.

Mathematics, science, and religion

It might seem odd to group religion with mathematics and science, because to modern people they are usually separate. But to ancient peoples such as the Babylonians, these concepts were linked. Indeed, Babylonian achievements in astronomy, the scientific study of the stars' movements, resulted from their interest in *astrology*.

Astrology is the study of the position of stars and planets that, according to believers in astrology, have a direct effect on a person's everyday life. Like people of ancient times, modern people read *horoscopes,* or astrological charts, in hopes of finding out who they will marry, or whether they will get rich, or what other things fate has in store for them. Astrology was and is an unscientific belief system, more like a superstition than a science. Yet it makes use of scientific data or information, and therefore the Babylonians' astrological studies yielded some advances in learning.

Though they did not have telescopes, which are essential to the work of a modern-day astronomer, Babylonian astrologers charted the movements of the heavenly bodies they could see with the naked eye. Each of these had an association with a god. The Moon was Sin, a *deity* (DEE-ih-tee) first worshiped by the Sumerians; the Sun was Shamash, who drove across the sky in a fiery chariot; and so on all the way to Jupiter, which they equated with the supreme god Marduk (MAR-duke).

Marduk was primarily a Babylonian deity, but most of their gods originated in Sumer. Ishtar (ISH-tar), associated with Venus, seems to have come from the Sumerian goddess Inanna. The Greeks and later the Romans worshiped deities with similar roles—and with the same planetary associations. Thus, for instance, the Greek and Roman Apollo, the sun god, drove a chariot across the sky every day. As for the planets, today these are known by the Roman names of gods whose function was typically the same as their Babylonian counterpart: Jupiter the supreme god, Venus the goddess of love, and so on.

By the time of Nebuchadnezzar II centuries later, Babylonian astronomy had progressed a great deal. The Babylonians were the first to recognize that planets and stars were not the same thing, and they made detailed observations of the Earth's movement around the Sun. They figured that the Earth took 360 days to revolve around the Sun. Their calculation of a year's length was off by 5.25 days, but the number 360 made for easy division. From the Babylonians comes the idea of a circle as having 360 degrees, each degree of which is divided into sixty minutes, which in turn are divided into sixty seconds.

These terms are still used for measuring angles and portions of a circle—but of course minutes and seconds are also used for measuring time in a day, which is one of the most notable of all Babylonian contributions to modern life. The Babylonians also divided the period of the Earth's movement around the sun into twelve signs of the astrological *zodiac* (ZOE-dee-ack) and divided the year into twelve months. Theirs were *lunar* months, however, meaning that they were based on the twenty-eight day cycle of the Moon.

Therefore in some years they had to add a thirteenth month to make the calendar work out right. To divide the month, they used the four phases of the Moon as it goes from a new moon to a full moon and back again. A twenty-eight day month divided by four yields a seven-day week—yet another Babylonian contribution to everyday life.

The Babylonians divided the period of the Earth's movement around the Sun into twelve signs of the astrological zodiac.
Archive Photos. Reproduced by permission.

A series of invasions (1749–625 B.C.)

Although Hammurabi was a strong leader, it would be many centuries before another king of similar strength emerged in Babylonia. In fact, the nation entered a period of decline soon after his death, and the next thousand years would be characterized by a series of invasions from all sides.

Hammurabi's son fought off an attack from a nation called the Kassites (KASS-ites), who came from the mountains to the east. The Kassite invasion did not succeed then, but they would return. In the meantime, a group known as the Sealand people swept into Babylonia from the south, taking over cities and establishing their own dynasty. Historians know little about the people of the Sealand, who were much less civilized than the Babylonians and made little cultural impact, but they remained a threat to Babylonia for many years. In 1600 B.C., the Hittites came down from the northwest and *sacked,* or destroyed, Babylon. Strangely, however, they did not remain in the area, and soon after they departed, the Kassites seized control of Babylonia in 1595 B.C.

Though their name is not nearly as well-known as that of the Babylonians, the Kassites in fact established the longest-running of all dynasties in Babylonia. Apparently they respected the civilization established by the people they had subdued, and over the next four centuries Babylonian culture flourished. It was a time of considerable construction, as Babylon and other cities were rebuilt from the ruins of the Hittite invasion. During this period cuneiform went through a great deal of development, thanks to the establishment of schools to teach *scribes* the art of writing.

The Kassites encouraged trade, and maintained relations with leaders of other powerful lands. A record of their *diplomacy,* or negotiations with other leaders, exists in the form of the Amarna Letters found in the Egyptian city of Akhetaton. These letters show that the Kassite kings exchanged gifts with the pharaohs, who sent them gold.

Despite their achievements, the Kassites lost control of Babylon to the invading Assyrians in 1225 B.C. Other parts of Babylonia remained under Kassite rule until 1158, when a nation called the Elamites (EE-lum-ites) invaded from the south. During the Elamite period, the only pocket of Babylonian resistance was in the city of Isin, which established its own independent dynasty.

The most powerful of Isin's kings was Nebuchadnezzar I (neb-you-cud-NEZ-ur), who reigned from 1125 to 1104 B.C. and eventually drove out the Elamites. Once again, Babylonia experienced a brief period of renewal. For a time it appeared that Nebuchadnezzar would establish a new empire. He even took on the powerful Assyrians, and invaded their territory all the way to within twenty miles of their capital. But he never went any farther; nor did the Babylonians get to fulfill their hopes of once again becoming a powerful nation. Nonetheless, Nebuchadnezzar became a legendary figure who inspired hope. It is perhaps fitting that the most famous Babylonian leader other than Hammurabi would later be named Nebuchadnezzar as well.

But the time of Nebuchadnezzar II still lay many centuries in the future. Before Babylonia reemerged, it would fall into the hands of more invaders. Notable among these were the Aramaeans (air-uh-MAY-uns) from the region of modern-day Syria to the west. Like the Kassites, they came as invaders but adopted Babylonian culture—with a major twist. Their language, Aramaic (air-uh-MAY-ick), gradually replaced Babylonian as the common language of the people. Because of the great influence of Babylonian civilization, Aramaic spread throughout the region until it became the *lingua franca* (LING-wah FRANK-uh), or common language, for much of the known world [see sidebar, "Lingua Franca Spoken Here"].

During much of the period from the 800s to the 600s B.C., Babylonia faced an off-and-on threat from the Assyrians, who took over in the 700s and in 689 sacked Babylon. This second destruction of their capital city enraged the Babylonians, who revolted against Assyria in 652 B.C. The Assyrians put down the rebellion after four years, but the Babylonians remained defiant. Two decades later, they established a new dynasty that would be the most powerful since the days of Hammurabi.

The Chaldean (Neo-Babylonian) Empire (625–539 B.C.)

This last and perhaps brightest phase of Babylonian history is sometimes called the Neo-Babylonian Empire. The prefix *neo-* simply means "new" and is often used to describe the new version of something. As for *Chaldean* (kal-DEE-uhn), it was the name for a group of people from southern Babylonia. They may have had Aramaic roots, but they consciously identified themselves with Babylonia: in this way, they established their own legitimacy as rulers through a connection with the past glory of the empire.

Reconstruction of the Ishtar
Gate from Babylon.
*The Granger Collection.
Reproduced by permission.*

The founder of this new dynasty was Nabopolassar (nab-oh-poe-LASS-uhr), who reigned from 625 to 605 B.C. Coming out of the Chaldean homeland in the south, his troops swiftly overran all of Babylonia, but they did not stop there. He formed an alliance with the Medes (rhymes with "beads") to the east, and together they took on the Assyrians. In 612 B.C., the combined forces of the Chaldeans and Medes attacked the Assyrian capital of Nineveh (NIN-uh-vuh). For three months, they conducted a *siege,* a sustained military attack against a city, until Nineveh fell to them. In spite of this success, the Assyrians still held on and retreated to the west, where they reestablished themselves with the help of Egyptian forces. Nabopolassar once again defeated the Assyrians, and in 605 B.C. his son Nebuchadnezzar completed the victory with a battle against the Egyptians at Carchemish (KAR-kuh-mish.) After this, Babylonia claimed most of the Assyrian Empire.

Nabopolassar died while his son was away at Carchemish. Nebuchadnezzar returned in haste to Babylon, where he was crowned king. Under his long reign (605–562 B.C.), his city and his nation flourished as never before. Nebuchadnezzar ordered immense building projects in Babylon, including a new temple to Marduk, new palaces, improved and extended walls, and magnificent gateways such as the Ishtar Gate.

The blue-tiled Ishtar Gate opened onto the Processional Way, along which parades went during Babylonian festivals. The gate and the parade route are legendary, but Nebuchadnezzar's Babylon included even more famous structures. There was the seven-story ziggurat of Etemenanki, which some archaeologists associate with the biblical Tower of Babel [see sidebar, "The Garden, The Flood, and The Tower"]. And there were the Hanging Gardens of Babylon, one of the Seven Wonders of the Ancient World. According to legend, Nebuchadnezzar built them for his wife, a Mede, who missed the mountains of her homeland; because Babylon was flat, he created man-made mountains complete with lush vegetation.

Under Nebuchadnezzar's rule, Babylon became a vast city of some 2,500 acres, or about four square miles. But Nebuchadnezzar did not only build, he also conquered. In 597 B.C., he launched a campaign against the Israelites in Judah, and took many prisoners, including their king. He left another king in charge as a *vassal*—a ruler who is subject to another ruler. When this king rebelled, he returned and destroyed the Israelites' capital at Jerusalem in 586 B.C. Thus began the Babylonian Captivity, one of the most important events in the history of the Hebrews. Though Nebuchadnezzar conquered the Israelites, the Bible treats him not as an enemy, but as someone who did God's will. He is a major figure in the biblical Book of Daniel, which tells how a gifted young Hebrew interpreted Nebuchadnezzar's dreams concerning his own future and that of his nation.

Daniel prophesied that the empire established by Nebuchadnezzar would be short-lived, and indeed it was. After the king's death in 562 B.C., there followed a succession of weak kings. Nabonidus (nab-oh-NIDE-us), who ruled from 555 to 539 B.C., was not so much weak as he was strange. Instead of paying attention to affairs of state, he devoted himself to studying the Sumerian past and its religion. For many years of his reign, he lived in a desert oasis, apparently unconcerned that the Persians from the east were about to conquer Babylon.

During this time, he left his son Belshazzar (bel-SHAZZ-ur) on the throne, and Belshazzar became the unfortunate main character in a chilling story from the fifth chapter of the Book of Daniel. In Daniel's account, while feasting and drinking, the king was surprised to look up and see a finger—apparently unattached to a hand—writing four strange words of the wall of his palace: "MENE, MENE, TEKEL, UPARSIN" (min-AY, min-AY, tek-UHL, oo-PAR-sin.) Terrified by words he did not understand, he called for Daniel, and Daniel interpreted the message: "God has numbered the days of your reign and brought it to an end.... You have been weighed on the scales and found wanting.... Your kingdom [will be] divided and given to the Medes and the Persians." Daniel concludes the chapter by saying, "That very night

The Code of Hammurabi

A code is a system of laws. The legal codes of the various United States are so large that they take up many volumes. By contrast, the Code of Hammurabi consists of just 282 laws. It begins with a short prologue, or introduction, in which he states that the gods appointed him "to rise like the sun over the black-headed people, and to light up the land." It ends with an *epilogue,* or conclusion, that offers blessings for those who obey—and curses for those who do not. Strictly speaking, the Code of Hammurabi is not a true code of law because it added to already existing laws. Nonetheless, it is the oldest statement of laws known to the world, and it formed the basis of later legal systems.

There are aspects of Hammurabi's laws that may seem harsh to modern people, including its most famous lines: "If a man destroys the eye of another man, they shall destroy his eye. If he break a man's bone, they shall break his bone." Likewise it established different degrees of punishment depending on the status of the person harmed.

According to Laws 196 through 199, for instance, a rich man who put out the eye of another rich man, or broke another rich man's leg, would indeed be subjected to having his own eye put out or his leg broken. By contrast, if he did the same to a common man, he would merely have to pay a fee in silver; and if he poked out a slave's eye or killed the slave, he would have to pay half the slave's value—presumably to the slave's owner.

Yet the law was remarkable in that it established protections for many

Belshazzar ... was slain [killed], and Darius the Mede took over the kingdom" (Daniel 5:26-28, 30).

Assyria (2000–612 B.C.)

Third among Mesopotamia's great civilizations was that of Assyria, which arose earlier than Babylonia and ended sooner. But it would be a mistake to assume that these groups—Sumerians, Babylonians, and Assyrians—were the *only* peoples of Mesopotamia. There were of course the Aramaeans, whose one contribution to the culture of the area, their language, was exceedingly important. There were the

Hammurabi, bas-relief stone carving.
The Library of Congress.

members of society, particularly "the widow and the orphan," who might not otherwise be protected. It also gave women much greater rights than was often the case in the ancient world, allowing them to divorce, own property, and conduct business. Hammurabi's laws even established rights for prostitutes.

Among the issues dealt with in the Code of Hammurabi are personal property, real estate, business, trade, agriculture, marriage, inheritances, adoption, contracts, and leases. Other important legal codes of the ancient world, all of which would have an impact on modern law, are the laws established by the Hebrew prophet Moses and the Roman emperor Justinian.

other groups that menaced Babylonia, including the Hittites and the Persians. Also there were the peoples at the fringe of Mesopotamia, who either threatened or were threatened by the Babylonians and Assyrians. Principal among these were the Israelites, who became captives of both nations.

Finally, there were the smaller groups of earlier times in Mesopotamia, who ultimately became part of larger cultures. Among these were the Akkadians, who became so completely tied to Sumerian culture that it is impossible to talk about the one without the other; and there were city-states such as Mari and Isin, ultimately absorbed in Sumer and Babylonia respectively. There were also the Hurrians, who entered the region in about 2000 B.C. and established the kingdom of

Mitanni (mi-TAHN-ee), which flourished briefly between 1500 and 1300 B.C. Caught between the powerful Hittites to the north and the even more powerful Assyrians to the south, Mitanni survived by making an alliance with Egypt; but eventually the Egyptians lost interest in this relationship, and courted favor with the Assyrians. That was the end of Mitanni, whose two threatening neighbors devoured it.

Despite the many names and the many cultures, however, there remained three primary Mesopotamian groups. But since the Sumerians disappeared from the scene much earlier, Mesoptamian history between about 1800 and 600 B.C. can be characterized as a great competition between two cultures, Babylonia to the south and Assyria to the north. Both had great capital cities along the rivers of Mesopotamia: Babylon on the Euphrates and Nineveh on the Tigris. Both grew out of Amorite groups who absorbed the Sumer-Akkad civilization, and they were similar in language, religion, and other cultural aspects. Perhaps because they were so similar in some ways, they were almost always in conflict, like two family members who cannot resolve their differences.

This pattern has repeated itself throughout history, from ancient times to the modern world. As ancient history is full of conflicts between related peoples, the twentieth century has been full of wars and conflicts between neighboring lands. Africa has been subject to countless struggles among and within nations of similar heritage. The countries that broke off from the nation of Yugoslavia entered a period of incredible struggle following the end of Communism there in 1992. Greece and Turkey have often been at odds with one another in the nineteenth and twentieth centuries, just as peoples of those two nations fought in the Trojan War more than 3,000 years before. The two greatest conflicts in history, World War I (1914-1918) and World War II (1939–1945) involved, among other issues, an age-old rivalry between Germany and France.

In some ways, the Assyrians and Babylonians can be compared with the German and French nations. Like the French, the Babylonians were noted for their splendid culture, which excited both the admiration and the scorn of other countries, who often tended to see them as people devoted to pleasure and high living. And like the Germans, the Assyrians were known for their talent at making war. For much of the first half of the twentieth century, Germany had an ambition of ruling the world, and it developed one of the most powerful military forces ever known. Similarly, Assyria wanted to rule the known world, and it created an army that terrorized many nations. This is not an entirely accurate comparison, of course, because Germany has produced all manner of cultural achievements in the arts and philosophy. Assyria is likewise remembered for its brilliant architecture. But the greatest talent of the Assyrians was the art of warfare.

Old Assyria (2000–1363 B.C.)

Assyria originated from three city-states: Nineveh, Arbela, and Ashur (AH-shoor). The latter, from which the Assyrians took their name, was also the name of their chief deity. Like the Egyptian Ra and the Babylonian Shamash, Ashur was a sun god. Aspects of his character say much about ancient Assyria: he was not a merciful god, but delighted in war, and took special pleasure in the execution of prisoners.

Settled by Amorites in about 2000 B.C., the region experienced its first military triumphs under Shamshi-Adad I (SHAHM-shee AH-dahd), who ruled from 1813 to 1781 B.C. Though other civilizations of about the same time can be described as empires, or large countries that united many groups of people, Shamshi-Adad's was perhaps the first true empire because he established a centralized and highly organized state to rule the conquered nations. For a brief time under his rule, he controlled everything from Babylonia in the southeast to the Mediterranean in the west.

But Shamshi-Adad's son lost his empire to Hammurabi of Babylon in 1760 B.C. It would be many years before Assyria reemerged. In the meantime, it was ruled by Mitanni, then a great power in the region. From the Hittites, the warriors of Mitanni had learned about using *chariots,* small and highly mobile open-air wagons drawn by horses, in warfare. Chariots might be called the tanks of their day, but with their speed they can also be compared with fighter planes. When the Assyrians learned about chariot warfare, they gained a valuable weapon. By 1363, the Assyrian ruler Ashur-uballit I (AH-sure-oo-BAH-lit) had driven out the armies of Mitanni and begun building a new empire.

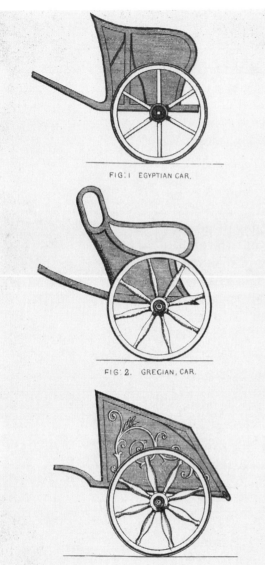

FIG. 1 EGYPTIAN CAR.

FIG. 2. GRECIAN, CAR.

FIG. 3. ROMAN CAR

Examples of war chariots. Top to bottom: Egyptian, Greek, and Roman.
Archive Photos. Reproduced by permission.

Middle Assyria (1363–934 B.C.)

Because Assyria as such had not emerged as a nation in the time of Shamshi-Adad, Ashur-uballit (reigned 1363–1328 B.C.) can be called the founder of the first Assyrian empire. He conquered Mittani and waged war against Babylonia.

Tukulti-Ninurta I (too-COOL-tee ni-NOOR-tah), who reigned from 1243 to 1207 B.C., sacked Babylon in 1225. He also started a practice that would be common among Assyrian conquerors to follow, the *deportation* or forced removal of defeated peoples. The deportees were relocated to another part of the empire, the idea being that they could not cause as much trouble to the rulers if they were removed from their homeland.

Once again, however, the period of Assyrian power did not last long. Tukulti-Ninurta's son led a revolt against him, and *usurped* (you-SURPD) or seized the throne. For the next few years, the area was ravaged by a variety of conquering peoples, most notably the Phrygians from what is now Turkey, as well as the Sea Peoples, who also threatened Egypt.

The next great Assyrian king was Tiglath-Pileser I (tig-LAHTH puh-LAY-zur). During his reign, from 1104 to 1076 B.C., he fought a seemingly endless series of wars against the Phrygians, Aramaeans, and Babylonians. At one point he reached the Mediterranean, where he washed his weapons in the water as a way of symbolically saying that his conquests were through. Assyria during this time developed the uses of chariot warfare and iron *smelting* (another Hittite contribution), and borrowed heavily from Babylonian culture in areas that ranged from literature to religion to its system of weights and measures. Indeed, much of Assyrian culture throughout its history was adapted from Babylonian roots.

After Tiglath-Pileser, the pattern of previous years continued as Assyria lost the gains made under his rule. For about a century, Aramaeans dominated, but by 934 B.C. the Assyrians were on the move again.

The Neo-Assyrian Empire (934–612 B.C.)

A series of kings from 934 B.C. onward began conquering territory for Assyria. During this time, they perfected their system of warfare, using chariots and cavalry units, deporting conquered peoples, and placing local areas under the rule of Assyrian governors. In 883 B.C., Ashurnasirpal II (AH-sure-nah-ZEER-pall) established what historians call the Neo-Assyrian Empire, and under his rule (883-859 B.C.), the Assyrian armies developed a particularly effective strategy for warfare.

This *innovation,* or new idea, had nothing to do with the actual fighting, but concerned a matter of equal importance to armies: supplying the troops. An old saying goes "An army travels on its stomach," meaning that men cannot fight if they have not been fed. Ashurnasirpal established local supply houses throughout the empire, where the Assyrians stored grain and other items with which to feed soldiers. This made it possible to move farther and to conquer more lands.

Ashurnasirpal was a great and ruthless leader who, in addition to his conquests and deportations of subject peoples, built many palaces and a capital city, Calah (cuh-LAHK) on the ruins of an old city called Nimrud (nim-ROOD). The next kings fought a series of wars, but the Assyrians' power declined while other nations, including the Babylonians and Aramaeans, had victories at their expense. During this time, Aramaic emerged as the language of the Assyrian people, and indeed the Aramaeans began to have an increasingly dominant role in the life of the empire. Ironically, this was a result of what had seemed an ingenious plan when it originated: the relocation of conquered peoples.

Another powerful force threatening Assyria was Urartu (oo-RAR-too) to the north, but the next great Assyrian ruler, Tiglath–Pileser III (r. 745–727 B.C.), dealt with the Urartians. In another military *campaign,* he drove as far southwest as the Sinai

The Bull guardian from the Palace of Ashurnasirpal II. The winged bull was often seen in Assyrian art.
The Granger Collection (New York). Reproduced by permission.

Desert, on the borders of Egypt. For a time, he tried to maintain good relations with the Babylonians, but he became suspicious of the Chaldeans' desire to rule the area, so he invaded and set himself up as king of both nations.

Surprisingly, given the record of conquest the Assyrians had already established, it was only under Tiglath-Pileser that they set up a *standing army*, or a full-time military. His successor was Sargon II (r. 721–705 B.C.), who carried on the work of conquering the world and reestablished Assyrian rule over Babylonia when the Babylonians made a bid to regain power. He also conquered Israel in 721 B.C., and repeating a familiar pattern, he carried off most of its people. This group became *assimilated*, or mixed, into the Assyrian Empire, and later became legendary as the "Ten Lost Tribes of Israel."

Sargon built himself a new capital, Dur-Sharrukin (door-shah-ROO-kin), whose name means "Fort Sargon." His palace there was a magnificent structure, which had on its gateway a pair of winged bulls that were characteristic of Assyrian art forms. But as in the case of the Egyptian pharaoh Akhenaton's capital at Akhetaton, his successor and son, Sennacherib (sin-ACK-uh-rib; r. 704—681 B.C.) later abandoned the city in favor of Nineveh. During a military campaign, Sargon was ambushed and killed, an event that deeply upset the Assyrians because it seemed like a bad sign from Ashur. Indeed, Assyria's days were numbered.

The Assyrian art of warfare had evolved further, with military roads and supply lines—including a military postal system for communications between generals—that were the envy of competing nations. Sennacherib also launched the first Assyrian navy. As was always the case, he could only maintain power through nearly constant warfare, and the threat from Babylonia became more and more severe. Still maintaining control over the other nation, he had set his son up as ruler over

Babylonia. But the Chaldeans joined forces with the Elamites and killed the son. Sennacherib, filled with rage, marched his troops into Babylon in 689 B.C., and sacked the capital city.

The Assyrians had sacked Babylon before, of course, but this time it was different. For one thing, they destroyed the city as they never had previously, even diverting (changing the course of) the Euphrates so that it flooded Babylon. In the long run, this so angered the Babylonians that it led to the rise of the Chaldean Empire under Nabopolassar sixty years later. Even in the short run, however, it proved a bad move, because the Assyrian people themselves were almost as upset over the destruction as the Babylonians. They may have been at war with Babylonia on a regular basis, but they still shared many things in common with the Babylonians, including much of their religion, and they considered the sacking of Babylon an offense to Marduk and the other gods.

Therefore Sennacherib's son, Esarhaddon (ee-sar-HAD-duhn), who ruled from 681 to 668 B.C., tried to improve relations with the Babylonians by rebuilding temples to Marduk and other parts of their capital city. He also waged war with Egypt, capturing the city of Memphis and setting up Necho as a vassal king. At this point, the Assyrian Empire reached its height in terms of the territory it controlled, all the way from the Persian Gulf in the east to the Nile Delta in the west, and from the mountains of Asia Minor to the deserts of Arabia.

But usually when something reaches its peak—whether it be an empire, a business, or even a person's career—it is most often past its prime, because that high point is usually a result of work that was put in before. After Sennacherib, the decline of the Neo-Assyrian Empire was swift, though there remained one last great ruler. This was Ashurbanipal (AH-sure-bah-NEE-pal), Sennacherib's son, who ruled from 669 to 627 B.C.

Sennacherib had made Ashurbanipal ruler over Assyria and his brother Shamash-shuma-ukin (SHAH-mosh shoo-MAH oo-kin) king of Babylonia. Shamash-shuma-ukin was the older of the two, and he probably did not care for the fact that his brother had the more powerful position. In 652 B.C., he led a revolt against Assyria. Ashurbanipal managed to subdue the Babylonian revolt in 648, and according to legend, Shamash-shuma-ukin committed suicide by burning down his palace with himself and his wives in it rather than surrender to his brother.

The Epic of Gilgamesh

An *epic* is a long poem that recounts the adventures of a legendary hero. Often, but not always, it involves a long journey, the most famous example being Homer's *Odyssey*. Usually the hero of an epic grows, becoming wiser or better than he was when he began, as is again the case with Odysseus.

The Gilgamesh Epic, too, involves a journey of growth. At the beginning of the story King Gilgamesh, apparently based on a real king in the Sumerian city of Uruk, treats his people so badly that they beg the gods to get rid of him. The gods respond by sending Enkidu (in-KEE-doo) to wrestle with him, but Gilgamesh wins—and the two become the closest of friends. Together they set out in search of the giant Humbaba (hoom-BAH-buh), who guards a nearby forest under the direction of the god Enlil (in-LEEL). They kill Humbaba, and on their way back to Uruk, they meet the goddess Ishtar. In spite of her beauty, Gilgamesh resists her charms, and that is the beginning of his troubles.

The scorned Ishtar goes to the chief god Anu (ah-NOO), who sends the Bull of Heaven against Gilgamesh and his kingdom. As a result of this curse, Uruk is subjected to seven years of *drought*—that is, a period of time when there is not enough water. Gilgamesh has already been changed by his friendship with Enkidu, and he is so upset by the wrong done to his people that he kills the Bull. That night, he learns in a dream that the gods will repay him either by killing him or Enkidu.

As it turns out, they kill his friend, and Gilgamesh is overwhelmed with grief. Wanting to bring Enkidu back from the dead, he goes in search of someone who can give him the secret to eternal life. That someone is a true survivor, Utnapishtim (oot-nah-PISH-tim), who lived through a great flood that destroyed most of the

Despite the fact that Ashurbanipal was a fighting man, like most other Assyrian rulers before him, he was also a man of culture. In those days, when scribes were the primary bearers of knowledge, illiteracy was common, even among kings. Ashurbanipal distinguished himself not only by his ability to read and write, but also by his contributions to learning. Under his direction, Assyrian scribes put together the first true library. The final version of the Gilgamesh Epic, Mesopotamia's greatest contribution to world literature, emerged during his reign.

Gilgamesh, from alabaster sculpture found in Khorsabad. *Corbis-Bettmann. Reproduced by permission.*

population long before. Utnapishtim gives him a branch from a plant that is said to restore life, and Gilgamesh heads for home. But on the way he stops for a swim, and while he is in the water, a snake steals the life-giving branch. In the end, Gilgamesh is forced to realize that no man can live forever.

Though it originated in Sumer as early as 2000 B.C., the Gilgamesh Epic was handed down by various Mesopotamian peoples, including the Babylonians and the Assyrians. The version prepared by scribes in the library of the Assyrian emperor Ashurbanipal (r. 669–626 B.C.) is the best known. But the story was lost for many centuries and not rediscovered by archaeologists until the A.D. 1800s.

There are several parallels between the Gilgamesh Epic and the Bible, most notably in its mention of a great flood that may be the same one described in the Book of Genesis. Likewise the branch offered to Gilgamesh by Utnapishtim resembles the Tree of Life in the Garden of Eden; and as with Adam and Eve, Gilgamesh ends up being tricked by a snake.

Assyrian art forms, particularly relief sculptures of great winged lions and other creatures, reached their height during this time as well.

Ashurbanipal's empire did not outlast him by a long time. Just fifteen years after his death, in 612 B.C., a combined force of Babylonians and Medes completely destroyed Nineveh. Assyrian rulers struggled to maintain a weak grip on power, aided by their allies in Egypt, but with the destruction of its capital city, the Assyrian Empire had come to an end.

Mesopotamia in modern times

Babylonia and Assyria fell first to the Persians and later to the Greeks under Alexander. Still later, Mesopotamia briefly became a part of the Roman Empire. In the A.D. 600s, like much of the Middle East, it fell to the conquering Muslims and flourished again as a part of their empire. The Muslims gave the area its religion, Islam, which is the faith of modern Mesopotamia. Again like most of the Middle East, it came under the rule of the Turkish or Ottoman Empire for many centuries, which only ended with the defeat of Turkey in World War I. Britain then took over, and for a time they revived the old name of the region.

In 1932, Mesopotamia achieved independence as Iraq. Kings ruled the country until 1958, when a revolution led by the military overthrew the monarchy. The Baath (buh-OTH) Party gained control in 1968, and in 1979 the Baath leader Saddam Hussein (suh-DOM hoo-SAYN; 1937–) assumed control. Meanwhile modern Syria, the land of the Aramaeans in ancient times, also came under the leadership of its own Baath Party, which like its counterpart in Iraq favored unity among Arab nations against their ancient enemy, Israel. But this was not the only theme from ancient times that was repeated: despite their similarities, the governments of Syria and Iraq remained opposed to one another. In 1980, Iraq went to war against another enemy from times past, Iran (ee-RAHN), formerly Persia. The Iran-Iraq war lasted for eight years, claimed more lives than any conflict since World War II, and did not result in a clear victory for either side.

On August 2, 1990, Saddam's troops swept into the oil-rich nation of Kuwait (coo-ATE) to the south. Not only did they slaughter many people, but with his hold on the combined oil fields of Iraq and Kuwait, Saddam threatened to bring the world to its knees. The United Nations, a world organization established for the primary purpose of maintaining peace, launched an attack on January 17, 1991. The Gulf War lasted only a few months, and United Nations forces—primarily those of the United States, which launched a powerful air attach on the Iraqi capital of Baghdad (BAG-dad)—forced the Iraqis out of Kuwait.

But Saddam was not removed from power, and he continued to threaten the region. Saddam, whose capital is close to the site of old Babylon and who has identified himself with the Babylonians, also maintained uneasy relations with an age-old rival, the Assyrians. The latter, who live in the northern part of the country as their ancestors did thousands of years before, maintain the Aramaic language and are Christians instead of Muslims.

Digging up the past

The Assyrians and Babylonians could not have known that their great gods Ashur and Marduk, along with the other deities they worshiped, would be largely forgotten in modern times; or that the god of the people they defeated, the Israelites, would be worshiped by hundreds of millions of people. Yet thanks to the Israelites and their holy book, the Old Testament, the memory of those two nations was preserved throughout the Middle Ages (A.D. 500–1500) By contrast, Sumer, though its city Ur was mentioned in the Book of Genesis, would be lost to history for many centuries.

In 1842, archaeologists from several countries who had been conducting an *excavation* (ex-cuh-VAY-shun), or archaeological dig, on Assyrian sites found a set of tablets in Akkadian cuneiform. Because the Assyrians had retained use of Akkadian for a time, the archaeologists knew how to interpret the writing, but parts of the tablets bore another language they could not identify. Gradually they became aware of a culture older than that of Akkad, and over time they conducted a series of excavations at Ur and other cities.

These archaeological digs, which continue to the present day, have established much of the region's early history, but the archaeologists have faced several problems. Sumerian inscriptions were on clay, which is much less durable than stone. Also they have had to deal with the Mesopotamian practice of building on top of the ruins of past buildings. Thus many of these archaeological sites are in the form of *tells,* or small mounds of earth heaped over layers of ruins.

The digging up of Assyria began much earlier than that of Sumer, and the recovery of Babylonia followed excavations at Nineveh and other Assyrian cities. Between 1899 and 1917, a team of German archaeologists was able to uncover most of the layers that represented the empire of Nebuchadnezzar. They

even reconstructed the Ishtar Gate, which stands in the Pergamum Museum in Berlin. Flooding from the Euphrates, however,
prevented them from reaching the level of Hammurabi's era.

Viewing the landscape of modern Iraq, it is perhaps
hard to believe that this region was once called the Fertile Crescent, a land of lush gardens and fruit trees maintained by the
extensive irrigation systems of the various Mesopotamian peoples. The delta of the Euphrates in southern Iraq is still green
in many places, but the constant fighting in ancient times
destroyed most of the irrigation systems, and much of the
country is dry, rocky desert.

Yet Mesopotamia lives on in modern culture, in the Gilgamesh Epic and in Hammurabi's Code, in the days of the week
and in the many other aspects of astronomy to which the Babylonians contributed. The building styles of the area, particularly in Assyria, have continued to fascinate architects. Among
these was an American, Frank Lloyd Wright (1867-1959), often

described as the greatest architect of the twentieth century, who included many Assyrian aspects in his designs.

Likewise it appears that the Romans made use of Assyrian styles in their monuments and other symbolism. Certainly the Romans, who built the greatest empire of the ancient world, must have been fascinated by the Assyrians' talent for warfare, which influenced military tactics for centuries to come. A less distinguished admirer may have been Adolf Hitler (1889–1945), who like the Assyrians waged a kind of "lightning warfare," as he called it, which stunned the conquered peoples. Architecture in Nazi Germany, too, seems to have reflected Assyrian as well as Roman themes.

In modern times, Saddam Hussein has often been likened to Hitler. His swift invasion of Kuwait seems to point back to Assyria, but he has clearly identified himself more with the legacy of Babylonia. During the Gulf War, the American media noted the fact that Nebuchadnezzar was his hero: thus, to carry on the theme of legitimacy, Saddam had reached back more than 2,500 years to identify himself with the past glories of his nation. In keeping with his admiration of Nebuchadnezzar's empire, in 1988 he began work on the restoration of ancient Babylon. Archaeologists there are reportedly piecing together the remains of Nebuchadnezzar's palace, Hammurabi's temple, and even the Hanging Gardens.

Saddam Hussein, painting on a wall. *Archive Photos. Reproduced by permission.*

For More Information

Books

Baumann, Hans. *In the Land of Ur: The Discovery of Ancient Mesopotamia.* Translated by Stella Humphreys. New York: Pantheon, 1969.

Butcher, Geoffrey. *Daniel and the Kings of Babylon.* Vero Beach, FL: Rourke Publications, 1984.

Dijkstra, Henk. *History of the Ancient & Medieval World,* Volume 2: *Egypt and Mesopotamia.* New York: Marshall Cavendish, 1996, pp. 217-70.

Finkel, Irving L. *The Hero King Gilgamesh.* Lincolnwood, IL: NTC Publishers, 1998.

Hassig, Susan M. *Iraq.* New York: Marshall Cavendish, 1993.

Landau, Elaine. *The Assyrians.* Brookfield, CT: Millbrook Press, 1997.

Landau, Elaine. *The Babylonians.* Brookfield, CT: Millbrook Press, 1997.

Landau, Elaine. *The Sumerians.* Brookfield, CT: Millbrook Press, 1997.

Lansing, Elizabeth. *The Sumerians: Inventors and Builders.* New York: McGraw-Hill, 1971.

Malam, John. *Mesopotamia and the Fertile Crescent, 10,000 to 539 B.C.* Austin, TX: Raintree Steck-Vaughn, 1999.

Martell, Hazel Mary. *The Kingfisher Book of the Ancient World.* New York: Kingfisher, 1995, pp. 16-27.

Moss, Carol. *Science in Ancient Mesopotamia.* New York: F. Watts, 1998.

Swisher, Clarice. *The Ancient Near East.* San Diego, CA: Lucent Books, 1995.

Web Sites

Assyria Online. http://www.aina.org/aol/ (February 25, 1999).

"Mesopotamian Civilization in the Tigris-Euphrates Valleys." http://www.ancientworld.simplenet.com/chapter2/index.html (February 25, 1999).

Mr. Donn's Ancient History Page. http://members.aol.com/donnandlee/index.html (February 25, 1999).

"The Near East." *Exploring World Cultures.* http://eawc.evansville.edu/egpage.htm (February 25, 1999).

Nineveh On-Line. http://www.nineveh.com/ (February 25, 1999).

Israel

3

Egypt had its monuments and its magnificent history of many thousands of years. Likewise Babylonia, Assyria, and Persia all had their great conquests, along with their many cultural achievements. But none of these ancient civilizations had nearly the same degree of impact on modern society as a tiny cluster of tribes called Israel. This group of people, which only existed for about 400 years as a full-fledged nation with a government and territory of its own, left behind almost nothing in the form of sculpture, architecture, or other artwork. Their conquests were modest compared with those of their powerful neighbors. Their contribution to other areas of life such as trade or science was insignificant. The Israelites' one major contribution to culture, however, made up for all other shortcomings. That contribution was a book called the Bible, which has had more influence on the history of the world than any book ever written.

Where to find Israel

Located at the center of the Middle East, Israel was and is a tiny nation about the size of New Jersey. To the west is the

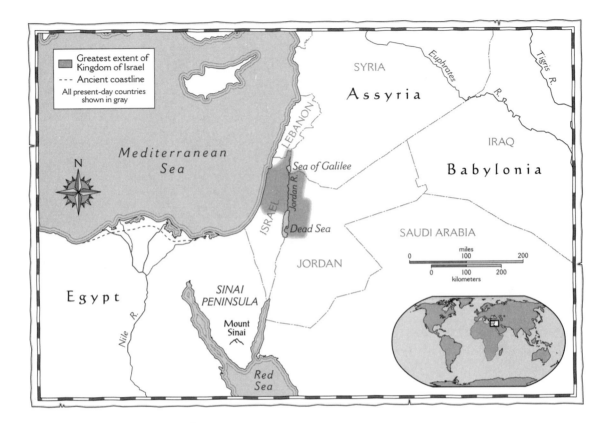

Map of Israel.

XNR Productions.
The Gale Group.

Mediterranean Sea; to the east, the Jordan River and the hills beyond. To the north it borders on Lebanon, which in ancient times was the home of the Phoenicians, and near its northeast corner is the Sea of Galilee. To the southeast, at the other end of the Jordan, is the Dead Sea, so named because it is full of salt and other minerals. Southward lies desert, which extends all the way down the Sinai (SIE-nie) Peninsula, an area of land that juts out into the Red Sea. In ancient times, Israel's location put it between the unfriendly nations of Egypt to the southwest and Babylonia and Assyria to the east, with many other hostile peoples in surrounding areas. The people of Israel today are called Israelis (iz-RAY-leez), but in ancient times they were known variously as *Israelites*, which referred to their nation; *Hebrews*, which referred to their language; or *Jews*, which referred to their religion. They are part of a larger linguistic group, called *Semites* (seh-MITES), which also includes the neighboring Arab nations.

History before Abraham

It is literally impossible to discuss the history of ancient Israel without referring to the Old Testament. The Jewish scriptures provide the main, and in some cases the only, source for certain aspects of that history. But this single source also creates problems, because the Bible is full of passages referring to events that many people find hard to believe. Did God really appear to Moses in the Burning Bush? Did a donkey really speak, as Numbers 22 reports? And did the Israelites really defeat Jericho (JARE-ih-koe) by blowing trumpets?

The answers to these questions are as much a matter of religious faith as they are of history. In the case of the Israelites it is not as important to distinguish fact from legend as it is when studying the histories of other ancient peoples. No one worships the gods of those other nations and therefore no one believes in the tales concerning them. Also, regardless of whether one believes something in the Bible actually happened, it is important to understand what the Israelites believed. One of the main themes in the Bible, after all—both in the Old Testament and the New—is faith. Therefore it is easiest, when studying the Israelites, to accept their account at face value, or if one finds it hard to do that, to treat certain events as symbolic.

Indeed the religion established by the Israelites relies heavily on symbols, a fact that is clear at the very beginning of the Old Testament. The Book of Genesis opens with an account of how God created the world and all living things; placed the first man and woman, Adam and Eve, in the Garden of Eden; and later drove them out of Eden when they disobeyed him. Most likely Adam and Eve were symbols for all of humanity, as the Garden was a symbol for the world. Symbolic or not, the story established certain themes, or basic ideas, essential to the Israelites' religion.

Adam and Eve in the Garden of Eden.
Archive Photos. Reproduced by permission.

Words to Know: Israel

Apocrypha: A term, meaning "writings of uncertain origin," used to describe seven books not included in all versions of the Christian Bible.

Align: To associate or line up with someone or something else.

Allah: The Arabic word for God.

Anoint: To pour oil over someone's head as a symbol that God has chosen that person to fill a position of leadership.

Anti-Semitism: Hatred of, or discrimination against, Jews.

Apostle: A religious figure who is sent out to teach, preach, and perform miracles.

Assimilate: To be mixed into a larger group of people.

Atone: To make up for something.

Baptism: To be lowered into water as a symbol of death and rebirth.

Bear false witness: To lie.

Chosen People: The name by which Jews are often known, meaning that they were chosen to fulfill God's plans on earth.

Coincide: To happen at the same time as something else.

Commemorate: To recall an important event or person.

Concubine: A woman whose role toward a man is like that of a wife's, but without the social and legal status of a wife.

Covenant: A sacred agreement.

Covet: To desire something that belongs to someone else.

Crucifixion: A Roman punishment in which the victim was nailed or tied to a cross until he died.

Crusade: "Wars for the cross," or so-called holy wars by European kings to recapture the city of Jerusalem.

Deity: A god.

Deportation: Forced removal of a person or a group of people.

Descendant: Someone who is related to an earlier person; an *ancestor.*

Disciple: A close follower of a religious teacher.

Epistle: A letter.

Exile: A situation of being forced to move away from the place in which one lives.

Exodus: The act of going out from a place.

Foreshadowing: An early sign of something that will appear later, either in history or in a story.

Fundamentalist: Someone who calls for a return to the basic traditions of a religion.

Ghetto: A place in which a group of people, separated by race, religion, or some other factor, are forced to live.

Hellenistic: Influenced by Greece.

Holocaust: The systematic murder of more than six million Jews by Nazi Germany during World War II (1939–1945).

Idol: A statue of a god that the god's followers worship.

Ironic: When something is intended to be one way, but turns out to be quite different from what was intended.

Islam: A faith that arose in Arabia in the A.D. 600s, led by the prophet Muhammad (A.D. 570?–632).

Koran: The holy book of Islam.

Locust: A type of insect similar to a grasshopper.

Millennium: A period of 1,000 years; its plural is *millennia*.

Morality: A code of right and wrong.

Mosque: A Muslim temple.

Muslim: A believer in Islam.

Notorious: Having a bad reputation.

Pagan: Worshiping many gods.

Peninsula: An area of land that sticks out into a body of water.

Pharaoh: The title for the king of ancient Egypt.

Plague: A disease or other bad thing that spreads among a group of people.

Prophet: Someone who receives communications directly from God and passes these on to the people.

Protestant: A group of Christians that split off from the Catholic Church in a series of movements about A.D. 1500.

Province: A political unit, like a state, that is part of a larger country.

Rabbi: A Jewish teacher or priest.

Ram: A male sheep.

Resurrect: Bring back to life.

Revolutionary: Someone who calls for an armed uprising against the rulers of a nation or area.

Sabbath: The seventh day, a holy day of rest. For Jews, this day is on Saturday; for Christians, Sunday.

Sacrifice: A symbolic offering to God.

Scriptures: Holy writings.

Shrine: A holy place for believers in a religion.

Symbol: Something that stands for something else.

Synagogue: A Jewish temple.

Talmud: A Jewish text that provides additional information on the law and other subjects covered in the Old Testament.

Vassal: A ruler who is subject to another ruler.

Western: A term referring to the cultures and civilizations influenced by ancient Greece and Rome.

Zealot: A group of Jewish revolutionaries who called for the overthrow of Roman rule; also, someone who is extremely committed to a cause.

Zoroastrianism: The religion of ancient Persia.

Cain kills his brother Abel and brings forth the wrath of God, who witnessed the murder. *Archive Photos. Reproduced by permission.*

Because of the wrong committed by those first two humans, the Israelites believed, all of humanity was guilty, which resulted in a fall from grace with God. But all hope was not lost, because God would again and again show his willingness to make *covenants* (CUH-vuh-nunts), or sacred agreements, with humankind. This willingness distinguished the Hebrew *deity* (DEE-ih-tee) from all others. Most ancient peoples worshiped gods who changed their minds on a whim, helping or hurting people depending on what suited them at the moment. The god of the Hebrews, on the other hand, was much more likely to judge people fairly. For example, when Adam and Eve's son Cain killed his brother Abel in Genesis 4, God placed a curse on Cain but then gave him a form of protection so that no one would kill him.

The incident that led to the murder involved a *sacrifice,* or a symbolic offering to God. Abel had offered up lambs, whereas Cain had brought only fruit or some other type of plant. This is the first mention of a practice that would become common: by shedding the blood of a lamb, a creature that symbolizes purity, men could *atone,* or make up, for their sins. Again, the sacrifice was a symbolic act whose most important aspect was not so much God's desire for the offering as it was the willingness of the worshiper to make that offering. This was another difference between the Hebrew god and other deities, who tended to be greedy and demanding.

It should be pointed out, however, that the Hebrew god had his demanding side as well. He was, as he often described himself throughout the Old Testament, "a jealous god," meaning that he expected to be the Israelites' only object of worship. This attitude extended to his name, which is often rendered as *Yahweh* (YAH-way) or *Jehovah* (je-HO-vah) [see sidebar, "God's Names"]. Despite his demand for worship, however, the offer of a covenant demonstrated a desire to treat man as a kind of equal. This may seem inconsistent, but Genesis says that God created man "in his own image"; likewise, he allowed human beings the freedom to choose between right and wrong, which he would not have done if he considered people mere slaves.

God's Names

The word "God," or *Elohim* (ee-loe-HEEM) in Hebrew, was a general term, like "man," and capitalizing it simply distinguished him as the one and only supreme deity. (Likewise Muslims worship *Allah* [ah-LAH], which is Arabic for "God.") Later, when Moses asked the name of the god who appeared in the burning bush, he was told simply, "I Am." The Israelites believed that God had a name; however, it was so sacred that it could not even be spoken. Therefore they usually referred to him by titles such as "Lord" or *Adonai* (a-doe-NIE.) The Hebrew scriptures sometimes represented his name as "YHWH," which was unpronounceable precisely because it was too sacred to be pronounced. Over time, however, he came to be called *Yahweh* (YAH-way), which later Christian scholars changed to *Jehovah* (jeh-HOE-vah).

But the sins of later generations made God so angry that he nearly destroyed his creation in the Great Flood, as described in the seventh and eighth chapters of Genesis. He spared Noah, along with Noah's families and the creatures in the ark with him, and afterward he made the first of many significant covenants, promising that he would never again destroy the earth. As important as this covenant was, however, it did not have as much bearing on the Israelites' later history as the covenants that he would make with a *descendant* of Noah, a man called Abraham.

From Abraham to Joseph (c. 1800–c. 1650 B.C.)

The true history of Israel begins in the Sumerian city-state of Ur around 1800 B.C. Abraham, or rather Abram (AY-brum)—he would only later receive his new name from God—was married to Sarai (suh-RYE), who also would be renamed later. Like many people in the region both then and now, Abram and Sarai lived with an extended family. The leader of their family was Abram's father Terah (TARE-ah), who apparently worshiped the gods of Ur. At one point Terah almost moved his family to Canaan (KAY-nun), which would later become the Israelites' Promised Land, but he decided to settle in a city close to Ur.

God did not allow Abram to remain there long but instead told him to "go to the land I will show you": Canaan. God told him that this land would be his and promised that Abram would become the father of many people. This seemed impossible, because Abram and Sarai had so far been unable to conceive even one child. Later God came to Abram in a dream and told him that his descendants would one day be enslaved in a foreign land for 400 years, but promised that they would come away "with great possessions." Soon afterward, he made his first true covenant with Abram (Genesis 15), promising him that his people would rule the lands from the Nile River in Egypt to the Euphrates in Mesopotamia.

Impatient for God to fulfill his promise of children, Abram and Sarai decided that Abram would conceive a child with Hagar (HAY-gar), her Egyptian maid. So Hagar gave birth to a son named Ishmael (ISH-may-el) when Abram was eighty-six years old. In spite of Abram's impatience, God blessed him with another covenant in which he broadened the scope of his earlier promises and gave Abram and Sarai their new names, Abraham and Sarah. As a symbol of their covenant, God directed that Abraham and all the males under his care—Abraham was a wealthy man, with many servants and others who looked to him for protection—should undergo *circumcision*. This delicate operation on the most sensitive spot in his body served to show that a man belonged to God, and thereafter the men of Israel would be circumcised.

Many more years passed, and both Abraham and Sarah doubted that God would ever make good on his promise—especially now that Sarah was more than ninety years old. But finally she gave birth to a son named Isaac, an event that both she and Abraham greeted with much joy. Soon afterward, however, she became jealous of Hagar, and convinced Abraham to send her and Ishmael away. Reluctantly Abraham agreed. Hagar and Ishmael wandered in the desert for many days, and just when she was about to give up, God came to her and told her that her son too would father a great nation. And indeed he did: today the Arab peoples, who consider Ishmael their ancestor, control the area from the Nile to the Euphrates, and virtually all of the Middle East except Israel.

There remained one last important episode in Abraham's life, and it was a powerful one. According to Genesis 22:2, God said, "Take your son, your only son, Isaac, whom you love, and go to the region of Moriah [more-AYE-uh.] Sacrifice him there as a burnt offering on one of the mountains I will tell you about." Abraham did not question this terrible demand. He went through with it to the point of drawing a knife to kill the son that God had promised for so long. But God stopped him and told him to sacrifice a ram (a male sheep) instead. Because of his faith and his willingness to do what God had asked him—though God apparently never intended to let him go through with the sacrifice—God said, "I will surely bless you and make your descendants as numerous as the sky and as the sand on the seashore. Your descendants will take possession of the cities of their enemies, and through your offspring all nations on earth will be blessed, because you have obeyed me."

Abraham waking with his son, Isaac. *Archive Photos. Reproduced by permission.*

Isaac, Jacob, and Joseph

Abraham would become the most important figure in the Old Testament other than Moses. Known by the respectful term "Father Abraham," he is held in the highest regard by Jews, Muslims, and Christians, and all three religions place great importance on God's promises to him. To Christians in particular, the episode involving the sacrifice of Isaac, as well as the promise that the world would be blessed through his descendants, was a *foreshadowing* of Christ and his sacrificial death on the cross.

By contrast, Isaac's chief significance is as the son of Abraham and the father of Jacob, to whom God would later give a new name: Israel. Abraham had his flaws, but Jacob was an outright rascal in his early years. He tricked his older brother Esau by pretending to be him, and thus received a blessing from Isaac, who had gone blind and did not realize that he was blessing his younger son. The blessing of a father to an oldest son was an important event that could determine a man's success for the rest of his life. To the people of the ancient Middle East, words were sacred: therefore they put a great deal of emphasis on blessings and covenants, and they did not dare to speak the name of God. Saying something was the same thing as doing it, so by stealing Esau's blessing, Jacob in effect stole his brother's future.

When Esau found out what Jacob had done to him, Jacob had to leave home in a hurry, and over the next years, a number of harsh experiences caused him to grow up. He was even tricked himself by a man named Laban (LAY-ban) when he fell in love with Laban's daughter Rachel and agreed to work seven years for her hand in marriage. At the end of seven years, a marriage ceremony was held. Presumably the bride was veiled, and there was probably a great deal of drinking at the celebration that followed. At any rate, Jacob woke up the next morning to discover that the wife he had slept with was not Rachel but her older—and much less attractive—sister, Leah. When he went to Laban to complain, Laban explained that he had to marry off his older daughter first; but if Jacob would work for another seven years, he could marry Rachel as well. It was an appropriate payback for Jacob's own trickery against Esau years before.

Though he still had to work the seven years, Jacob married Rachel after spending a week with Leah. Probably Laban's intention was to let Leah conceive children, since he knew that Jacob would probably not spend many nights with her after he had Rachel. The Old Testament says that God had mercy on Leah, and that she had six sons and a daughter; Rachel, on the other hand, could not conceive for many years. In the meantime, Jacob fathered four other sons by two *concubines,* but he still wanted a child with the wife he loved most. Finally Rachel became pregnant, and she bore a son named Joseph, whom Jacob loved more than all the rest. She later gave birth to Benjamin, bringing the total of Jacob's sons to twelve. The descendants of these sons would become the twelve tribes of Israel.

Later Jacob had a remarkable experience. One night in a time of great trouble—he was about to face his brother Esau again—he lay down beside a stream to sleep, but an angel came and wrestled with him. They fought until dawn, neither of them overpowering the other. Toward daybreak Jacob demanded that the angel bless him. The angel's blessing was this: "Your name shall no longer be Jacob, but Israel"—which means "he struggles with God"—"because you have struggled with God and with men and have overcome." Suddenly realizing that the angel was God in human form, Jacob asked him his name, to which the angel replied, "Why do you ask my name?" Then Jacob knew for sure that it was God.

The focus of Genesis eventually shifts from Jacob to Joseph. Jacob had pampered his beloved son so much that the boy's brothers began to despise him. Joseph did not help matters by telling his brothers that he had dreams in which they all bowed down to him. Finally, a group led by Leah's son Judah (JEW-duh) ganged up on him and sold him to slave traders from Egypt.

In Egypt, Joseph went through a series of difficult experiences, but eventually he gained favor with the *pharaoh* (FAIR-o) by interpreting his dreams for him. Clearly dreams had a great deal of meaning for the Israelites, as they did for people throughout the Middle East in ancient times. Joseph won the pharaoh's admiration even though the interpretation itself was not pleasant: Egypt was about to experience seven years of famine (a period of time when food is scarce). But he also offered

The Structure of the Bible

The scriptures of the Jewish faith are contained in what Christians call the Old Testament, which consists of thirty-nine separate books. The Christian scriptures also include the New Testament, an additional set of twenty-seven books. Some Christians also recognize seven more books, sometimes referred to as the *Apocrypha* (uh-POCK-riff-uh), or writings of uncertain origin. ("Apocrypha" is a negative term, but it is easier to remember—and pronounce—than the other name for these books, which is *deutero-canonical* [DOO-tuhr-o kuh-NON-i-kul].)

The books are in turn broken up into chapters (or psalms in the case of the book by that name). The chapters are further broken into verses, usually designated with a colon separating chapter and verse. Hence the first verse of the Bible is Genesis 1:1, meaning Chapter 1, Verse 1. However, the books were not originally written in verse form; those divisions were assigned later.

To make it easier to understand the scope of the Bible, the books of the Old and New Testaments are often divided into groups. These divisions vary between Jews and Christians, and between the Catholic and Protestant branches of Christianity. What follows is one way of dividing the books:

Old Testament

Pentateuch ([PIN-tuh-tuke] or Law; a record of the period from the creation of the world to the death of Moses.)

Historical Books (The history of Israel from the conquest of Canaan to the end of the Captivity.)

Poetic Books

Prophetic Books (Prophecies, and records of prophets' lives, from the time of the divided kingdom through the Captivity. Prophetic Books are divided into "major" and "minor," which refer to the size of the book, not the importance of the prophet involved.)

Apocryphal Books

(The origin of these writings is not known; Apocryphal Books can be found in various places throughout the Old Testament.)

New Testament

Gospels (The life of Jesus according to Matthew, Mark, Luke, and John.)

Acts (The acts of Jesus's apostles after his lifetime.)

Epistles (Letters from the apostles to churches they established throughout the ancient world. The first group are by the Apostle Paul, the second group by various authors.)

Revelation (A prophecy of the world's end.)

a solution in the form of a plan to store up grain and other food-stuffs, so the pharaoh put him in charge of the operation.

Thanks to Joseph, Egypt survived the famine, and he became a very powerful man in the Egyptian government. Meanwhile, the famine forced Jacob's sons to go to Egypt to see if they could buy any food. By now many years had passed since Judah and the others had sold Joseph into slavery; therefore, when they went to see a great Egyptian official, they had no idea he was their brother. As was customary when meeting an important person, they bowed down to him—just as Joseph had dreamed they would.

The most respectful of them all was Judah, who had emerged as the leader among Jacob's sons even though he was not the oldest. He had clearly repented of his earlier deeds, and God blessed him for this by ultimately making Judah's the most notable of the twelve Israelite tribes. The word *Jew*, in fact, comes from the name *Judah*, which means "praise."

After a series of meetings, Joseph finally revealed his identity, but he had no interest in taking revenge. Instead, he welcomed his brothers and invited the entire family to come to Egypt and live. So Jacob and all his sons and their families settled in Egypt, where they would remain for 400 years—as God had told Abraham long before.

From Moses to Samuel (c. 1250–1020 B.C.)

Many historians believe that the movement of Jacob's family into Egypt may have *coincided* with (occurred at the same time as) the Hyksos invasion. If so, it is perhaps easy to understand how the Egyptians came to despise the Israelites, as they later did. Thus by the beginning of the Book of Exodus (which means "to go out from a place"), the Israelites' situation had become very different than it was in the time of Joseph. Fearing their growing numbers, the Egyptians had made slaves of them, and the pharaoh set out to kill all boys born to the people of Israel.

But a woman from the tribe of Levi (LEE-vie) devised a plan to save her own son. She put him in a basket made of reeds and let it float down the Nile past the pharaoh's palace. The pharaoh's daughter found the basket and decided to adopt the boy, who eventually came to live in the pharaoh's house. She named the child Moses, which comes either from a Hebrew word meaning "to draw out" (of the water) or from an Egyptian word meaning "is born."

The boy would grow up to become Israel's greatest leader, the true founder of the Israelite nation. But he was raised as an Egyptian, and he might have had an easy life if he had not grown concerned about the harsh treatment of his people. When he saw an Egyptian beating an Israelite, he killed the Egyptian and had to flee to the land of Midian (MIH-dee-uhn), a desolate place on the Arabian Peninsula.

Moses lived in Midian for a long time, taking a wife and starting a family. The Book of Exodus says that one day while he was tending a flock of sheep for his father-in-law, God appeared to him in a burning bush and ordered him to go lead the Israelites out of Egypt. Moses was extremely reluctant to do this, but God promised that he would be with him, so finally he returned to Egypt. There he enlisted the help of his brother Aaron, and together they went to the pharaoh and demanded the release of the Israelites. This must have taken a great deal of bravery, because Moses did not yet have any great power. The pharaoh's response was to make conditions even worse for the people of Israel.

Moses and Aaron kept going back to the pharaoh, and each time the pharaoh refused to yield. Therefore God sent ten *plagues* (PLAYGZ) against Egypt. First he turned the Nile into blood, and then he infested the land with frogs, gnats, and flies in turn. He killed livestock, or farm animals; caused boils, or intense sores; sent a rain of hail; brought another infestation in the form of *locusts;* and turned daytime into darkness. Each time, the pharaoh's resistance simply increased.

Then came the tenth and worst plague, the killing of all the Egyptians' firstborn sons—just as the earlier pharaoh had tried to kill the sons of the Israelites. On the night when this happened, the Israelites protected themselves from the angel of death by placing the blood of a lambs on the frames of their front doors; then they ate a solemn feast. This was called the Passover. Jews still celebrate it each year to commemorate the way that God passed over their houses and did not take their sons.

The pharaoh was not so fortunate. When he lost his firstborn son, he finally gave in. Moses, by now recognized as the leader over all the Israelites, led them out of Egypt. The Bible reports that when they came to the Red Sea, God parted the waters and let them walk on dry land; but when the pursuing army of the pharaoh—who had meanwhile changed his mind—tried to follow them, the sea swallowed them up.

Forty years in the wilderness

Despite this triumphal exodus from Egypt, it would be forty years before the Israelites finally claimed the Promised Land, as they called Canaan. During this time, they made their way through what the Bible calls a *wilderness,* the Sinai Desert. Of course it would not even take forty days to cross such a relatively small area, but this long period of wandering was God's punishment for disobedience, according to the Book of Exodus.

The most significant event during this time occurred when the people stopped at Mount Sinai. Leaving Aaron in charge of the people, Moses went up to the top of the mountain. There he received from God the Ten Commandments [see sidebar, "The Ten Commandments"], which were carved into two stone *tablets*. He also received a long, long series of laws, chiefly concerning the ways that God should be worshiped. The Book of Leviticus (luh-VIT-i-cus) consists of many more laws concerning everything from diet to the settlement of disputes between neighbors. Dietary restrictions, in fact, would become very important to Judaism (JOOD-ee-izm), as the faith of Israel came to be called: even in modern times, people who strictly follow the Jewish scriptures refuse to eat pork and other foods.

Moses remained on the top of Mount Sinai for so long that the people of Israel became impatient and proceeded to make a golden calf and worship it. When Moses saw this, he became so furious that he broke the two stone tablets. God later replaced these, but he dealt severely with the Israelites, killing many of them. This was the first of many violent acts that would follow as Israel became a nation. God called the Israelites his *Chosen People,* but that did not stop him from responding with swift fury when they disobeyed him.

Later, as they approached the Promised Land, Moses sent twelve spies to observe the military strength of the Canaanites. All but two of them came back and said that Canaan

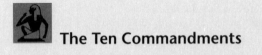

The Ten Commandments

The Ten Commandments formed the basis of Israelite law and have greatly influenced the legal traditions of many civilizations that followed. The first three command respect for God, the fourth respect for one's parents, and the remainder respect for one's neighbors. The commandments begin with a reminder that "I am the Lord your God, who brought you out of Egypt, out of the land of slavery." Adapted here from Exodus 20, the commandments are:

1. You shall have no other gods before me.

2. You shall not make or worship any *idols*.

3. You shall not misuse the name of God.

4. Remember the *Sabbath* day and keep it holy.

5. Honor your father and your mother.

6. You shall not commit murder.

7. You shall not commit adultery.

8. You shall not steal.

9. You shall not *bear false witness* against your neighbor.

10. You shall not *covet* anything that belongs to your neighbor.

appeared too powerful to defeat. This lack of faith and courage, too, enraged God, and he condemned the Israelites to wander for forty years. Moses himself never entered the Promised Land but died within sight of it.

Conquest and conflict

Aaron had been Moses's closest associate, but he was a priest. In fact the entire tribe of Levi became the priests of Israel from that point on. The task of actually leading the people fell to Joshua, who was one of the two spies who had come back from the Canaanite cities with a good report. Under Joshua, the Israelites conquered the ancient city of Jericho, which may well be the oldest city yet discovered by archaeologists. According to the biblical account, Israel destroyed Jericho by marching around the city for seven days, shouting and blowing trumpets. More conquests of Canaanite cities followed, until the Promised Land belonged to the Israelites.

In spite of these great victories, the period that followed was one of great conflict. Thus the Bible says at the end of the Book of Judges, "everyone did as he saw fit." The dozen leaders called judges were not judges as that term is normally understood, but simply powerful rulers. It is interesting that one of them was a woman, Deborah, since the number of well-known female leaders in the ancient world can probably be counted on one hand [see sidebar, "Women in the Old Testament."]

A less admirable female figure of this time was Delilah, who tricked the judge Samson into giving up the secret of his incredible strength. Delilah was a Philistine (FILL-i-steen). The Philistines—one of the many Canaanite peoples already living in the area when the Israelites arrived—were almost always in conflict with Israel. (Some archaeologists believe that the Philistines were also among the Sea Peoples who threatened Egypt.) Samson killed many of them, and they could not defeat him until he confessed to Delilah that his strength came from the fact that he had never cut his hair. Therefore she cut it while he was sleeping one night and rendered Samson powerless.

After the time of the judges, Israel came under the leadership of the prophet Samuel. Moses, too, had been a *prophet,* or someone who receives communications directly from God and passes these on to the people. Samuel would be the only other prophet to exercise a direct leadership role over Israel. Later, in the time of kings, prophets such as Isaiah and Jeremiah existed outside the circles of power and were often at odds with the leaders.

All the other peoples of the area had kings, but God had decreed that Israel would be different. The people, however, demanded a king, and finally God granted their wish. He sent Samuel to *anoint* Saul, a tall and handsome donkey-handler from the tribe of Benjamin. To anoint means to pour oil over someone's head, a symbol that God has chosen that person to fill a position of leadership. At first Saul appeared to be a great and capable leader; but another leader was on the rise.

From Saul to the Exile (1020–587 B.C.)

Only at this point in Israel's history can historians assign accurate dates to events. Saul, who ruled from about 1020 to 1000 B.C., won a number of victories in battle against the Philistines and other enemies. On several occasions he disobeyed orders from God delivered through Samuel. God became increasingly displeased with him. Meanwhile, the Bible says, God was raising up a new and unlikely leader.

David, who ruled from about 1000 to 960 B.C., would be Israel's greatest king. Under his leadership, Israel's territory would reach its largest point, and David would win victory after victory. Though he started as a mere shepherd boy, from an early age he showed signs of future greatness. He is said to have killed a lion with his bare hands, and his victory over the Philistine giant Goliath caught the attention of King Saul.

At first Saul treated him almost like a son, and gave him one of his daughters as a wife. David also began a close friendship with Saul's son Jonathan, which would continue even after Saul turned against him. But Saul eventually became jealous of David, and for many years David was a hunted man. During this time, he wrote a number of the *psalms* (SAULMS), or songs to God, contained in the book of that name, and assembled a fighting force of his own that would become known as "the Mighty Men of David."

Saul met his end in a battle that claimed three of his sons, including Jonathan. Saul himself committed suicide by falling on his sword. An aging Samuel then anointed David king. The new king distinguished himself with numerous victories over Philistines, Canaanites, and other hostile peoples. More important than these conquests, however, was his capture of Jerusalem, an ancient city that became the new capital of the Israelites. He celebrated its capture by giving the Ark of the Covenant, a sacred box containing the stone tablets of the Ten Commandments, a place of honor in the new capital city. The Israelites considered the Ark sacred; stories were told of terrible things that happened to men who touched it. Later, during the conquest by other nations that led to the Captivity, the Ark was lost and has never been seen again."

God made a covenant with David, promising that his descendants would rule forever. Christians have taken this as a promise regarding Christ, who descended from David. David composed many songs of praise to God, for example Psalm 119, the longest chapter in the Bible. He was called "a man after God's own heart" despite occasional lapses into sin, as when he coveted another man's wife [see sidebar, "The Ten Commandments."] That desire led him to break another commandment, against murder, when he sent the woman's husband to certain death in battle. He married the woman, Bathsheba (bath-SHEE-buh). Out of this union came his successor, Solomon; however, David had to pay heavily for his sins.

Because of David's checkered past, God denied him an honor that he gave instead to Solomon (reigned c. 960–922 B.C.): the building of a great temple in Jerusalem. The temple would house the Ark of the Covenant in a place called "The Holy of

Holies." The Bible records a great deal about the building of the temple and about Solomon's legendary wisdom, in Proverbs and Ecclesiastes (ee-klee-zee-AS-teeze), biblical books attributed to him. Ecclesiastes is unusual among books of the Bible for its world-weary philosophical tone. Another unusual book is "Song of Solomon," likewise traditionally attributed to the king. It is a love poem from a man to a woman and has no equal in ancient literature (certainly not in the Bible) for the intensity of the desire it expresses. Solomon, incidentally, is said to have had some 800 wives. According to legend he had a love affair with the Queen of Sheba from the African country of Ethiopia.

The divided kingdom (922–721 B.C.)

The reign of David and later Solomon marked Israel's high point. Afterward came years of decline, followed by disaster. After Solomon's death, in about 922 B.C., Israel divided into two kingdoms. To the south was Judah, which consisted of that tribe as well as Benjamin's and part of the Levite priestly tribe. It was ruled by members of David's dynasty. To the north was Israel, which consisted of the remaining ten tribes and was ruled by elected kings. Over the coming years, Judah had a number of wicked rulers, along with some good ones; by contrast, *all* of Israel's kings, according to the Bible, were evil.

Without a doubt the most *notorious* (no-TORE-ee-us; unfavorably well-known) rulers over Israel were the royal couple Ahab (AY-hab) and Jezebel (JEZ-uh-bell.) For years, the Israelites' god had been at war with other deities of the region, including the Canaanites' Baal (BAIL); the Phoenicians' Astarte (uh-STAR-tay), a variation on the Mesopotamian love goddess Ishtar; and others. Jezebel attempted to replace worship of Yahweh with that of Baal. Ahab tried to *align* (associate) Israel with its neighbors, something God had clearly forbidden. They committed various other evil deeds, such as killing a man to steal his vineyard (VIN-yurd.) God, through the prophet Elijah, another major figure of the Old Testament, dealt harshly with them.

Much of the Old Testament is devoted to the troubled centuries between the death of Solomon and the Captivity. As 1st and 2nd Samuel recorded events involving Saul and David, the books of Kings and Chronicles preserve the period from

Women in the Old Testament

Though it would be a mistake to say that women in Israel enjoyed anything like equality with men, their status was much higher than in most ancient societies, even the supposedly more advanced cultures of Greece and Rome. Thus there were few prominent women in Rome, and fewer still in Greece, whereas the Bible is full of important females. There was Ruth, for instance, who lived around the time of the judges and whose story is told in a very short book that bears her name.

But not all female figures were as positive as Ruth, Deborah the judge, or Abraham's wife Sarah. There was Eve; there was Delilah, who tricked Samson into giving up the secret of his strength; and there was Jezebel, who was so cruel that her name has become a negative word in the English language.

Also it should be noted that not many females had a reputation like that of Deborah, who is remembered purely in her own right rather than as the mother, wife, sister, or daughter of a more famous man—as is the case with many of the women named below. Nonetheless, few other ancient historical texts mention so many different females of importance; and as for the Jezebels and Delilahs, it should be pointed out that there were plenty of wicked *men* in the Old Testament as well.

Other famous women of the Old Testament, in order of their appearance, include:

Hagar: Sarah's maid and mother of Ishmael.

Rebecca: Mother of Jacob.

Leah: Wife of Jacob and mother of Judah.

Rachel: Wife of Jacob and mother of Joseph.

Dinah: Daughter of Jacob.

Miriam: Moses's sister, who assisted him in leading the people.

Zipporah: Moses's wife.

Rahab (RAY-hab): A prostitute from Jericho who helped the Israelites conquer the city and whose life was spared in return.

Abigail: Wife of David.

Bathsheba: A woman with whom David fell in love, even though she was another man's wife.

The Queen of Sheba: A great queen, perhaps from Ethiopia, with whom King Solomon fell in love.

Esther: The wife of a Persian emperor during the Captivity, who helped save her people.

Solomon through the Exile and Captivity. Likewise most of the Prophetic Books [see sidebar, "The Structure of the Bible"] are devoted to the works of men sent by God to criticize the wickedness of Israel and Judah. These prophets include Isaiah, Jeremiah, Micah (MIKE-uh), Hosea (ho-ZAY-uh), and Amos.

The end of Israel and Judah (721–587 B.C.)

During this time, Judah at least had a few bright periods, but Israel was threatened by conflict with the Syrians or Aramaeans, Egyptians, and Assyrians. Isaiah warned Ahas (AY-hass), the king of Israel, not to make an alliance with Assyria against the Aramaeans, but he did. Tiglath-Pileser III, the Assyrian king, drove out the Aramaeans, but in return for the favor he grabbed large portions of the Israelites' territory.

Finally, in 721 B.C., Tiglath-Pileser's successor, Sargon II, completed the conquest of Israel. As was the Assyrians' policy, he deported large numbers of the Israelites to another part of his empire. Most likely these people became *assimilated* into the Assyrian Empire; however, "The Ten Lost Tribes of Israel" became a legend. In later centuries, people would claim that they had ended up in Africa or even America.

Judah managed to hang on for another century and a half, led by kings such as Hezekiah (hez-uh-KIE-uh; r. 715–687 B.C.), a righteous leader according to the Bible. But after his time, the kingdom came under the influence of Assyria. King Josiah (joe-SIE-uh; r. 640–609 B.C.) worked against the Assyrians' influence in the government and religion of Israel, but he died in an unsuccessful attempt to stop an Egyptian invasion of Mesopotamia.

By the time of Josiah's death in 609 B.C., Assyria had fallen to Babylonia, and Judah fell under Babylonian influence. Babylonia and Egypt now went to war, and Judah took Egypt's side—which turned out to be a mistake. In 587 B.C., Nebuchadnezzar II of Babylonia conquered Judah and carried many of its people into captivity in Babylon.

The Captivity and aftermath (587–63 B.C.)

In the history of Israel, the period from 587 to 538 B.C. is known as the Captivity or the *Exile*. (Because the divided kingdom had ended, the distinction between Judah and Israel no longer had any meaning. Therefore one can refer to "Israel" as a whole again.) This was the period of prophets such as Ezekiel (ee-ZEKE-ee-uhl) and Daniel, who wrote their works while living in Babylonia.

During this time, the Israelites went through a great deal of soul-searching as they considered the reasons why Yahweh had abandoned his covenant with their people. They came to recognize the importance of worshiping the one god and began to believe that he would send a leader to rescue their people. This figure, known as the Messiah (meh-SIY-uh), is described in later passages from the Book of Isaiah that were probably written during the period of the Captivity rather than by Isaiah himself. Some Israelites believed that the Messiah would reestablish Israel as a political nation, whereas followers of Christ would later come to believe that the Messiah came to establish a spiritual rather than a political leadership.

With the fall of the Babylonian Empire to Persia in 539 B.C., the Israelites came under a new master. The period of captivity under Persia, like the earlier Babylonian Captivity, would have an enormous influence on Israel. The books of Job and Esther were written during this time. According to Jewish tradition, Esther saved her people from slaughter by a cruel official of the Persian Empire, and this event is *commemorated,* or remembered, in the festival of Purim (POOR-im).

The religion of the Israelites also experienced the influence of Zoroastrianism [zo-ro-AS-tree-uhn-izm] from Persia. Before this time, the writings of the Old Testament contained few references to the idea of a devil. One of the most curious aspects of Judaism (JEW-day-izm), as the Israelite religion came to be called, was its scriptures' suggestion that evil things, as well as good, came from God. The Zoroastrian religion, however, had an idea of an evil god continually at battle with the good. From this came the concept of Satan or Lucifer, which developed over later centuries. Incidentally, the three famous *Magi* (MAY-jie) or wise men, who according to the New Testament traveled to see the baby Jesus, were probably Zoroastrian priests.

Another particularly significant aspect of Persian rule was the respect the emperor Cyrus had for other peoples' religions. He allowed the leaders Ezra and Nehemiah (nee-huh-MIYE-uh) to return to Jerusalem and begin rebuilding the city. This led also to a reconstruction of the Israelites' way of life, and by the 300s B.C. the population of Jerusalem began to return to its pre-Captivity levels.

The Hellenistic Period and the Maccabees (333–63 B.C.)

Alexander the Great marched through the area of Israel, which by then had come to be called Palestine, in 333 B.C. After Alexander conquered the Persian Empire, Palestine became Greek, and this began a phase known as the Hellenistic (hell-in-IS-tick), or Greek, Period. First the Ptolemies, the Egyptian inheritors of Alexander's empire, ruled Palestine, but from 198 B.C. the area came under the control of the Seleucids (suh-LOO-sidz), a Hellenistic group that had also emerged from Alexander's conquests.

Several important things happened in these centuries. No longer known by their nation but by their religion, the people of Israel were called simply Jews, and they began to spread throughout the region. This spreading of the Jews, known as the Diaspora (dee-AS-pour-uh), would continue for many centuries, as they remained a people without a homeland of their own. Some of them went to Egypt, where they made the first translations of the Old Testament from the Hebrew language into Greek.

The Seleucids tried to force the Greek religion on the Jews, and this led to a revolt by a priest named Mattatias (matt-uh-TIE-us) and his son Judas Maccabeus (mack-uh-BEE-us) in 164 B.C. They reconquered Jerusalem, an event that Jews commemorate in the festival of Hanukkah ([K]ON-oo-kuh). Under the Maccabees, whose history is recorded in the Apocryphal book by that name [see sidebar, "The Structure of the Bible"], the people of Israel enjoyed their last period of freedom for more than 2,000 years. But a later Maccabean ruler attempted to combine the functions of king and priest, an unpopular move with his Jewish subjects. This made it easy for the Romans to conquer the region in 63 B.C.

Roman rule (63 B.C.–A.D. 135)

In 34 B.C., a Roman *vassal*—that is, a king who is subject to a more powerful king—began to rule the area, which under the Romans had come to be known as Judea (jew-DEE-

uh). This ruler's name was Herod the Great, and though he is remembered for his cruelty, he also began the rebuilding of the temple in Jerusalem, which was not completed until A.D. 64.

Part of Herod's bad reputation comes from the New Testament. The period of the Old Testament had ended with the restoration of Jerusalem under Ezra and Nehemiah. The New Testament begins with the birth of Jesus in about 4 B.C. (Although B.C. means "Before Christ," due to changes in the calendar, the original estimate of Jesus's birth was off by about four years.) According to the Gospels [see sidebar, "The Structure of the Bible"], Herod heard rumors that a new and rival king was about to be born. Therefore, like the pharaoh who had tried to stop Moses centuries before, he ordered the killing of firstborn sons.

But of course Jesus was born. Though his parents were the carpenter Joseph and his young wife Mary, Christian belief holds that Mary conceived Jesus through an act of God's spirit without having sexual relations with Joseph. Stories of Jesus's birth form a significant part of the Western tradition in the form of Christmas, a holiday celebrated by Christians and non-Christians alike.

The New Testament tells little about the first years of Jesus's life, but at about the age of thirty, he went to his cousin John for *baptism.* To be baptized is to be lowered into water as a symbol of death and rebirth. John, better known as John the Baptist, had been preaching baptism. He had also preached the coming of the Messiah. He saw Jesus not only as that leader, but as God in human form—which Jesus himself claimed to be.

As Jesus embarked on his ministry, his main opposition came from scholars of the Jewish scriptures known as Pharisees (FAIR-uh-seez). For his disciples, or close followers, he chose twelve men quite different from the Pharisees: several, including Peter and John, were fishermen; one was a hated tax collector; and another, Judas Iscariot, belonged to a group of anti-Roman political revolutionaries in the tradition of the Maccabees. (A *revolutionary* is someone who calls for an armed uprising against the rulers of a nation or area. An important group of revolutionaries at that time were the *Zealots* [ZELL-uhts], whose name is still a part of the English language as a term for someone who is extremely committed to a cause.) Nor did Jesus choose to keep the kind of company the Pharisees would expect of someone who claimed to be a religious teacher. Instead, he spent his time with prostitutes and other sinners. Although he did not approve of their sin, he taught that God's grace was for them as well.

It is important to note that Jesus was a Jew and that he was known as *rabbi* (RA-bye), a Jewish term for a teacher or priest. He did not attempt to remove the Old Testament, but to build on it. He angered the Pharisees by telling them that he was the promised Messiah. For three years, he conducted his ministry, teaching, preaching, and—according to the New Testament—healing and performing miracles. Nothing he did won the admiration of the Pharisees, who criticized him, for instance, for healing a man on the Sabbath, the day of rest according to the law of Moses [see sidebar, "The Ten Commandments"].

Ultimately the Pharisees captured Jesus, with the help of Judas Iscariot, who had turned against his teacher, perhaps because Jesus proved not to be the political leader he had hoped he would be. Jesus was brought before Pontius Pilate, the Roman governor of Judea, who allowed the Jerusalem crowd to decide Jesus's fate. The crowd called for him to be crucified, a Roman punishment in which the victim was nailed or tied to a cross until he died.

The meaning of the crucifixion, and what happened afterward, is the basis for Christianity. Christians believe that by dying on the cross, Jesus took on the sins of the world, just as in the Old Testament a lamb took on the sins of those who sacrificed it to God. As the son of God, Jesus became, in Christian belief, the sacrificial lamb for all mankind's sins; and after being dead for three days, he overcame sin and death and returned to life. Christians celebrate his *resurrection* at Easter.

The New Testament went on to record that Jesus, after being resurrected, gave his disciples power to perform miracles as great or greater than his own. The disciples became apostles (uh-POS-uhls, from a Greek word meaning "to send"). They went out into the world to preach about Jesus. Initially the apostles were persecuted by a Pharisee named Saul of Tarsus, but he had a dramatic conversion and, under the new name of Paul, became the most important of the apostles.

Paul and the others traveled around the known world, starting churches and, through their *epistles* (ee-PIS-uhls) or letters to those churches, directing the faithful. At that point, the Roman authorities still opposed Christianity, and Christians were subjected to persecution both at home and abroad. Paul and Peter apparently died at the hands of the Romans, while John, a disciple of Jesus, had a less severe fate, being exiled to an island in the Aegean (uh-GEE-uhn) Sea near Greece. There he had a series of visions concerning the future, of which he told in the Book of Revelation, the last book of the Christian Bible.

Revelation was written in about A.D. 90, and by that point the history of Judea had become tied with that of Rome. The country had become a *province* of Rome in A.D. 44, but there was continual unrest among the people. In A.D. 70, the Roman emperor Titus (TIE-tus) destroyed Jerusalem and its temple, but a group of Zealots still held on to a fortress at Masada (muh-SOD-uh.) Forces under Titus destroyed Masada in A.D. 73, and 400 Zealots committed suicide rather than surrender. In A.D. 135, the Roman emperor Hadrian (HAY-dree-uhn), responding to more Jewish unrest, declared that no Jew could live in the city of Jerusalem.

Israel to the present day

The focus of Christianity shifted from Palestine to Greece and Rome as those societies, formerly committed to *pagan* religions, eventually accepted the new faith. Ironically, the Roman Empire that had crucified Jesus would one day adopt Christianity as its state religion. Christianity would long outlast the Roman Empire.

The Israelites would lose control over Jerusalem and surrounding areas not just for centuries, but for *millennia*. During the Middle Ages (A.D. 500–1500), the Jews spread throughout Europe, North Africa, and Asia. Muslims took over Palestine in the 600s A.D. Jerusalem was a holy place both to Christians and Muslims, as well as to Jews. The Christian kings of Europe led a series of *Crusades,* or so-called holy wars, to retake Jerusalem during a period of nearly two centuries starting in 1095. The Crusades were anything but holy; they resulted in much bloodshed and cruelty on both sides. In the end, Jerusalem remained under Muslim control.

Emperor Hadrian, right profile.
The Library of Congress.

The Europeans did, however, gain valuable exposure to the advanced culture of the Arabs during the Crusades. This exposure helped bring Europe out of the ignorance and superstition that characterized much of the early Middle Ages. But it did little to help the situation of the Jews, who were persecuted throughout Europe. Europeans prevented Jews from holding most jobs and forced them to live in specific areas called *ghettoes* (GEH-toze). They forced Jews out of their countries, for instance from Spain in 1493, and killed many of their people.

The justification for this *anti-Semitism* was that the Jews had crucified Christ. Some anti-Semites even claimed that

The Bible in the Arts

Signs of the Bible's influence on Western culture can be found in the biblical themes that appear in many of the arts, including painting, sculpture, architecture, music, literature, and film.

Most painters in the Middle Ages and the *Renaissance,* a period of renewed commitment to learning that began in about A.D. 1500, used Bible stories as their subjects. Perhaps the most striking examples are the paintings on the walls and ceiling of the Sistine (SIS-teen) Chapel, located in the Vatican, the center of the Catholic faith in Rome. Painted over a period of four years by Michelangelo (mick-ul-AN-jel-o; 1475–1564), it depicts events ranging from the Creation to the Great Flood.

Michelangelo also created many notable works of sculpture, including a statue of David and one of the Virgin Mary holding her son, Jesus, after his death on the cross. Many other painters and sculptors, including Leonardo (lee-o-NAR-do) da Vinci (1452–1519) and Raphael (rah-fie-EL; 1483–1520) composed works depicting Jesus as an infant in the arms of his mother. This particular scene is so well known that it has a name, Nativity (nuh-TIV-i-tee), which means "birth."

The influence of the Bible in architecture can be found in the numerous great churches and Jewish temples of the world. The style of these buildings draws on concepts contained in the Bible. For instance, the front of a Jewish *synagogue* (SIN-uh-gog) often bears a copy of the original Ten Commandments. Great cathedrals such as Notre-Dame (NO-truh DOM) in Paris, completed in 1345, are often called "sermons in stone" because they contain numerous statues depicting events from the Old and New Testaments.

The Bible's influence in music extends from classical to popular forms. Each year at Christmas, audiences around the world are treated to performances of the *Messiah,* a work for vocals, chorus, and symphony composed by George Frideric (FREE-drick) Handel (1685–1789) in 1742.

persecution of Jews was an act of Christian obedience. (The New Testament paints a very different picture, suggesting that all of humanity, and not just one group of people, is guilty of killing the son of God. It also teaches that all people are to be treated with kindness.) Anti-Semitism sank to its depths under Adolf Hitler (1889–1945) and the Nazi Party, which controlled Germany from 1933 to 1945 and killed more than six million Jews in the *Holocaust* (HOE-loh-cost).

Equally well known is the work of Johann (YO-hahn) Sebastian Bach (BOCK; 1685–1750), who created numerous Christian works including *Jesu, Joy of Man's Desiring* and the music for the Christian hymn "A Mighty Fortress Is Our God." (The latter contains words written by Martin Luther, 1483–1546, the most significant leader of the Reformation. The Reformation was the revolt against Catholicism that created the Protestant churches.) Among popular works based on biblical themes are such well known songs as "Go Tell It on the Mountain" and "Rivers of Babylon."

The Bible itself, of course—particularly the beautiful King James Version, a translation completed in 1611—is often studied in literature classes. So too is *Paradise Lost,* a long poem by John Milton (1608–1704) portraying the revolt against God by the angel Lucifer, who became Satan. Many other literary works do not specifically depict biblical events but involve so many references to the Bible that a reader who knew nothing about the religion of the Israelites would be lost. A great example is *Moby Dick* (1851), a classic of American literature by Herman Melville (1819–1891). It is no mistake that the narrator is named Ishmael, the wanderer, or that the captain of his ship is the evil Ahab. The story itself is closely related to the biblical Book of Jonah.

Even film, the most recently developed of all the major arts, has drawn heavily on biblical themes. Among the best "Bible epics" is *The Ten Commandments* (1956), produced at a time when Hollywood was churning out movies on biblical subjects. A less notable example is *The Bible* (1966). Films about Christ include *The Robe* (1953), *The King of Kings* (1961), *The Greatest Story Ever Told* (1965), and *Jesus of Nazareth* (1977). *Jesus Christ Superstar* (1973), based on a musical of the same name, and *The Last Temptation of Christ* (1988) both raised a great deal of discussion among Christians, many of whom disagreed with the ways in which these two films portrayed Jesus.

Ironically, the Holocaust resulted in the creation of Israel, the first official Jewish nation in 2,000 years. For centuries, there had been a great deal of disagreement as to whether the Jews could reclaim Palestine, since large numbers of Arabs had settled in their former homeland. At one time, the British government even suggested a Jewish state in what is now the African nation of Uganda. But worldwide sympathy after the Holocaust paved the way for the establishment of the State of Israel in 1948.

Independence was one step toward the restoration of Israel, but far from the last one: Israel had to fight wars with Egypt, Syria, and other Arab neighbors in 1948, 1967, and 1973. In spite of an agreement between Israeli and Egyptian leaders in 1977, tensions have remained high, particularly on the West Bank of the Jordan River. This area, taken from the nation of Jordan in the 1967 war, includes Jerusalem, and has a large population of Palestinian Arabs. During the 1990s, hopes for a peace settlement were continually frustrated by outbreaks of violence on all sides.

The legacy of ancient Israel

With the exception of Greece and Rome, no other ancient society has so directly affected the course of modern life as did the tiny nation of Israel. It is virtually impossible for a person in the United States, Europe, or any other part of the

Western world to go a day without experiencing the effects of Israel, Greece, and Rome. People seldom think about ancient Greece or Rome in their everyday lives, however, but events in ancient Israel are commemorated every weekend and on many holidays throughout the year. Names from the Old and New Testaments, too, are a part of day-to-day life: everyone knows a David or a Deborah, a Mark or a Mary.

Dead Sea Scrolls, the manual of discipline, on display at the Special Museum, House of the Book in Jerusalem.
Corbis-Bettmann. Reproduced by permission

People continue to disagree over the meaning of the Bible. At one time, some scholars had come to believe that Abraham, Moses, David, and even Jesus did not really live, but rather were legendary figures like the Greek heroes in the *Iliad*. Over the years, however, considerable archaeological evidence has surfaced regarding the Bible, including the Dead Sea Scrolls, a collection of ancient biblical texts found in Palestine in the late 1940s and early 1950s. Historians have come to treat Biblical figures as historical. Certainly there is plenty of outside evidence for events and people from the time of David onward.

As for the truth of the Bible, however, that continues to be an area of disagreement. As noted earlier, Muslims hold much of the Bible sacred and respect biblical figures ranging from Abraham to Jesus. However, they have their own holy book, the *Koran* (core-AN). Likewise Jews have a number of sacred texts in addition to the Old Testament, including the Talmud, which provides additional information on the law and other subjects covered in the Old Testament. Catholics and Protestants, as well as other major branches of Christianity such as the Greek and Russian Orthodox (ORE-tho-dox) churches, all believe that Jesus was the son of God, but they disagree about other aspects of Christianity.

And of course, Christians disagree with other groups in Western society. The latter part of the twentieth century in the United States, for instance, saw the rise of religious and political groups sometimes described as "Christian fundamentalists" (fun-duh-MEN-tul-ists), who called for a return to biblical traditions in American society at large. Fundamentalists have been sharply opposed by others who favor a nonreligious basis for government and public *morality*. But all sides can agree on at least one fact: the traditions of a small group of people, who existed only briefly as a nation more than 2,500 years ago, continue to influence the world.

For More Information

Books

Connolly, Peter. *The Jews in the Time of Jesus: A History.* Oxford, England: Oxford University Press, 1983.

De Paola, Tomie. *The Miracle of Jesus: Retold from the Bible and Illustrated by Tomie de Paola.* New York: Holiday House, 1987.

Dijkstra, Henk. *History of the Ancient & Medieval World,* Volume 3: *Ancient Cultures.* New York: Marshall Cavendish, 1996, pp. 313-36.

Harker, Ronald. *Digging Up the Bible Lands.* Drawings by Martin Simmons. New York: Henry Z. Walck, 1972.

Kent, David. *Kings of Israel.* Illustrated by Harry Bishop, John Keay, and Rob McCaig. London: Kingfisher, 1981.

Kuskin, Karla. *Jerusalem, Shining Still.* Illustrations by David Frampton. New York: Harper, 1987.

Odijk, Pamela. *The Israelites*. Englewood Cliffs, NJ: Silver Burdett, 1990.

Sasso, Sandy Eisenberg. *But God Remembered: Stories of Women from Creation to the Promised Land*. Illustrated by Bethanne Andersen. Woodstock, VT: Jewish Lights Publishing, 1995.

Smith, F. LaGard, ed. *The Narrated Bible*. Eugene, OR: Harvest House, 1984.

Tubb, Jonathan N. *Bible Lands*. New York: Knopf, 1991.

Web Sites

"Canaan and Ancient Israel @ University of Pennsylvania Museum of Archaeology and Anthropology." *University of Pennsylvania*. http://www.upenn.edu/museum/Collections/ canaanframedoc1.html (February 26, 1999).

"Canaanite/Ugaritic Mythology FAQ." *University of New Hampshire*. http://pubpages.unh.edu/~cbsiren/canaanite-faq.html (February 26, 1999).

"History of Jerusalem." *Virtual Jerusalem*. http://www.virtual.co.il/ communities/jerusalem/history.htm (February 26, 1999).

The Jerusalem Biblical Zoo. http://www.itmi.com/jeruzoo/english/ index.htm (February 26, 1999).

Temple News. http://members.tripod.com/~faithibmfaith/index-37.html (February 26, 1999).

Phoenicia, Syria, and Arabia

The term "Middle East" usually describes a vast stretch of lands from Morocco in North Africa to Afghanistan on the edge of the Indian subcontinent. But the very middle of the Middle East consists of countries that lie south of Turkey, west of Iran, and east of Egypt and the Red Sea. They extend all the way south to the bottom of Arabia, a huge, boot-shaped expanse of land that sticks out 1,400 miles (2,253 kilometers) into the waters that separate Africa from the Indian subcontinent. This region includes nine modern nations: Lebanon, Syria, Jordan, Saudi Arabia, Yemen, Oman, the United Arab Emirates, Qatar, and Kuwait. The first three countries lie to the north, between Israel, Iraq, and Turkey, in an area that ranges from the fertile Mediterranean coast in Lebanon to the rocky deserts of Jordan and Syria. As for the other six countries, except in a few areas, they are almost purely desert and dry, rocky mountains.

The importance of Phoenicia, Syria, and Arabia

With regard to Phoenicia, Syria, and Arabia—that is, the entire Arabian Peninsula—it seems that the smaller the region,

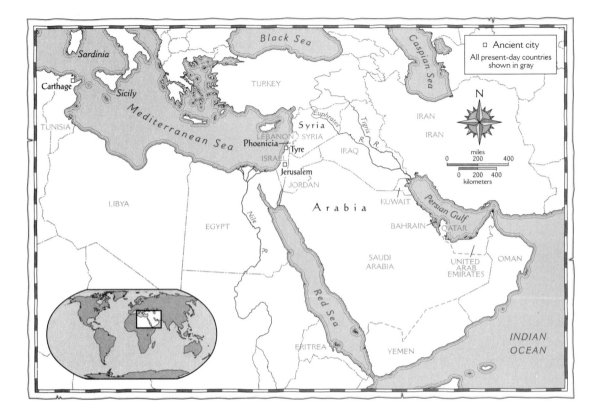

Map of Phoenicia, Syria, and Arabia. *XNR Productions. The Gale Group.*

the greater its influence on the ancient world. Arabia is an area of more than 1.75 million square miles (4.53 square kilometers, or almost half the size of the United States), but it played little role in ancient history; later, however, it would have an enormous impact on world events. As for Syria, which in modern times is a nation of more than 70,000 square miles (or 181,300 square kilometers; about the size of Missouri), its language, Aramaic, spread throughout the ancient world. When Jesus Christ brought his message of salvation to the Israelites, the language in which he spoke was Aramaic. Finally, there was tiny Phoenicia. In modern times, it is called Lebanon, a nation that covers fewer than 4,000 square miles (10,360 square kilometers), meaning that it is geographically smaller than Los Angeles County, which contains the northern portion of greater Los Angeles, California. Small it may have been, but its contribution to civilization was great: Phoenicians gave the world its first alphabet; established *colonies* in Spain, France, and North Africa; and sailed all the way around the African continent.

Phoenicia (c. 2000–64 B.C.)

On the eastern coast of the Mediterranean (med-ih-tur-ANE-ee-uhn) Sea lay Phoenicia (foh-NEE-shuh), a narrow strip of land just 200 miles (322 kilometers) long and 30 miles (48 kilometers) wide—much smaller, in fact, than modern-day Lebanon (LEB-uh-nahn). It is not clear how the Phoenicians got their name, though it may have come from a Greek word for red or purple, a reference to the dyed cloth that the Phoenicians wore and sold. The Phoenicians spoke a *Semitic* language and were probably a Canaanite (KAY-nuhn-ite) people; certainly they lived in the same region as the Canaanites, and worshiped Canaanite gods such as Baal and Astarte.

Phoenicia was never a single country, but a loose collection of *city-states* of which the most notable were Tyre (pronounced like "tire"), Sidon (SIE-duhn), and Byblos (BEEB-lohs). Unlike the city-states of Sumer, these towns were never at war with one another. In fact the Phoenicians are almost unique among ancient peoples in that they did not maintain an army or attempt to conquer other peoples; rather, their focus was on trade.

Conquest through trade

Trade is a term used to describe the exchange of goods for units of value (money, gold, or other goods) between two individuals or two countries. Trade is different from production, which occurs when a farmer grows a crop or raises of group of animals for sale, or when a *craftsman* manufactures goods for sale. A merchant, someone who engages in trade, sells the goods produced by farmers and tradesmen (or, in modern times, by factories) to *consumers*—that is, ordinary people who buy things they need. Rather than having to sell directly to the public, it was easier for producers of goods to sell their items to merchants, who then sold them to the consumers. As a result, the *economy* of Phoenicia grew, and so did its wealth.

The Phoenicians had little choice but to engage in trade. Though their soil was not bad for agriculture, the mountain ranges to the east meant that the available area for raising crops or animals was limited. Nor did Phoenicia have the kind of military power that would make it possible to conquer others; instead, the Phoenicians established their influence through business.

Words to Know: Phoenicia, Syria, and Arabia

Archaeology: The study of the material evidence left behind by past cultures.

Bronze: A type of metal made from a mixture of tin and copper.

City-state: A city that acts as an independent country.

Commerce: Buying and selling of goods on a large scale.

Consumer: A person who buys things from a merchant or businessperson.

Cuneiform: A type of wedge-shaped writing used in Mesopotamia.

Dynasty: A group of people, often but not always a family, who continue to hold a position of power over a period of time.

Economy: The whole system of production, distribution, and consumption of goods and services in a country.

Export: Selling goods to another country.

Fundamentalist: A person who strictly follows a basic set of (often religious) principles.

Goods: Items that are bought and sold.

Hegira: Muhammad's escape from Mecca with his followers in A.D. 622; the beginning of the Muslim calendar.

Hieroglyphics: A system of symbols, called hieroglyphs, which made up the Egyptians' written language.

Import: Buying goods from another country.

Ironic: When something is intended to be one way but turns out to be quite different from what was intended.

Islam: A faith that arose in Arabia in the A.D. 600s, led by the prophet Muhammad (A.D. 570?–632).

Koran: The holy book of Islam.

Literate: Able to read and write.

Mariner: A sailor.

Ports, ships, and trade

Beginning in about 2000 B.C., the peoples of Phoenicia established great port cities such as Tyre. There they engaged in *import,* bringing in goods from other countries such as Egypt, and *export,* selling goods from Phoenicia to the rest of the known world. Among Phoenician-produced items were cloth goods, dyed in the reddish-purple color produced by a type of shellfish plentiful along the Mediterranean coast.

Another important item was wood, one of the country's only *natural resources.* Phoenician cedar (SEE-duhr), was a reddish wood so prized that the "cedars of Lebanon" became

Merchant: Someone who sells goods.

Middle Ages: The period from the fall of the Roman Empire to the beginning of the Renaissance, roughly A.D. 500 to 1500.

Migration: Movement by a large group of people from one place to another.

Muslim: A believer in Islam.

Natural resources: Materials from nature, such as trees or minerals, that are useful to the operation of business or a society.

Nomadic: Wandering.

Peninsula: An area of land that sticks out into water. Examples include Arabia, Italy, and Florida.

Pictograms, phonograms: Two types of written symbol. A pictogram looks like the thing it represents; a phonogram represents a specific syllable.

Province: A political unit, like a state, that is part of a larger country or empire.

Scribes: A small and very powerful group in ancient society who knew how to read and write.

Semitic: A term describing a number of groups in the Middle East, including the modern-day Arabs and Israelis.

Services: Actions that are bought and sold—for example, cleaning a house or serving food.

Spherical: Shaped like a ball.

Terrorism: Frightening (and usually harming) a specific group of people in order to achieve a specific political goal.

Trade: The exchange of goods for units of value (money, gold, or other goods) between two individuals or two countries.

Trade route: Roads or paths along which goods are regularly moved for export and import.

Vassal: A ruler who is subject to another ruler.

famous throughout the ancient world. Phoenician cypress wood was a popular export as well. (The flag of modern Lebanon depicts a cypress tree.) Phoenician craftsmen were also known for their ability at woodworking: thus when Solomon was building his temple in Jerusalem, he brought in Phoenician craftsmen. The Bible also indicates that Phoenicians were talented at working with *bronze,* a type of metal made from a mixture of tin and copper, which was used both for everyday items and for decorations.

It appears that the Phoenicians enjoyed generally good relations with their Israelite neighbors to the south. Both

Solomon and his father, David, made *treaties*, or agreements between nations, with the Phoenician king Hiram (HIGH-rum) of Tyre in the 900s B.C. These agreements with Israel, which at that point was a powerful force in the region, helped make it possible for Phoenicia to establish a number of *trade routes*—roads or paths along which goods are regularly moved for export and import—over both land and sea.

Phoenician colonies and voyages

Trade routes alone, however, were not enough: particularly in faraway places, the Phoenicians needed warehouses where they could store goods for later sale as well as trading posts where they could conduct business with the local peoples. For this reason, they established a number of overseas colonies in the period from about 900 to about 600 B.C.

To call a place a *colony* means that it is a territory belonging to another country. When people from the ruling country go to a foreign place in large numbers and begin to bring that place under their control, they are *colonizing*. For instance, the Egyptians colonized Kush, and the British colonized North America in the 1600s and 1700s A.D. Phoenician colonization was somewhat unusual because, as always, the Phoenicians' main concern was not political or military power, but business. They were not interested in making foreigners speak their language or worship their gods; all they wanted to do was conduct trade.

The most famous of all Phoenician colonies was Carthage (KAHR-thej), located in what is now the nation of Tunisia (too-NEE-zhuh) in North Africa. Established some time after 800 B.C., Carthage possessed a fine harbor that made it a favorite port of call for trading ships. Eventually it would become a great city, so great it challenged the most powerful empire of the ancient world: Rome.

Across the Mediterranean, Phoenician traders founded cities on the islands of Sicily and Sardinia (sar-DEEN-yuh) off the coast of Italy. They also established cities on the European continent, including Marseilles (mar-SAY) in France, as well as the Spanish cities of Barcelona (bar-suh-LOH-nuh), Cadiz (kah-DEEZ), Malaga (muh-LAH-guh), and Algeciras (al-juh-SEER-uhs). Farther away, at the edge of the known world, were what the Phoenicians called "the tin islands": Britain, as well as the region of Britanny (BRIT-uh-nee) on the northwest coast of France. The Phoenicians brought in purple cloth and traded it with the locals for tin, essential for making bronze.

To appreciate the vast distances covered, and the bravery of *mariners* (MARE-uh-nurz) or sailors who crossed the Mediterranean to parts beyond, it is important to remember how little ancient people knew about the Earth. As far as most people knew, the entire world consisted of what can now be identified as the Middle East, southern Europe, and northern Africa. Some had guessed that the Earth was *spherical* (S'FEER-ih-kul)—that is, shaped like a ball—but nobody had any idea what lay on the other side of the planet. Beyond the farthest edge of Spain, at the rock of Gibraltar (ji-BRAWL-tur), lay an ocean, known today as the

Drawing of Vasco da Gama. *Archive Photos. Reproduced by permission.*

Atlantic, which was so wide that many believed it surrounded the entire world. The modern equivalent of Phoenician mariners would be astronauts, who likewise go bravely into unexplored regions.

The greatest of Phoenician voyages took place in about 600 B.C., when the Egyptian pharaoh Necho II (NEE-koh; r. 610—595 B.C.) hired a group of Carthaginians (kar-thuh-GIN-ee-unz) to sail around the coast of Africa. For some time, the Phoenicians had been trading with Africans, but this voyage took them from Carthage all the way around the continent. Hugging the coastline as they went, the Phoenician sailors rounded the southern tip of Africa and came back up the coast along the Indian Ocean. They sailed around the "Horn of Africa" to the east, and up the Red Sea coast of Egypt and Ethiopia. It would be more than 2,000 years before anyone else would make such an extraordinary voyage, when the Portuguese explorer Vasco da Gama sailed around the African continent in the A.D. 1400s.

Phoenician trade with Africa

The Phoenicians regularly traded with Africans who lived on the Atlantic coast below the Sahara (suh-HAIR-uh) Desert, probably in the area of the present-day nation of Senegal (SIN-uh-gahl). They would land their ships on the coast, and because they could not communicate with the Africans, they developed an unusual method of trade.

The Phoenicians would set out a certain amount of goods on a beach, then return to their ships. The Africans would then place an amount of gold, which was plentiful in their area, next to the Phoenicians' goods. If the Phoenicians judged that it was a fair exchange, they would take the gold and depart. If they did not, however, they would leave their goods on the shore until the Africans brought out more gold. Once they had agreed on an exchange, the Phoenicians would take their gold and sail away.

Other African lands with which the Phoenicians traded were Ophir (OH-fur), which may have been located where Mozambique (moh-zam-BEEK) is now, on the southeastern coast of Africa; and Punt, the location of present-day Somalia (soe-MAHL-ee-uh) on the "Horn of Africa" to the east.

The alphabet and other contributions

Exploration, trade, and crafts-manship were not the Phoenicians' only achievements. Perhaps the greatest of all their contributions to civilization was the development of the alphabet. Though the Phoenicians did not claim to have invented the alphabet they used, they certainly developed it, and through their many voyages extended it to the known world. The Phoenician alphabet, which appeared between 1700 and 1500 B.C., originally used only nineteen symbols, roughly equivalent to the letters of the English alphabet, except for *I* and the last six letters, *U* through *Z*.

Before the alphabet, all writing had been in the form of *pictograms,* symbols that looked like the thing they represented, or *phonograms,* symbols that represented a syllable. To use *hieroglyphics,* as the Egyptians did, or *cuneiform* as did the people of Mesopotamia, one had to memorize hundreds of symbols. Therefore only *scribes,* highly learned men trained in the use of pictograms and phonograms, were *literate* (LIT-uh-ret)—that is, able to read and write.

To use an alphabet, by contrast, one only had to remember a small number of symbols—twenty-six in the alphabet used by English-speakers. Thus the alphabet led to a great increase in learning, because ordinary people were able to become literate as well. Eventually almost all the civilizations of the Western world began to use some form of alphabet. Today only the peoples of the East, such as the Chinese and Japanese, use pictograms and phonograms.

After the development of the alphabet, the next great advance in expanding people's ability to read and write did not come until about A.D. 1450, when the invention of the printing press made it possible to spread the written word throughout the world. The first book printed was the Bible. It is no mistake, perhaps, that the word *Bible,* which is Greek for "book," comes from the name of the Phoenician city-state of Byblos.

Caught between warring nations

Phoenician civilization did really die out; rather, the Phoenicians were absorbed into the empires of conquering nations. Assyria had begun threatening Phoenicia as early as 868 B.C., but when the Assyrian monarch Tiglath-Pileser attempted to capture Tyre in 734 B.C., he ran into trouble. Because the city was built on an island about a mile offshore, it was a mighty fortress; in fact its name means "rock." After two years, the Assyrians finally captured Tyre, but they did not attempt to turn the region into a *province* (PRAH-vints) of their empire—not yet, at least.

In 701 B.C., Sennacherib led another Assyrian invasion of Phoenicia. He drove out the king of Tyre, replacing him with a *vassal* (VAH-sul), and conquered the other important cities of Phoenicia, including Sidon. A later king of Tyre attempted a revolt against the Assyrians, and this action resulted in the destruction of Sidon in 677 B.C. Still Tyre remained rebellious, protected by its location. The Assyrians tried once more to capture it, but they had troubles of their own at home and eventually lost their empire to the Babylonians. Finally in 587 B.C., the Babylonian king Nebuchadnezzar conquered Tyre.

Just as Babylonia replaced Assyria as the dominant power in the region, the Persians replaced Babylonia in about

GREEK ALPHABET.	HIERATIC SIGNS.	PHOENICIAN ALPHABET.	GREEK ALPHABET.	HIERATIC SIGNS.	PHOENICIAN ALPHABET.
A			Λ		
B			M		
Γ			N		
Δ			Ξ		
E			O		
F			Π		
Z			Ϙ		
H			P		
Θ			Σ		
I			T		
K					

Table comparing the Greek, Hieratic Greek, and Phoenician alphabets.
Corbis. Reproduced by permission.

539 B.C. As part of the Persian Empire, the Phoenician fleet helped wage war on the Greeks. Later, the armies of Alexander the Great conquered the Persians' empire, and Phoenicia passed into Greek hands in 333 B.C. Like much of the Middle East, it then fell under the Seleucid Empire before becoming part of the Roman province of Syria in 64 B.C.

Syria (A.D. c. 1200–600s)

The Syrians, whose kingdom lay to the north of Phoenicia, shared much common history with their seafaring neighbors. They too were a Canaanite people speaking a Semitic language, and they likewise often found themselves caught between a number of great powers in the region.

Syria had been populated since at least 8500 B.C., and for thousands of years it was controlled by a people known to archaeologists as the Halaf (huh-LAHF) civilization. The latter established the city of Ugarit (YOO-guh-rit), which would remain an important center until its destruction by the mysterious Sea Peoples in about 1200 B.C. Halaf culture, however, ended in about 4500 B.C., for reasons that are unclear, and over the next few thousand years, Syria was controlled by groups from Mesopotamia.

During the 1700s B.C., the Mesopotamian city-state of Mari (MAHR-ee) held power over the area, extending its territory all the way to Ugarit on the Mediterranean coast. Mari was followed by a number of other small civilizations. By the 1300s B.C., the Hittites were on the move, and they often clashed with the Egyptians for control of the region. Another force was Mitanni (mi-TAHN-ee) to the east. The Mitannians attempted to play the Hittites and Egyptians against one another until they were crushed by the Hittites in the mid-1300s B.C.

The Hittites finally did battle with the Egyptians at the Syrian city of Kadesh (KAY-desh) in about 1285 B.C., and with the apparent victory of the Hittites, Syria came under Hittite control. The trading city of Ugarit, however, remained independent and established ties both with Egypt and the Hittites. The city flourished from about 1400 to about 1200, and the Ugaritic language spread throughout the region. After the Sea Peoples destroyed the city, Phoenicians took over the trade that had once passed through Ugarit.

The Aramaeans

Syria truly came into its own under the control of the Aramaeans (air-uh-MAY-uhnz), a Semitic-speaking group from Mesopotamia who had briefly controlled Babylonia. In about 1200 B.C., however, they moved westward, rushing into the power vacuum created by the Sea Peoples' destruction of the Hittites. The most powerful group of Aramaeans established themselves in the city of Damascus (duh-MAS-kuhs). Damascus would become an important city and remains the capital of Syria in modern times.

The kings of Aram (AY-ram), as Syria at this time was called, regularly did battle with the Israelite kings Saul and David in the late 1000s and early 900s B.C. Though David defeated the Syrians, after the division of Israel following the death of Solomon, the kings of Judah and Israel were often on friendly terms with the Aramaean kings. Ben-Hadad II (bin HAY-dad; r. 879—842 B.C.), persuaded the Israelites and others to join him in making war on Assyria. For a time, this alliance seemed to work, but in about 732 B.C., the Assyrians won control over Syria.

Later history

Like much of the region, Syria would pass from empire to empire over the next few centuries, first falling into Babylonian hands, then Persian, until it was conquered by Alexander the Great in the 330s B.C. But because of their earlier conquest of Babylonia, the Syrians left a powerful legacy in the form of their language, Aramaic. The Babylonians had spread it throughout the region until it became the *lingua franca* (LING-wuh FRANK-uh), or common language, for much of the known world.

Later in ancient times, Syria would rise to prominence as a central part of the Seleucid Empire that developed in the wake of Alexander's conquests. The Seleucids founded Antioch (AN-tee-ahk), a city in northern Syria that became a major commercial area. In the early years of Christianity, Antioch also served as a center for missionaries going into the world to preach Christ's gospel.

By that time, the city had fallen under the control of the Roman Empire, which in its declining years faced a signif-

Lingua Franca spoken here

The term *lingua franca* (LING-wah FRANK-uh), meaning "common language," is derived from Latin. Latin, like Aramaic before it and English afterward, would become a language that allowed people of different native tongues to communicate. In the modern world, for instance, if a pilot from Korea is landing a plane in Germany, it is likely that he or she will speak to the control tower in English.

In the Middle Ages (A.D. c. 500–1500), Latin served a similar function. Learned men from England, Germany, Spain, and other parts of Europe could all communicate in the language, which by then was no longer spoken by common people. Even in the twentieth century, Latin is still often used in the High Mass (church service) of the Catholic Church. (The term *Catholic,* incidentally, means "universal.") Likewise Latin terms are used by doctors and scientists all over the world.

Aramaic became established in the Middle East long before the rise of the Roman Empire and its Latin language. Thanks to its adoption by the Babylonians,

Jesus Christ preaching to his disciples.
Archive Photos. Reproduced by permission.

Aramaic spread from Palestine to Persia. It offered a useful means of communication in the empires that covered those widely separated lands. Jesus Christ, who brought a universal message of salvation and who commanded his disciples to "go into the world and preach the Gospel," spoke in Aramaic.

icant problem in Syria: the kingdom of Palmyra (pal-MEER-uh). The latter was actually just a city-state on the edge of the Syrian desert, but under Queen Zenobia (zeh-NOH-bee-uh) between A.D., 267 and 272 Palmyra began building an empire at a time when Rome was troubled by a long series of bad emperors. The emperor Aurelian finally captured Zenobia and partially destroyed the city in 273.

Syria would remain a part of the Roman and Byzantine empires until its capture by the Sassanians of Persia in 611. Less than 25 years later, however, it fell under a new force sweeping the Middle East. That force was Islam, and its origins lay to the south, in barren Arabia.

Nomads travelling through the desert.
AP/Wide World Photos. Reproduced by permission.

The Arabian Peninsula

Maps of the Middle East in ancient times show a continuing record of settlement and conquest—but not on the Arabian *Peninsula* (peh-NIN-soo-luh), which remained unconquered. Few ancient armies could wage war in the barren desert landscape, nor did many conquerors have any real reason to want to control the region. It was a land good neither for raising crops or flocks, and indeed one of the few animals that could live there was the camel. Not many people lived in Arabia, and the sparse tribes of the interior were *nomads*.

The only settled areas were at the fringes of Arabia. To the north, in what is now Jordan, was Petra, a stunning city of temples and tombs carved out of solid rock. Founded prior to 400 B.C., Petra flourished as an important trading center for many centuries. Another area of settlement was on the coast, particularly in the southwestern corner of the peninsula. In this area, part of the modern country of Yemen (yeh-MAHN), the Red Sea meets the Gulf of Aden (AY-den), making it an ideal spot for trading between Egypt, sub-Saharan Africa, and India. For many centuries, the region remained under the control of various Arab kingdoms, and because of the many spices grown and sold on the Arabian coast, this part of the peninsula gained the nickname "the incense states."

As for the interior of the Arabian Peninsula, however, an event in 24 B.C. says much about conditions there. In that year, the Romans made their one and only bid to gain control of Arabia, and not surprisingly, they went for the relatively wealthy southwestern corner. Equally unsurprising was the fact that they got lost on their way through the desert—their Arab guides led them astray on purpose—and Rome gave up hopes of adding the Arabian Peninsula to its empire.

In the early centuries A.D., the Himyarite (HIM-yah-rite) kingdom in Yemen accepted Judaism, and the Himyarites often found themselves at odds with the Aksumites across the Red Sea in Africa. The Aksumites had adopted Christianity, so their political and economic conflict with the Himyarite Arabs acquired religious overtones. For that reason, the Byzantine Empire supported the Christian Africans, while the Sassanids in Persia, who were Zoroastrian, took the side of the opposing force. Aksum took over the incense states for a time, but by A.D. 575, Persia had assumed political power over the region.

Persia also had a sort of "big brother" relationship with a group of Arabs called the Lakhmids (LAHK-midz) centered in a town called Hira (HEE-rah) in the far northeastern corner of Arabia. They were united in their opposition to the Roman Empire, but like other Arab groups of ancient times, the Lakhmids had little real impact on the course of history.

Tradition holds that the Arab peoples descended from Ishmael (ISH-may-el), the first son of Abraham in the Bible. The Book of Genesis records that Ishmael's mother, the Egyptian maidservant Hagar (HAY-gar), received a promise from God that her son would produce a great nation. To the tribes who inhabited the windswept lands of the Arabian Peninsula, the promise must have seemed hard to believe.

Phoenicia, Syria, and Arabia in later times

In the A.D. 500s and early 600s, new powerful forces arose on the Arabian Peninsula. There were the Ghassanids (GAHS-uh-nidz), who *migrated* from Yemen northward to the area of modern-day Jordan. They became allies of the Byzantine Empire, which used their help in battling the Persians and Arabs in Hira to the east. At about the same time, a group called the Kinda, loyal to the kings in Yemen, conquered parts of central Arabia as well as Bahrain (BAH-rain), a small kingdom on the Persian Gulf to the east.

Muhammad standing, holding open book.
Archive Photos. Reproduced by permission.

By A.D. 600, most of the eastern coast of Arabia, including Oman (oh-MAHN), was either controlled by the Persians, or at least on friendly terms with them. Cities of the western coast either were allied with Yemen or were independent. In the interior of Arabia, it was every tribe for itself, as they waged almost constant war with each other. As with the feuds between the Hatfield and McCoy families in the mountains of West Virginia during the nineteenth century, or the wars between gangs such as the Bloods and the Crips in large cities during the late twentieth century, the causes of these conflicts were unclear to outsiders.

Into this very unpromising environment was born one of the most extraordinary figures in human history, Muhammad (moo-HAH-med; A.D. 570?–632). A merchant from the town of Mecca (MEH-kah) on the western side of the peninsula, he is said to have received a vision from God, or Allah (uh-LAH), which led him to establish a new religion, Islam (IZ-lahm). In 622, a group of his enemies in Mecca tried to murder him, and he and his small group of followers fled to a town that came to be known as Medina (meh-DIE-nah). There Muhammad founded a government based on the teachings of the Koran (koe-RAHN), Islam's holy book.

The birth and spread of Islam

Just as Christians begin their modern calendar with the birth of Christ, Muslims (MUZ-limz), or believers in Islam, date their calendar from Muhammad's *hegira* (heh-ZHIE-ruh) or flight from Mecca in 622. After that date, Islam spread rapidly, and for more than 600 years, various *dynasties* of Arabic origin held sway over the area. During this period, leadership moved to the older, more sophisticated cities of the north, particularly Damascus in Syria and Baghdad in Iraq. Because of the Islamic conquests that began in Muhammad's time, however, all of these areas had adopted the Arabic language and many aspects of Arab culture.

Thus Arabia, a barren region of forgotten people, came to rule much of the world, establishing a civilization that kept learning alive while much of Europe was mired in darkness and superstition during the Middle Ages (A.D. c. 500–1500). The age-old prophecy concerning Ishmael had been fulfilled.

The modern Arab world

By the end of the Middle Ages, the Arab influence spread from Morocco (muh-RAH-koh) in the far west of North Africa to Iraq, and from northern Syria to Sudan (soo-DAN), south of Egypt on the Nile River. It was truly a vast territory, but it was not united—and Arabs no longer controlled it. For nearly a thousand years, beginning in the 1000s A.D. and not ending until after World War I (1914–1918), Turks held the vast majority of the region. First there were the Seljuks (sel-JOOKZ), who ruled from the 1000s to the 1300s; and later there was the Ottoman (AH-tuh-man) Empire, which did not cease to exist until 1924.

Between the world wars, much of the region was controlled by France and Britain, which had defeated the Ottoman Empire (along with Germany and other countries) in the First World War. Syria and Lebanon became French possessions, while Palestine, Jordan, and Iraq fell under British rule.

Liquid gold

Meanwhile, the Arabian Peninsula had begun to emerge yet again as a powerful force in world history, thanks to the discovery of oil in the 1930s. The desert lands of Arabia, worthless for agriculture, could hardly have been more valuable if they were covered in gold dust instead of sand: with the spread of automobiles, particularly in Europe and America, the world had an unquenchable thirst for gasoline, and the once-poor nations of Arabia became fabulously wealthy.

As in Muhammad's time, it was *ironic* that the forgotten nations of Arabia came to have enormous power. Also ironic was the fact that most of the powerful countries of ancient times had little oil, whereas the poorest regions were now rich. Thus Syria had much less oil than Arabia, and Lebanon less still; likewise Yemen, the one relatively powerful Arab nation in ancient times, proved to have little oil.

Photograph of a city street in Beirut, Lebanon in the mid-twentieth century. *Archive Photos. Reproduced by permisison.*

Hussein I (King of Jordan).
Archive Photos/Archive France.
Reproduced by permission.

Oil wealth, along with the guidance of the powerful Saud (sah-OOD) family, led to the independence of Saudi (SOW-dee) Arabia, by far the largest nation on the Arabian Peninsula. The Sauds were sheikhs (SHAYKZ), or desert kings, as were the rulers of many other oil-rich nations such as Bahrain and Oman that became independent in the years following World War II (1939–1945). But Israel, too, became an independent country in 1948. This development led to great tension with its Arab neighbors.

This tension was increased by the rising movement for an independent Arab state in Palestine—the same land that Israel claimed for its own. The Palestine Liberation Organization (PLO) and its leader, Yassir Arafat (yah-SEER AIR-uh-fat; 1929–), were not above using *terrorism* to achieve their aims. Thus at the 1972 Olympics in Munich, a Palestinian group killed eleven Israeli athletes.

The Palestinians in 1978 attacked Israel from bases in Lebanon. The Israelis responded by occupying part of Lebanese territory to establish a protective buffer zone. In 1982, Israel launched a major attack against Palestinian strongholds in Lebanon, particularly in the capital city of Beirut (bay-ROOT). Beirut, a favorite tourist spot during the 1950s and 1960s, became a war-torn shell of a city. On October 25, 1983, a terrorist drove a truck filled with explosives into barracks that housed U.S. peacekeeping forces in Beirut; the resulting explosion killed more than 200 Marines.

The terrorists were allied not with the PLO, but with another, even more violent, force in the region: Iran under the Ayatollah Khomeini. Nor were the Palestinians and the Islamic *fundamentalists* in Iran the only threat to peace: another was Hafez al-Assad (hah-FEZ ahl uh-SAHD; 1928–), who took power in Syria in 1971. A fierce enemy of Israel, he supported the PLO and began occupying parts of Lebanon in 1976. Even more frightening was Saddam Hussein of Iraq, who in 1990 invaded the oil-rich sheikhdom of Kuwait. Like many leaders in the region, Saddam claimed to desire unity among all Arabs, but his ruthless attack on his neighbors to the south sent another message.

A quite different leader—and certainly no relation of Saddam's, though they had the same last name—was King Hussein I (hoo-SAYN; 1935–1999) of Jordan. Hussein, who became ruler in 1952, initially supported the PLO, but like Anwar Sadat of Egypt, he came to desire better relations with Israel. From the 1970s onward, he actively supported the cause of peace in the region. When he died in 1999, people all over the world mourned his passing.

For More Information

Books

Burrell, Roy. *Oxford First Ancient History.* New York: Oxford University Press, 1991, pp. 82-83.

Dijkstra, Henk. *History of the Ancient & Medieval World,* Volume 3: *Ancient Cultures.* New York: Marshall Cavendish, 1996, pp. 295-312.

Dué, Andrea, editor. *The Atlas of Human History: Cradles of Civilization: Ancient Egypt and Early Middle Eastern Civilizations.* Text by Renzo Rossi. New York: Macmillan Library Reference USA, 1996, pp. 16-19, 40-43.

Dué, Andrea, editor. *The Atlas of Human History: Civilizations of Asia: India, China and the Peoples of Southeast Asia and the Indian Ocean.* Text by Renzo Rossi and Martina Veutro. New York: Macmillan Library Reference USA, 1996, pp. 48-51.

Foster, Leila Merrell. *Lebanon.* Chicago: Childrens Press, 1992.

Long, Cathryn J. *The Middle East in Search of Peace.* Brookfield, CT: Millbrook Press, 1996.

Martell, Hazel Mary. *The Kingfisher Book of the Ancient World.* New York: Kingfisher, 1995, pp. 90-91.

Mulloy, Martin. *Saudi Arabia.* New York: Chelsea House, 1987.

Mulloy, Martin. *Syria.* New York: Chelsea House, 1988.

Odijk, Pamela. *The Phoenicians.* Englewood Cliffs, NJ: Silver Burdett Press, 1989.

Tubb, Jonathan N. *Bible Lands.* New York: Knopf, 1991, pp. 22-23.

Web Sites

"The Ancient Phoenicians." *St. Maron Parish of Cleveland.* http://www.stmaron-clev.org/phoenicians.htm (April 13, 1999).

A Bequest Unearthed, Phoenicia. http://phoenicia.org/ (April 13, 1999).

"The Phoenicians." *Lebanon2000.Com.* http://www.lebanon2000.com/ph.htm (April 13, 1999).

Asia Minor and the Black Sea Region

The regions and groups discussed in this chapter have certain elements in common, not the least of which is geography. First among these regions is Asia Minor, site of the modern-day nation of Turkey, which in ancient times was the home of the Hittites, the Phrygians, and the Lydians. Asia Minor, which forms a bridge between the European continent and Asia, is bounded by the Mediterranean Sea on the south and the Black Sea on the north. North of the Black Sea lies the Ukraine, controlled by groups such as the Cimmerians and Scythians in ancient times. To the southeast of the Ukraine, between the Black Sea and the Caspian Sea, is the Caucasus, whose most notable ancient civilizations were Urartu and Armenia.

The importance of Asia Minor and the Black Sea region

The Hittites, who lived in central Turkey from about 1750 to about 1200 B.C., created a great empire that rivaled

Words to Know: Asia Minor and Western Asia

Archaeology: The study of the material evidence left behind by past cultures.

Barbarian: A negative term used to describe someone as uncivilized.

Barter: Exchange of one item for another.

Chariot: A small and highly mobile open-air wagon drawn by horses.

Commerce: Buying and selling of goods on a large scale.

Communism: A political and economic system in which the government owns virtually all property in the name of the people.

Concentration camp: A camp where political prisoners or prisoners of war are held.

Dictator: A ruler who holds absolute, or complete, power.

Dynasty: A group of people, often but not always a family, who continue to hold a position of power over a period of time.

Economy: The whole system of production, distribution, and consumption of goods and services in a country.

Islam: A faith that arose in Arabia in the A.D. 600s, led by the prophet Muhammad (A.D. 570?–632).

Linguist: A scholar who studies the historical development of languages.

Medieval: An adjective describing the Middle Ages.

Middle Ages: The period from the fall of the Roman Empire to the beginning of the Renaissance, roughly A.D. 500–1500.

Muslim: A believer in Islam.

Nomads: Wandering groups of people.

Peasants: A farmer who works a small plot of land.

Peninsula: An area of land that sticks out into a body of water.

Sack (verb): To destroy.

Semitic: A term describing a number of groups in the Middle East, including the modern-day Arabs and Israelis.

Smelting: Refining a metal, such as iron.

Soviet Union: A country that combined Russia and fourteen other nations under a Communist government from the end of World War I to the early 1990s.

Strait: A narrow passage of water.

Sultan: A type of king in the Muslim world.

Systematic: Planned and orderly.

Tumulus: A burial mound.

Usurp: To seize power.

Vassal: A ruler who is subject to another ruler.

Westerner: Someone from a culture or civilization influenced by ancient Greece and Rome.

Map of Asia Minor and the Black Sea Region.
XNR Productions. The Gale Group.

Egypt and the nations of Mesopotamia, with whom it was often at war. The two greatest achievements of the Hittites were the development of iron *smelting* and *chariot* warfare, skills that their enemies adapted and used against them. Their language also provided an important historical link for scholars studying the relation between the peoples of Europe and India. Later came the Phrygians, known for their great wealth; and the Lydians, the first nation to coin money. As for the Cimmerians, Scythians, and Sarmatians of the Ukraine, they were notable not so much for their civilizations as for their conquests. Among the nations they threatened were Urartu and Armenia to the south, civilizations that became heavily involved in the affairs of Mesopotamia, Persia, and even Rome.

Asia Minor

Asia Minor, or modern-day Turkey, covers more than 300,000 square miles (777,000 square kilometers), making it a bit smaller than the states of Texas and Oklahoma combined. Its western portion is part of the European continent, and a narrow passageway of water, called a *strait,* separates this portion from the majority of Turkey, which is part of Asia.

Its location between Europe and Asia made Asia Minor an important crossroads. Many of the ancient world's most important civilizations developed along the Mediterranean to the south and west: Egypt, Israel, Phoenicia, and later Greece and Rome. To the southeast was Mesopotamia, a constant source of conflict for the civilizations of Asia Minor. Likewise conflict came from the nations across the Black Sea to the north, people who were considered *barbarians* (bar-BARE-ee-uhnz), or uncivilized peoples.

The Hittites (c. 1750–c. 1200 B.C.)

For centuries, the principal source of knowledge about the Hittites (HI-tytz) was the Bible, which refers to them throughout the Old Testament as one of many nations that made war on Israel. Many historians believed that the Hittites never really existed, especially because their neighbors to the west, the Greeks, knew nothing of them. But the Hittite culture flourished and died long before Greek civilization came into being, so the omission is understandable. Beginning in the late A.D.1800s, as archaeological evidence of the Hittites' existence mounted, historians were forced to recognize the truth of the Biblical account.

Like the peoples who founded later civilizations in Persia and India, the Hittites were descendants of the Indo-European tribes who came from the region of the Caucasus (KAW-kuh-sus) around 2000 B.C.. When they arrived in Asia Minor, there was already a *Semitic* people there called the Hatti (HAH-tee), from which the name "Hittite" comes. This has created some confusion for students of history, because the people later referred to as the Hittites simply took over the lands belonging to the Hatti and adopted their name, but in fact they were a new and distinct culture.

Around 1750 B.C., the Hittites established their capital at Hattush (hah-TOOSH), about 100 miles (161 kilometers) east of the present-day Turkish capital of Ankara (ANG-kuh-rah). From there, they began conquering neighboring peoples,

Assyro-Babylonian Empire, 479 B.C. *Archive Photos. Reproduced by permission.*

expanding all the way to the Mediterranean, more than 500 miles west of Hattush. In about 1600 B.C., they *sacked* Babylon but did not stay around to make it a Hittite possession. As it turned out, they had run out of supplies for their army and had to return home. On their retreat, they were defeated by the Hurrians, whose kingdom of Mitanni (mi-TAHN-ee) was briefly a great power in the region. This began a period of decline for the Hittites.

The Hittites always had trouble staying organized, which is why they are usually referred to in the plural form, rather than as "the Kingdom of Hatti" or some other term that would indicate a firmly established nation. King Telipinus (teh-li-PIE-nus) in about 1525 B.C. tried to bring a measure of organization to his people, but after his death the land of the Hittites became unstable again. A new *dynasty* arose in the mid-1400s B.C., however. From this line would come the greatest of the Hittite kings, Suppiluliumas I (suh-pil-oo-LEE-uh-mus), whose reign began around 1380 B.C.

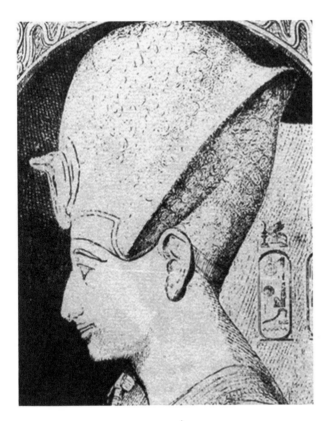

Ramses II.
The Library of Congress.

There followed a century of conquest, during which time the Hittites continually threatened Egypt and Babylonia, the world powers of the time. The Hittites conquered the Hurrians, paying them back for their defeat centuries before and establishing a *vassal* (VA-sul) king in Mitanni. They maintained their power through such vassals—that is, a king who is subject to another king—and by marrying their princesses to the rulers of other lands. In about 1285 B.C., they fought the Egyptians under Ramses II at Kadesh (KAY-desh), and it appears that the Hittites gained the upper hand. They did not conquer Egypt, but the fact that Ramses agreed to marry a Hittite princess suggests that he was eager to develop and maintain good relations with them.

For many years, the Hittites controlled most of Asia Minor and Syria, and faced only occasional trouble from the Assyrians to the southeast. But their enemies had also learned from the Hittites, who at the time possessed the most advanced military technology in the world. Not only were they the first people to discover how to smelt iron, an important advancement for any civilization—particularly one that was almost constantly at war, as the Hittites were—but they also became the first to use chariots in warfare. Later the Egyptians and especially the Assyrians would make great use of these horse-drawn wagons, which gave them the advantage over armies on foot.

By all appearances, however, the group that brought an end to the Hittites came neither from Egypt nor Assyria; rather, it appears that in about 1200 B.C., they were destroyed by the mysterious "Sea Peoples." Historians do not know the exact origin of the Sea Peoples, though it is possible they came from the land of Canaan (KAY-nun) conquered by the Israelites. The Sea Peoples may have included the Philistines. In any case, the Sea Peoples threatened much of the region before vanishing, probably by inter-marrying with the peoples they con-quered; and afterward, the Hittites ceased to exist as a distinct group.

Despite their warlike character, which is symbolized by the fact that their principal contributions to civi-lization were military in nature, the Hittites also had a highly developed culture. Theirs was the first Indo-Euro-pean language known to scholars. Study of Hittite inscriptions has helped *linguists* (LING-gwistz) better under-stand how the languages of Europe and India developed. The Hittites were also unusual among most ancient peoples in that Hittite queens often had as much power as kings. Among notable female leaders was Puduhepa (poo-doo-HAY-pah), who ruled alongside her husband Hattusilis III (hah-tuh-SIL-us) in about 1250 B.C. She contin-ued to reign even after he died.

Many centuries later, Alexander the Great would travel to the city of Gordian. *Corbs Corporation (Bellevue). Reproduced by permission.*

Phrygia (1100s–695 B.C.)

The Hittites occupied the central part of Asia Minor, whereas the Phrygians (FRIJ-ee-unz) lived on the Black Sea in the northern part of the region. Related to the Greeks, they came into the area from Macedon (MAS-uh-dahn), the part of Greece from which Alexander the Great would emerge many centuries later. In fact, one of the great events of his early life occurred in the Phrygian city of Gordian (GOHR-dee-uhn). Far to the west of Phrygia was the city-state of Troy, with which the Greeks did battle in the famous Trojan War in about 1260 B.C. The *Iliad*, the Greek story of the war, men-tions the Phrygians.

In fact the Phrygians probably settled in the region in about 1200 B.C., or around the time the Hittites' kingdom fell. They did not emerge as a powerful kingdom, however, for more than 400 years. The king who united them, in about 725 B.C., was Mita (MIE-tuh), who perhaps because of

The legend of King Midas

King Mita of Phrygia (fl. 725 B.C.) may have been the basis for the Greek legend of Midas. Supposedly Midas pleased the god Dionysus (die-oh-NY-sus) so much that Dionysus offered him an extraordinary gift: everything he touched would turn to gold.

At first this seemed like a good thing, and his wealth grew rapidly: Midas had only to touch an ordinary object such as a twig or a rock, and suddenly it became priceless. But as soon as he became hungry, Midas discovered that this gift was not as wonderful as it had seemed. He tried to eat a piece of bread, but it turned to gold and became hard as a rock. Worse, when he tried to drink a glass of wine, it became melted gold in his throat.

Midas begged Dionysus to take back his "gift," which now seemed like a curse. Dionysus had mercy on him, and told him to go bathe in the River Pactolus (PAK-tuh-lus). When he did, washing away his power, the sands of the river turned to gold.

In modern times, people say that someone with a great ability for earning money has "the Midas touch."

his great wealth later became famous as King Midas (MIE-dus) in the Greek legends. Mita established his capital at Gordian, about sixty miles west of modern-day Ankara. Gordian had a great palace and a huge entrance gate, designed to impress visitors and subjects with the power of King Mita.

Outside the city were a number of burial mounds called *tumuli* (TOOM-you-lie; the singular form is *tumulus*.) These were similar in concept to the Egyptian pyramids, except that they were made of heaped earth instead of stone. One of these, called "The Great Tumulus," stands 174 feet high, making it taller than the Statue of Liberty, which is 151 feet tall without its base. The Great Tumulus, the second-tallest tumulus yet discovered by archaeologists, holds the remains of a man who may have been the great Mita himself.

Phrygia suffered an invasion by the Cimmerians (si-MARE-ee-unz) from the Caucasus in 695 B.C., but the conquerors did not maintain their control. Eventually Gordian and other cities regained their independence, but they remained subject to the next great power in the region, Lydia.

Lydia (c. 685–546 B.C.)

Lydia (LIH-dee-uh) lay on the far western edge of Asia Minor, facing Greece across the Aegean (uh-JEE-un) Sea. Its culture was even more closely tied to that of Greece than that of the Phrygians. According to legend, the dynasty that founded Lydia descended from the Greek hero Heracles (HAIR-uh-kleez), more commonly known as Hercules.

This early dynasty ruled for many centuries, but Lydia truly emerged as a civilization only under the Mermnad (MAIRM-nad) dynasty, established in about 685 B.C. Its founder was named Gyges (GY-jeez), a palace guard who, according to the Greek historian Herodotus (hur-AHD-uh-tus), murdered the king, Kandaules (KAN-duh-les), married his wife, and *usurped* (yoo-SURP'D) the throne. Gyges made Lydia a great power. His *successor,* Ardys (ARR-dis; r. 651–625 B.C.) managed to drive the Cimmerians out for good.

Later kings tried to conquer the Ionian (ie-OH-nee-un) colonies, Greek city-states along the Aegean coast. Only under Croesus (KREE-sus), who ruled from about 560 to 546 B.C., was the conquest complete. Like Mita, Croesus was known for his exceptional wealth, which gave rise to the expression "rich as Croesus," which has survived into modern times.

It was fitting, then, that Lydia under Croesus became the first nation in history to coin money, producing gold and silver coins. Before this time, businesspeople had *bartered,* or simply traded goods; now coins gave them an easy method of exchange. Instead of having to trade cattle for cloth, for instance, a farmer could sell his cattle and pay a cloth merchant in coins.

Croesus, King of Lydia, illustration. *Archive Photos. Reproduced by permission.*

The Lydians' capital was Sardis (SAR-dis), a great city that would long outlast their empire. It, too, had its tumuli, including the world's tallest, which stands 210 feet (64 meters) high. For a time, Lydian wealth and power seemed secure. Its stability as an empire was reinforced by the fact that Croesus's brother-in-law was king over the powerful Medes (MEEDZ) to the east. But when the Persians overthrew the Median king, it spelled the end for Croesus. In 546 B.C., the Persian armies defeated the Lydians, and Sardis became an important western city in the Persian Empire.

Four later kingdoms

The centuries that followed would see the rise and fall of the Persians and, later, the takeover of Asia Minor by Alexander the Great and his successors. Eventually four kingdoms would develop, only to be absorbed later by Rome.

Pergamum (PUR-guh-mum), in the western part of Asia Minor, flourished as an independent state during the period from 263 to 133 B.C. After the latter year, it became a part of the Roman Empire. Pergamum was an important cultural center and later came under the influence of Christianity: Revelation, the last book of the Bible, begins with messages to seven churches, among them the church at Pergamum.

Cappadocia (kap-uh-DOH-shuh), a mountainous region in the eastern part of Asia Minor, also functioned as an independent state, in this case during a period of about 300 years beginning with the time of Alexander. Long an ally of Rome, Cappadocia became a Roman province in A.D. 17.

Pontus (PAHN-tus), whose name is Greek for "sea," was a Black Sea kingdom to the north of Cappadocia. Established in the 300s B.C., it began to grow its empire during the centuries that followed. But another, much more powerful, empire was also on the rise, and this eventually led to a showdown between Mithradates the Great of Pontus (mith-ruh-DAY-teez; r. 120–63 B.C.) and the Roman general Pompey. By 63 B.C., Pontus also belonged to Rome.

For many years, Pontus was at war with another kingdom, Bithynia (buh-THIN-ee-uh). A mountainous and heavily wooded region in the northwest part of Asia Minor, Bithynia began its existence as a kingdom in 264 B.C. Continued warfare with Pontus, however, weakened it and made it ripe for Roman conquest in 74 B.C.

The Black Sea region

Though the Ukraine (you-KRAIN) is not part of the Caucasus (KAW-kuh-sus), both regions are noted for their rich, black soil, which makes the area one of the best places for farming in the world. Spanning the northern shore of the Black Sea, the Ukraine is a land of about a 250,000 square miles (647,500 square kilometers), nearly twice the size of Texas. The Caucasus, a mountainous region which in modern times consists of the extreme southern part of Russia, along with Armenia (ahr-MEEN-ee-uh), Georgia, and Azerbaijan (ah-zur-BAY-zhahn), is equally large. The word "Caucasian," which in modern usage typically refers to a person of European heritage, comes from the name of the Caucasus, and can also be used to refer to people from that region.

In ancient times, the Ukraine was inhabited in turn by the Cimmerians (sih-MARE-ee-unz), Scythians (SITH-ee-unz), and Sarmatians (sar-MAY-shunz). The Caucasus was controlled first by the Urartians (oo-RAR-shunz) and later by the Armenians. Other notable civilizations of the area, primarily in what is now Georgia, included Colchis (KOHL-kis) and Iberia (ie-BEER-ee-uh—not to be confused with the Iberian Peninsula, where Spain and Portugal are located.)

A series of tribes (900s B.C.–A.D. 300s)

The Cimmerians, Scythians, and Sarmatians were nomadic groups who originated deep in Central Asia and moved westward beginning in about 1000 B.C. First came the Cimmerians, who drove out the Trypilians (tri-PEEL-ee-unz), a group who had settled in the Ukraine as early as 6000 B.C. The Cimmerians occupied the region until they, too, were driven out, by the Scythians in the 700s B.C. They spread out to Asia Minor and Assyria, where they posed a threat for many years, and in about 600 B.C. took part in the destruction of Urartu.

People in the civilized countries of Europe and Asia considered these groups of people barbarians, but the Scythians, while not truly civilized—that is, they did not possess great cities and did not produce any notable literature—did engage in *commerce* with the Greeks. They spread their influence through military expeditions, and at one point their lands extended as far as the Balkan (BAWL-kun) Mountains in southeastern Europe. They managed to ward off attacks by the Persians in 512 B.C. and the Greeks under Alexander the Great in about 325 B.C.

By about 300 B.C., however, the Scythians had been driven back to their adopted homeland in the Caucasus. They were eventually overtaken by the Sarmatians, a closely related group. The Sarmatians retained control over the area until about A.D. 200, and joined forces with Rome against the various Germanic (jur-MAN-ik) tribes swarming over Europe at that time. Eventually the Huns, who brought down the Roman Empire, would push the Sarmatians out of the region in the A.D. 300s.

Urartu and Armenia (880 B.C.–A.D. 66)

Urartu and Armenia were not two different places; rather, they are the names of two different civilizations that occupied more or less the same location around Lake Van, between the Black Sea and the Caspian Sea. This area lies in what is now eastern Turkey and northwestern Iran, near Mount Ararat (AIR-uh-rat), which is mentioned in the Bible as the site where Noah's Ark came to rest. Parts of Armenia are quite fertile, giving rise to a legend that the Garden of Eden was located there, though the Bible places the Garden in Mesopotamia.

From records uncovered by archaeologists, it appears that there was already a civilization in the region as early as 1350 B.C. Urartu probably did not become united until a king named Aramu (uh-RAHM-oo) took the throne in 880 B.C. Some time after the end of Aramu's reign in 844 B.C., the Assyrians overran the area, but by the 700s B.C. Urartu was on the rise again. It briefly controlled lands from Colchis in the Caucasus, far to the north, to Syria in the west. But in 714 B.C., Sargon II of Assyria conquered Urartu. By about 600 B.C., it had ceased to exist.

In the next century, a new civilization, Armenia, began to take hold in the area once controlled by Urartu. Darius the Great mentioned the Armenians in his Behistun Inscription, and Armenia eventually became part of the Persian Empire. In 331 B.C., Armenia fell under the control of Alexander the Great.

Armenia taken by Romans

Armenia flourished under Artaxias I (ahr-TAK-shuhs; r. 190–159 B.C.) and Tigranes (ti-GRAY-neez; c. 140–c. 55 B.C.), who conquered a great empire that stretched into southern

The Caspian Sea and other Great Lakes

The Caspian Sea separates the Caucasus from Central Asia and is bounded on its southern shore by Iran. Despite its name, the Caspian Sea is actually a lake, because it contains fresh, as opposed to salt, water and does not empty into an ocean. In fact it is the world's largest lake, at more than 143,000 square miles (370,370 square kilometers)—which means that this "lake" is about the size of Montana. No wonder, then, that geographers called it a "sea."

By contrast, the second-largest lake in the world, Lake Superior on the U.S.-Canadian border, is 31,700 square miles (82,103 square kilometers), or less than one-fourth the size of the Caspian Sea. Lake Victoria in Africa, at the mouth of the Nile River, is the third largest, at just under 27,000 square miles (69,930 square kilometers). Fourth is the Aral Sea, about 200 miles east of the Caspian in Central Asia, at slightly less than 25,000 square miles (64,750 square kilometers); fifth is Lake Huron (23,000 square miles or 59,570 square kilometers), which like Lake Superior is one of the Great Lakes. All four of these lakes, plus the fifth- and sixth-largest in the world—respectively, Lake Michigan of the Great Lakes and Lake Tanganyika (tahn-gahn-YEE-kuh) in Africa—could fit inside the Caspian Sea, and there would still be almost 2,000 square miles (5,180 square kilometers) to spare!

Europe. But the empire did not last long: the Romans took most of Armenia's lands in the years between 69 and 66 B.C.

Nor was this the end of Armenia's unfortunate dealings with Rome: Tigranes's son, Artavasdes III (ahr-uh-VAZ-deez; c. 55–34 B.C.), found himself caught in the middle of a struggle between the Roman consul Octavian (later Caesar Augustus) on the one hand and Cleopatra and Mark Antony on the other. Antony and Cleopatra had him captured and executed.

In A.D. 66, the Roman emperor Nero crowned a prince of the Parthians, then ruling over Persia, as vassal king of Armenia. Later, in A.D. 303, Armenia became the first country in the world to adopt Christianity as its national religion. During the period from the 200s to the 600s A.D., Armenia changed hands between the Persian and Roman/Byzantine empires many times.

Empire, revolution, and genocide

During the first half of the Middle Ages (A.D. c. 500–1500), Asia Minor belonged to the Byzantine (BIZ-un-teen) Empire, which emerged from the eastern half of the Roman Empire. Geographically, the empire tied together Europe and Asia, and in terms of history, it linked the ancient and *medieval* (med-EE-vul) worlds. The Byzantine capital was at Constantinople (kahn-stan-ti-NOH-pul), just across a narrow strait from Asia Minor.

The Byzantine Empire was Christian, but with the rise of *Islam* (IZ-lahm) in the A.D. 600s, much of Asia Minor became Islamic. Around A.D. 1000, the region was invaded by the Turks, a group of people who came ultimately from Central Asia. A group of Turks called the Seljuks (sel-JOOKZ) established control over most of Asia Minor in the A.D. 1000s. Having adopted Islam as their religion, the Seljuks fought against the Crusaders from Europe who were attempting to gain control of Palestine.

In about A.D. 1300, another group of Turks called the Ottomans (AH-tuh-munz) established an empire on the Asian portion of Turkey. After the Byzantine Empire came to an end in the 1400s, they united Asian and European Turkey under their rule. They went on to conquer a region that stretched from Hungary in southeastern Europe to the Arabian Peninsula, and from Persia to Egypt. The Ottoman Empire lasted a long time—until 1924—but by the 1500s it was already in decline. By the early 1900s it had become known as "The Sick Man of Europe." Though it was still technically ruled by a *sultan* (SUL-tun), or king, in 1908 the real power shifted to an enthusiastic group of reformers known as the Young Turks. When World War I began in 1914, the Ottoman Empire joined Germany and Austria against Britain, France, Russia, and the United States.

Genocide in the Ukraine and Caucasus

During the Middle Ages the Ukraine had flourished as an independent kingdom, but it did so in the shadow of its powerful neighbor to the north, Russia. Russia also took an interest in the nations of the Caucasus, and Russia and the Ottoman Empire both sought to gain power over Armenia, controlled by the Ottomans after the 1600s. In 1915 the Ottoman Turks, attempting to crush Armenian hopes of independence, rounded up millions of Armenians and moved them to *concentration camps* in the Syrian Desert. There, more than 1.5 million Armenians were starved to death, the first instance of large-scale *genocide* (JEN-uh-side) in history.

Genocide is the *systematic* (that is, planned) murder of a whole group of people on the basis of race, class, or nationality. Though there had always been cruelty in the world, only in the twentieth century did nations have the power to commit wholesale acts of genocide. Although the massacre of the Armenians was the first, it was far from the last. The most famous instance of genocide, or course, was the Holocaust, the killing of six million Jews by Adolf Hitler (1889–1945) and the Nazis in Germany during World

Joseph Stalin sent millions of peasants to slave-labor camps for their refusal to give their land to the government. *Archive Photos. Reproduced by permission.*

War II (1939–1945). But a crime on an even greater scale has barely received any attention by historians: the massacre of some 10 million people in the Ukraine and Caucasus by Josef Stalin (STAH-lin; 1879–1953), *dictator* of Soviet Russia.

In 1917, Russia experienced a *revolution,* a political uprising to bring about rapid social change. The revolution and its aftermath, which established *communism* in Russia, was a violent one. Communism is a political and *economic* system that calls for the joint ownership of all property by the people of a nation; in practice, however, Communist governments—which are controlled by a very small group of leaders—own everything. Stalin, who was a Georgian, took power over the *Soviet Union* in 1929. He demanded that the *peasants* of the Ukraine and Caucasus give up their land to the government. They refused, so his troops sent millions of them to slave-labor camps, where they died. Stalin starved millions more by withholding food from them.

Kemal Ataturk helped move Turkey into the company of the United States and Western Europe.

Archive Photos. Reproduced by permission.

Hope for the future

After World War I, Turkey came under the leadership of a different kind of revolutionary: Mustafa Kemal (moo-STAH-fuh ki-MAHL), sometimes known as Kemal Atatürk (a-tuh-TOORK; 1881–1938). Kemal also ruled as a dictator and dealt harshly with his enemies, but his aim was to bring about genuine progress for Turkey. He helped move his nation into the twentieth century. As a result, Turkey became increasingly tied with the United States and Western Europe.

Progress took much longer in the Ukraine and the Caucasus, which suffered under Soviet rule. The Ukraine also endured a brutal invasion by the Nazis in World War II. Communism came to an end in the early 1990s, and the four nations—the Ukraine, Armenia, Georgia, and Azerbaijan—finally received their independence. These countries have continued to be plagued by war, however, including a conflict between Armenia and Azerbaijan in 1992 and 1993.

For More Information

Books

Bator, Robert. *Daily Life in Ancient and Modern Istanbul.* Illustrated by Ray Webb. Minneapolis, MN: Runestone Press, 1999.

Burrell, Roy. *Oxford First Ancient History.* New York: Oxford University Press, 1991, pp. 74-75.

Dijkstra, Henk. *History of the Ancient & Medieval World,* Volume 3: *Ancient Cultures.* New York: Marshall Cavendish, 1996, pp. 337-48.

Dué, Andrea, editor. *The Atlas of Human History: Cradles of Civilization: Ancient Egypt and Early Middle Eastern Civilizations.* Text by Renzo Rossi. New York: Macmillan Library Reference USA, 1996, pp. 24-27.

Hotham, David. *Turkey: The Land and Its People.* London: Macdonald Educational, 1975.

Martell, Hazel Mary. *The Kingfisher Book of the Ancient World*. New York: Kingfisher, 1995, pp. 24-25.

Wren, Melvin C. *Ancient Russia*. Drawings by Elizabeth Hammond. New York: John Day Company, 1965.

Web Sites

"About Indo-Hittite Languages." *Mansfield Library at the University of Montana.* http://www.lib.umt.edu/guide/lang/indohih.htm (April 13, 1999).

The Armenian Genocide. http://www.scf-usc.edu/~khachato/index1.html (April 13, 1999).

Armenia Resource Page. http://www.soros.org/armenia.html (April 13, 1999).

"ARMENIANS." http://www.calpoly.edu/~pkiziria/pub-files/history.html (April 13, 1999).

"History of Ancient Armenia and Urartu." http://www.usd.edu/~clehmann/ pir/arm_hist.htm (April 13, 1999).

"The Hittite Civilization." *Explore Turkey.* http://www.exploreturkey.com/ hitit.htm (April 13, 1999).

Hittite Home Page. http://www.asor.org/HITTITE/HittiteHP.html (April 13, 1999).

"Hittite/Hurrian Mythology REF 1.2." http://pubpages.unh.edu/~cbsiren/ hittite-ref.html (April 13, 1999).

"Phrygia." *Greek Mythology Link.* http://hsa.brown.edu/~maicar/ Phrygia.html (April 13, 1999).

"Sardis." *Explore Turkey.* http://www.ExploreTurkey.com/sart.htm (April 13, 1999).

Persia

6

Iran, which in its ancient version was called Persia, lies to the east of Iraq, or Mesopotamia. Shaped like a snail, the country has a number of *frontiers,* or borders. On its northwest frontier is Turkey—called Asia Minor in ancient times. Iran is bounded by water on both its northern and its southern edges: to the north is the Caspian Sea, the world's largest lake; and to the south are the Persian Gulf and the Gulf of Oman. Northeastern Iran borders the central Asian republic of Turkmenistan. In ancient times this area belonged to various *nomadic* (wandering) tribes originating north of China; during much of the twentieth century Turkmenistan was part of the Soviet Union. To the east is Afghanistan, a mountainous land with close *ethnic* ties to Iran. To the southeast is Pakistan, where the Indus Valley civilization flourished thousands of years before Persia came into being. A broad band of mountains runs through central Iran and along the Caspian shore. At the heart of the country is a desert; and eastward, the lands rise toward the high mountains of Afghanistan.

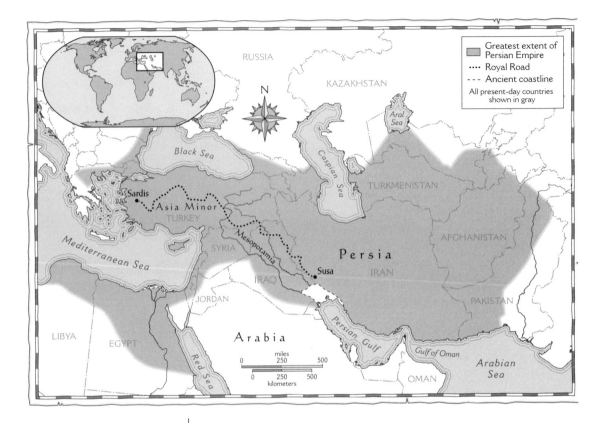

Map of Persia.
XNR Productions.
The Gale Group.

Why Persia is important

The *empire* established by the Persians in the 500s B.C. was as powerful and as brilliant as it was short-lived. The early Persian Empire was known for its religious *tolerance*: unlike most invaders before or afterward, the Persians respected the traditions of the people they conquered. For instance, they allowed the Jews to rebuild their city of Jerusalem. Another important aspect of Persian rule was their system of organization, which allowed them to build what was then the largest empire in history. The Persians built roads, dug canals, and established the first important postal system in history to maintain communications between the emperor and his *satraps,* or governors. They also brought about advancements in law. Among their most notable contributions to civilization was a religion few people in modern times have ever heard of: Zoroastrianism. Certainly people have heard of the Devil, however, and of the idea that good and evil, *symbolized* by God and Satan, are continually at war with one another—all these were Zoroastrian beliefs that greatly influenced Christianity.

Before the Persians (c. 4000 B.C.–550 B.C.)

Historians believe that as early as 4000 B.C., there was village life in what is now Iran, though it is not entirely clear who lived there. Perhaps these early peoples were relatives of the groups who established the Sumerian civilization to the west at about the same time. In any case, they disappeared from history in the face of a mighty invading force from the north.

These were the *Aryans* (AIR-ee-uhnz), a group within the larger collection of Indo-European tribes that originated somewhere in south-central Russia after 4000 B.C. Little is known about these groups, who ultimately spread out from India to Europe (hence the name "Indo-European"). In fact, the only evidence of their existence is the strong relationship between the languages of Iran, India, and Europe.

The Aryan invasion

Based on the clues historians can piece together from the *linguistic* (ling-GWIS-tik; language-based) evidence, it appears that in about 3000 B.C., the first Indo-European *migrations* began. Some tribes moved westward, into Europe, and some moved south into what is now northeastern Iran and Afghanistan. These were the Aryans, and between 2000 and 1500 B.C., they split into two groups. Some of their tribes moved eastward, crossing the Hindu Kush (HIN-doo KÜSH) Mountains into India, where they conquered groups living there. Some migrated southward, deeper into Iran.

Actually, the modern name of Iran is a much older one than "Persia" (PUR-zhuh). The term "Iran" comes from *Aryan,* whereas "Persia" refers to Fars, the area in southwestern Iran from which the Persians later emerged to rule the entire region. As for the word "Aryan," it would come to have a significance quite removed from its original meaning, thanks to the racist notions promoted by Adolf Hitler as dictator of Nazi Germany.

Words to Know: Persia

Assassination: Killing, usually of an important leader, for political reasons.

Communism: A political and economic system in which the government owns virtually all property in the name of the people.

Communists (cap.): Persons belonging to political parties that were usually associated with the Soviet Union.

Convert (n.): A new believer in a religion.

Cremation: The burning, as opposed to the burying, of a dead body.

Cult: A small religious group, most often with highly unusual beliefs.

Deify: To turn someone or something into a god.

Dynamic: Powerful or energetic.

Dynasty: A group of people, often but not always a family, who continue to hold a position of power over a period of time.

Economy: The whole system of production, distribution, and consumption of goods and services in a country.

Empire: A large political unit that unites many groups of people, often over a wide territory.

Ethnic: Relating to a group of people who share a common racial, cultural, national, linguistic, or tribal origin.

Frontier: Border.

Fundamentalist: Someone who calls for a return to the basic traditions of a religion.

Hostage: Someone who is taken captive and held in order to force someone else to meet certain demands.

Ironic: When something is intended to be one way, but turns out to be quite different from what was intended.

Islam: A faith that arose in Arabia in the A.D. 600s, led by the prophet Muhammad (A.D. 570?–632).

Isthmus: A narrow piece of land, with water on either side, which connects two larger areas of land.

Legitimacy: The right of a ruler to hold power.

The Medes

The Aryans who conquered Iran eventually divided into groups, the most notable of which were the Medes (MEEDZ) along the Caspian Sea in the north and the Persians across the mountains to the south. For a long time, the Medes were the dominant group. Beginning in the 700s B.C., they

Linguistic: Relating to language.

Mercenary: A professional soldier who will fight for whoever pays him.

Middle Ages: The period from the fall of the Roman Empire to the beginning of the Renaissance, roughly A.D. 500–1500.

Migrate: To move in large numbers.

Mujahideen: Islamic "holy warriors."

Muslim: A believer in Islam.

Namesake: Someone with the same name as someone else.

Nobleman: A ruler within a kingdom who has an inherited title and lands but who is less powerful than the king or queen.

Nomads: Wandering groups of people.

Peninsula: An area of land that sticks out into a body of water.

Province: A political unit, like a state, that is part of a larger country.

Satrap: A governor in the Persian Empire.

Sect: A small group within a larger religion.

Shah: A king of Iran before 1979.

Shiite: Someone who belongs to the Shiite sect of Islam, which is dominant in Iran.

Soviet Union: A country that combined Russia and fourteen other nations under a Communist government from the end of World War I to the early 1990s.

Stalemate: A situation in which a conflict ends without either side being able to claim victory.

Standard: A battle flag or banner.

Symbol: Something that stands for something else.

Theme: A basic idea in a story.

Theocracy: A government controlled by religious leaders.

Tolerance: Acceptance of other people and their different ways of doing things.

Treaty: An agreement between nations.

Uniform (adj.): Having the same form.

Usurp: To seize power.

Zoroastrianism: A religion, founded in Persia, based on a belief in a continuing struggle between the good god Ahura-Mazda and the evil god Ahriman.

threatened the Assyrians, but from 653 to 628 B.C., the Scythians controlled much of Iran.

In 625 B.C., however, a Median king named Cyaxares (kee-ax-ARE-eez) drove out the Scythians and resumed warfare against Assyria. He later joined forces with the Babylonians, and a combined force of Medes and Babylonians destroyed

Assyria in 612 B.C. After that, the Medes and Babylonians divided the Middle East between them. For a time, the Medes controlled much of Asia Minor, including Lydia.

But a new force was rising among the Medes' Persian cousins to the south, who were ruled by the Achaemenid (ah-kay-MEN-id) dynasty. In 559 B.C., a powerful Achaemenid king named Cyrus II [SIE-rus], whom history would remember as Cyrus the Great, came to the throne. Cyrus united the Persians against the Medes and after a long hard fight defeated them in 550 B.C. Thus was born the Persian Empire.

The Persian Empire (550–330 B.C.)

Cyrus next waged war against Lydia, defeating it and capturing its king, Croesus, in 546 B.C. After a successful campaign against the Ionian [eye-OH-nee-uhn] city-states of Greece, he turned his attention to Babylonia, and in 539 his armies captured Babylon. This was one of the most important events of ancient history, because now Persia controlled the largest empire that had existed up to that time. In ancient times, only the empire of the Greeks under Alexander, and later the Roman Empire, would be larger.

Equally important was the nature of Persian rule under Cyrus. Most conquerors before and since have attempted to impose their way of life on others, but Cyrus was willing to let conquered peoples maintain their religions and customs. Perhaps this was because the Persians, before they won their vast empire, possessed little in the way of culture, having been forced to live a hard existence in the rugged southern Iranian highlands. Therefore they were willing to adapt and borrow, and they allowed their new subjects to go on with their lives much as before. Thus the Assyrians and Babylonians continued to worship their gods. Cyrus even restored the Babylonians' temples. He also permitted the Jews to return to Israel and begin rebuilding their temple and their holy city, Jerusalem.

Cyrus met his end in battle in 529 B.C. and was succeeded by his son, Cambyses II (kam-BEE-sis). The latter managed to defeat the Egyptians in 525 B.C., adding that powerful nation to the growing empire. In 522 B.C. he learned that forces back home were plotting against him. On his way back to Persia, Cambyses died—possibly by suicide—and a general named Darius (DARE-ee-us) took the throne.

Darius becomes king

Darius I (r. 522–486 B.C.) began his reign by crushing the revolt against Cambyses, which had spread to many parts of the Persian Empire. It took a year to complete this task, after which Darius marched into northern India and added large areas of land to the empire. His biggest interests, however, lay to the west, in Greece. In 516 B.C. he marched against the Scythians to stop them from supplying the Greeks with grain.

He already controlled the Greeks of Ionia, but when they revolted against Persia in 499 B.C., this temporarily stopped him from advancing against Greece. Eventually the Greeks of Athens joined their neighbors in Ionia against him. The conflict came to a head in 490 B.C. with the Battle of Marathon, which ended with a Greek victory. Darius retreated, hoping to attack Greece again, but he died four years later without ever achieving his goal.

Darius I, walking in a procession with his attendants.
Library of Congress.

Zoroastrianism

Because he came from outside the Persian royal house, it was important for Darius to establish his *legitimacy* (lej-JIT-uh-meh-see), or his right to rule. He left behind a remarkable document, the Behistun (beh-hi-STOON) Inscription, a stone pillar telling of his deeds as king. According to the Behistun Inscription, Darius gained victory because he "was not wicked, nor a liar" and he "ruled according to righteousness." His power, the Behistun Inscription indicates, came by the grace of God—and that god had a name.

Unlike Cyrus, who does not seem to have held a strong religious belief, Darius—and through his influence, much of

Zoroaster, engraving.
Corbis-Bettmann. Reproduced by permission.

Persia—was Zoroastrian (zohr-oh-AS-tree-un). The roots of the faith went back several centuries, but the prophet who gave it its name did not appear until the 600s B.C. His name was Zoroaster (zohr-oh-AS-tur), sometimes rendered as Zarathushtra (zahr-uh-THOO-sh'truh). Zoroaster proclaimed that the god Ahura-Mazda (ah-HOOR-uh MAHZ-duh) was supreme above all other gods. The opposite of Ahura-Mazda was Ahriman (AH-ree-mahn), who was pure evil—in other words, the Devil.

In fact, the Christian idea of Satan (a name derived from a Persian word) came through the Zoroastrian influence on the Jews then under Persian rule. Although the Old Testament certainly discusses the nature of evil, there is little mention of a devil as such: rather, there is the Serpent who tempted Eve in the Garden of Eden, and there is Lucifer (LOO-si-fur), the leading angel, whose revolt against God is described in the Book of Isaiah. Generally, however, Judaism maintains that all things, both good and evil, come from God.

Not so with Zoroastrianism, which held that all existence was a constant struggle between the forces of light and the forces of darkness. This idea would have an enormous influence on Christianity, which likewise views the world as a battleground between God and his angels and Satan and his demons. It is interesting to note, then, that the "three kings," or "three wise men," who according to the New Testament followed a star to find the baby Jesus, were probably Zoroastrian priests.

The story of Zoroaster

The Zoroastrian holy book is called the *Avesta* (uh-VESS-tah), and most of it was probably written before Zoroaster's time. Little is known about Zoroaster's life. Some historians have doubted whether or not he really lived, but he was probably born about 630 B.C. Like many great prophets such as the Buddha, he left his home in search of truth, and along the way, he studied the beliefs of different peoples he met. These included his neighbors in the mountains of eastern Persia, who worshiped cattle; and others, who belonged to the "*cult* of fire." The latter treated fire as sacred, and indeed fire would become an important part of Zoroastrian religious services.

For a long time, Zoroaster met with very little success. It was ten years before he finally won his first *convert,* his cousin. Two more years passed, and he won over the king of a nearby city, who became an enthusiastic believer in the new religion. Soon Zoroastrianism began to spread, aided by wars of conquest, but it appears that Zoroaster himself was murdered in about 550 B.C.

He may have been killed by a group of magician-priests called the *Magi* (MAY-zhiy). The Magi belief system originated among the Medes, and as its name suggested, it relied on ideas of magic and evil spirits—concepts Zoroaster had been opposed to during his lifetime. After his death, however, many things happened to Zoroastrianism that probably would not have pleased its founder. Not only did the Magis' beliefs work their way into the Zoroastrian faith, but Zoroaster himself was *deified,* or made into a sort of god.

The organization of the Persian Empire

As the Behistun Inscription makes clear, Darius believed that his rulership was a reflection of the heavenly order controlled by Ahura-Mazda. This basic idea, a common *theme* in many kingdoms, relates to the concept of legitimacy. For example, the Israelite kings were judged on the basis of whether they followed the guidance of Yahweh and his prophets; likewise the Chinese believed their emperor to be the "Son of Heaven," whose rule would come to an end if he defied the gods.

Just as Darius believed that there were laws governing heaven and that his leadership was in line with those laws, he worked to establish an earthly order. The Persians created by far the most organized empire that had existed up to that time. Thanks to the superior military strength of the Persian army, it was seldom necessary for Darius to actually send in his troops to bring a group of subject peoples into line. The threat of military action was enough.

Besides, even under the less open-minded Darius, Persian rule was not perceived as a hardship by most of the conquered nations. In the area of law, Darius set out to establish a system of justice that would be *uniform*, or the same, throughout the empire, yet would also take into account local customs. Under his legal reforms, the provinces had two types of courts: one court to administer law under the Persian legal code and one court to deal with local matters according to the local system. In theory, this is not so different from the legal system in the United States today: a person who breaks the law may be charged under the local, state, or federal laws, depending on the nature of the crime.

The system of *satrapies* (SA-trap-eez), or provinces, also allowed a measure of local rule. The Persian Empire was divided into about twenty satrapies, each ruled by a satrap, or governor. The satrap, who was usually a member of the royal family, had a free hand in ruling his local area, but of course he was expected to remain loyal to the emperor in Susa (SOO-suh), the Persian capital.

Susa lay at the end of the "Royal Road," which ran for 1,500 miles from Sardis [see sidebar, "'The Royal Road' and the Persian Postal System"], but Darius built his palace and many other great structures at Persepolis (pur-SEP-oh-liss) to the southeast. Not only was the Royal Road a great feat of engineering in itself, but it made possible the world's first real postal system. The Persians also dug a canal between the Nile River in Egypt and the Red Sea to the east.

Taxes cripple the Persian economy

As in most countries then and now, the Persians paid for these great public works through taxes on the people. Their system of taxation was relatively liberal, at least at first. Subjects of the Persian Empire were taxed a flat ten percent of their income, which is much less than most people in the United States pay—and far less than the ancient Egyptians, who paid fully one-third of their income to the government.

But there were unfair aspects to the tax system as well. Only subject peoples, not Persians, had to pay taxes. Further-

The "Royal Road" and the Persian postal system

Under the emperor Cyrus (r. 559–529 B.C.), the Persians built a 1,500-mile road from Sardis in Asia Minor to the Persian capital at Susa. At the time of its building, the "Royal Road" was the longest in the world. Even compared with the interstate highways of the United States today, it is impressive. Interstate 75, which runs from the Canadian border in Michigan all the way to the southern end of Florida, is barely as long. One of the few U.S. interstates longer than the Royal Road is I-80, which runs for nearly 2,500 miles from New York City to San Francisco, California.

The Royal Road made possible one of the world's first postal systems. Along it lay some 80 stations, where one horsebound mail carrier could pass the mail on to another, a system not unlike the Pony Express used in the American West during the 1860s.

Mail in the Persian Empire, however, was not just for anyone: only the king and important leaders such as the satraps could use the postal system. The idea of ordinary people being able to mail letters did not take hold until the 1600s in England.

Nonetheless, the Persian messenger system was so efficient—the mail carriers did their job so well—that the Greek historian Herodotus wrote of them, "Neither snow, nor rain, nor heat, nor gloom of night stays [prevents] these couriers from the swift completion of their appointed rounds." These lines are inscribed on the front of the central post office building in New York City.

more, the official view of taxes was that everything belonged to the king and that the people who owned houses or lands were simply "renting" them from him. Later, as taxes rose, this had a crippling effect on the Persian *economy* and helped to bring about the empire's downfall.

Xerxes and the decline (486–330 B.C.)

After Darius came his son Xerxes (ZURK-seez; r. 486–465 B.C.). Though Xerxes is considered a great king along with Cyrus and Darius, he was less tolerant of the conquered peoples than his father had been, just as Darius was less tolerant than Cyrus. In 485 and 482 B.C., he suppressed revolts in Egypt and Babylonia. In both cases he replaced the local lead-

Leonidas, King of Sparta,
leading the charge at
Thermopylae.
*Corbis-Bettmann. Reproduced
by permission.*

ers with direct Persian rule. He even carried away the Babylonians' statute of their god Marduk, something Cyrus would never have done. Xerxes made clear his policies in his Daiva (DIE-vah) Inscription, which indicated that he would destroy the statues and temples of all gods other than Ahura-Mazda.

Finally, in 480 B.C., Xerxes launched the second attack against Greece that his father had hoped to make. He defeated the Spartans at the Battle of Thermopylae (thur-MAHP-uh-lee) and burned Athens, but his navy lost the Battle of Salamis (SAHL-uh-mis), and in 479 B.C. the Greeks were victorious. After that, Xerxes lost interest in imperial expansion and spent most of his time in his palace. In 465 B.C., he was *assassinated*.

Egypt breaks from Persia

Three minor kings followed, and later the Greek city-states of Athens and Sparta became engaged in the long Peloponnesian (pel-uh-puh-NEE-zhun) War, which lasted from

431 to 404 B.C.. At times the Persians supported Athens, at times Sparta, but in 412 B.C. they made a treaty with Sparta and assisted it in defeating Athens. In 400 B.C., Artaxerxes II (art-ag-ZURK-seez; r. 405–359 B.C.), again went to war in Greece, this time on the side of the Athenians, then revolting against the Spartan victors. After defeating the Spartans in 387 B.C., the Athenians and Persians signed an agreement respecting Persia's control over Asia Minor.

In the meantime, however, Egypt broke away from Persia, and a number of satraps almost succeeded in tearing the empire apart. The biggest threat came from Cyrus the Younger, the king's brother, who hired 10,000 Greek *mercenaries* (mur-sin-AIR-eez) to help him. Artaxerxes defeated him in battle but allowed many of the other rebellious satraps to remain in power. Artaxerxes III (r. 359–338 B.C.) also faced almost constant revolt, a sign that the empire was in decline. Although he managed to reclaim part of Egypt, the Egyptian rulers simply retreated upriver to Nubia or Kush and continued as before.

Artaxerxes III had *usurped* (yoo-SURP'D) the throne, and he killed off anyone who might try to claim it from him. But when it came to Persia's more long-term interests, he was not so careful. In 338 B.C., Athens begged Persia for help in pushing back a new force threatening Greece from the west, a king named Philip of Macedon (MAS-uh-don). Artaxerxes refused to assist the Athenians, and four years later—after he was dead and a king named Darius III was on the throne—Philip's son Alexander defeated the Persian forces in battle. After four more years, in 330 B.C., Persepolis fell to the new conqueror, better known as Alexander the Great. The Achaemenid empire was no more; a new power controlled the world.

Three Empires (332 B.C.–651 A.D.)

The career of Alexander (356–323 B.C.) was as short as it was brilliant. After conquering more land in less time than any military force had before—or ever has since—he died at the age of thirty-three in Babylon. Afterward, his generals divided his empire: just as Ptolemy took control of Egypt, Seleucus (seh-LOO-sus; c. 358–281 B.C.) won Persia, Mesopotamia, and much of the Mediterranean coast. He established the Seleucid (seh-LOO-sid) Empire in 312 B.C.

The next two centuries were a period rich in learning and knowledge, as the Greeks absorbed the vast knowledge of mathematics and astronomy gained by the Babylonians and Indians. The Persians and others enjoyed the influence of Greek philosophy, literature, and art. The spread of Greek ideas throughout the world was called *Hellenism* (HELL-en-ism). In Persia in particular, the interaction of Western and Eastern ideas created great opportunities for learning.

However, the Seleucid Empire itself proved weak. Threats from all sides would bring a speedy end to it. To the northeast, in Bactria (BAK-tree-uh, now part of northern Afghanistan and southern Russia), a Greek governor named Diodotus (dee-uh-DOH-tus) broke away from the Seleucids in 238 B.C. Around 150 B.C. Menander (meh-NAN-dur), a later Bactrian ruler, invaded India. For a short time, Bactria ruled extensive lands on either side of the Hindu Kush Mountains.

Kushans take the Bactrian kingdom

Even more powerful than the Bactrians, however, were the Kushans, who were originally called Kuei-shuang-wang (KWAY shoo-AHNG WAHNG). As their name suggested, they came originally from China, where they had been displaced by the building of the Great Wall. Between 130 and 35 B.C., the Kushans took over the lands formerly controlled by the Bactrian kingdom. The Kushans were often in conflict with the Sakas (SAH-kuhz), a Scythian tribe that had wandered down into the Bactrian areas in about A.D. 100. The Sakas established a small kingdom in India that held on until the A.D. 300s.

Another force was Rome, which dealt a fatal blow to the western portion of the Seleucid Empire by defeating it in battle in 192 B.C. But it was not Rome that ultimately replaced the Seleucids as the ruling power in Iran; the new conquerors were the Parthians (PAHR-thee-unz), a dynasty that began in 247 B.C. when it seized control of a former satrapy of the Persian Empire. Under the leadership of Mithridates I (mith-ri-DAY-teez; r. 171–138 B.C.), Parthian holdings rapidly expanded to include parts of Mesopotamia as well as most of Iran. One of his successors defeated the Seleucids for good in 129 B.C., ushering in nearly three centuries of Parthian rule.

The Parthians (129 B.C.–A.D. 165)

Parthia was not an empire like Persia; it was too loosely organized for that. Mithridates II (r. 124–87 B.C.) called himself "King of Kings," a title used by the Persian rulers and even in the twentieth century by the *shahs,* or rulers, of Iran. He expanded the empire to its furthest extent, bringing it into conflict with Rome in Mesopotamia. Parthia and Rome, then the two most powerful countries in the Western world, would struggle for the next two centuries. After an agreement in 95 B.C. that established the Euphrates River as its western border, Parthia ceased to expand. In 53 B.C., however, the Parthians dealt Rome a humiliating blow by defeating it in Syria and seizing the Roman standards, or battle flags.

In 20 B.C. the Parthians, by then growing weaker and weaker, returned the standards to Rome. As a token of his thanks, Caesar Augustus gave the Parthian ruler, Phraates IV (fray-AY-teez), a gift of a beautiful Roman slave girl named Musa (MOO-suh). Phraates and Musa had children together, and he agreed to allow them to be educated in Rome; but when her son Phraates V had come of age, Musa had his father murdered. Nor was this the most outrageous thing Musa did: once she had made her son king, she married him. Portraits of this strange couple appeared side-by-side on Parthian coins.

That Musa would marry her son was just further evidence that Parthia was rapidly spiraling to its downfall. In spite of this, the arts in Parthia, which skillfully combined Western and Eastern ideas, were flourishing. As time went on, some Parthian leaders still remained faithful to the traditions of the West (that is, Greece and Rome), whereas others rejected these traditions. One king, for instance, upon ordering his portrait for a coin, required that he be portrayed from the front, a break with the Greek and Roman tradition of depicting rulers from the side.

Caesar Augustus, engraving. *Archive Photos. Reproduced by permission.*

By A.D. 35, differences of opinion over the future of Parthia's relations with the West led to open conflict as the city of Seleucia (suh-LOO-shuh), former capital of the Seleucids, attempted to break away and establish a Hellenized kingdom. In fact, Greek ways were on the decline, but so was Parthia itself. It came to an end with the Romans' destruction of a later Parthian capital, Ctesiphon (TES-i-fahn), in A.D. 165.

The Sassanians (A.D. 165–637)

The Sassanian (suh-SANE-ee-uhn), or Sassanid (SA-suh-nid), kingdom originated in about A.D. 226 in the region of Fars, from which the Persians had emerged more than 700 years before. Founded by Ardashir I (AHR-duh-shuhr; r. 224–241), it was greatly expanded by his son Shapur I (shah-POOR; r. 241–272). The empire of Shapur I included not only Iran but also Afghanistan, virtually all of the Caucasus, and the coast of the Arabian Peninsula along the Persian Gulf.

Shapur went to war with the Roman Empire over Syria, which he conquered in the A.D. mid-200s. He won victories over several Roman emperors, and he even captured and killed one, Valerian (vah-LEER-ee-un). To the east, Shapur defeated the Kushans and added their lands to his empire as well.

During the late A.D. 200s, however, the kings who followed Shapur managed to lose much of what he had gained. As a result of their losses, which included Armenia and most of Mesopotamia, a number of noblemen decided to promote a new king from outside the royal family. His name would be Shapur as well—Shapur II—and he would be even more powerful and dynamic than his *namesake*. For five years, from A.D. 353 to 358, Shapur fought against the Huns from the east, who were also having an enormous impact on Rome. Facing a weakened Roman Empire, Shapur succeeded in winning back all of Mesopotamia and Armenia.

Except for Khusrau (kohs-ROW), a reformer who became king in the late 500s, the Sassanians would never again produce a figure as strong as the two Shapurs were. For two centuries, their royal house would face increasing pressure from noblemen eager to gain a share in the power, as well as from Kushans and Huns on the border. Nonetheless, Khusrau's attempts to reorganize everything from the tax system to the military to the nobility—and to usher in a return to Zoroastrianism when people were tempted by a variety of religious *sects*—helped stabilize the Sassanian Empire for a time.

But a later Khusrau, Khusrau II in the early 600s, was a ruthless and corrupt leader. Though he conquered vast new areas at the expense of the Byzantine Empire, he spent most of his time living it up in his palace in Ctesiphon, which was renowned for its wealth and its lavish way of life. In A.D. 628 he was assassinated, and by 651 a new, powerful force had gained control over Persia.

Persia and Afghanistan to the present day

Like most of the Middle East, Persia became part of the empire conquered by the *Muslims* (MUZ-limz) from Arabia during the A.D. 600s. The Persians took on the Arabs' religion, *Islam* (IZ-lahm), which sent Zoroastrianism into decline, but unlike Mesopotamia and other regions, Persia did not adopt the Arabic language. Also, its people remained *ethnically* (ETH-nik-lee) distinct from the Arabs.

In the A.D. 1000s, Persia came under the rulership of the Turks, and in the 1300s it fell to the Mongol (MAHNG-gul) conquerors from the east. The Safavid (SAH-fuh-vid) dynasty restored Persian rule in 1502; meanwhile, the *Shiite* (SHEE-ite) form of Islam had established itself as the dominant faith in the country. From the 1700s onward, Persia was ruled by a variety of local dynasties, but the real power lay in the hands of Western nations, particularly Britain, as well as Russia.

Britain and Russia continued to struggle for control over Iran and Afghanistan, where their contest was called "the Great Game," in the 1800s and early 1900s. The discovery of oil in Iran during the early twentieth century led to an intensified struggle and helped bring about the rise of the Pahlavi (pah-LAH-vee) dynasty in 1925. The Pahlavi dynasty played the British and the Russians, along with the Germans—who also took an interest in the region—off against one another, and helped establish Iran as a modern nation.

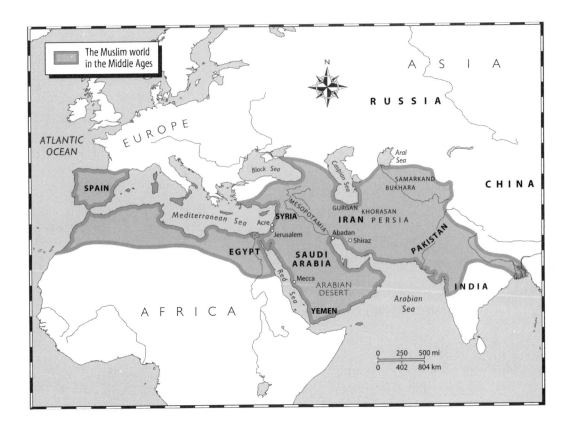

The Muslim world
in the Middle Ages

ATLANTIC
OCEAN

EUROPE

SPAIN

Mediterranean Sea

Black Sea

Caspian Sea

Aral
Sea

RUSSIA

ASIA

SAMARKAND
BUKHARA

CHINA

MESOPOTAMIA

SYRIA

GURGAN
KHORASAN
IRAN PERSIA

Acre
Jerusalem

Abadan
Shiraz

AFRICA

EGYPT

SAUDI
ARABIA

Mecca

ARABIAN
DESERT

YEMEN

Red Sea

Arabian
Sea

PAKISTAN

INDIA

0   250   500 mi
0   402   804 km

Map of the Muslim world in the Middle Ages.

XNR Productions. Gale Research.

The twentieth century

The Pahlavis ruled as *shahs,* or kings, but the figure known to modern history by the title "Shah of Iran" was Muhammad Reza Pahlavi (moo-HAHM-ed RAY-zah; 1919–1980), who assumed power in 1941. (In a reference to ancient traditions, the shahs also used the titles of "King of Kings" and "Light of the Aryans.") The Shah tried to rapidly modernize his country, both by building roads, airports, and schools and by making its culture more Western. The latter aim placed him at odds with Shiite *fundamentalists,* who demanded that the country maintain its Islamic traditions [see sidebar, "Shiite Fundamentalism"].

Nor were the fundamentalists the only people the Shah managed to anger: he maintained a powerful secret police force and dealt severely with student groups that wanted to bring about a *revolution* to establish *communism.* The Communists had the support of the Soviet Union to the north, which in 1978 also helped bring about a Communist revolution in neighboring Afghanistan.

Once in power, the Afghan Communists began killing off their enemies, and their opponents—who were also Islamic fundamentalists, though not Shiites—took to the mountains to wage war against them. Meanwhile, unrest was growing in Iran. In 1979 the Ayatollah Ruhollah Khomeini (ie-uh-TOHL-uh roo-HOHL-uh hoh-MAY-nee; 1900–1989), a powerful Shiite priest, led a revolution that overthrew the Shah. The Shah fled the country and died a year later.

A number of groups, including the Communists, helped bring about the Iranian revolution. Each hoped to achieve their own aims. But the Ayatollah's forces rounded up all opponents, killing or jailing them, and seized control of the U.S. embassy, where they held hundreds of American citizens as *hostages* for more than a year. Also in 1979, the Soviet Union invaded Afghanistan in order to deal directly with the Islamic enemies of the Communist government. The Islamic forces called themselves *mujahideen* (moo-ZHAH-hi-deen) or "holy warriors." For the next decade they waged a bloody war against the Soviets.

Muhammad Reza Pahlavi's attempts to modernize Iran conflicted with the Shiite Fundamentalists' traditional beliefs. *AP/Wide World Photos. Reproduced by permission.*

The holding of the U.S. hostages and the Soviet invasion of Afghanistan had effects felt in the United States. Many Americans perceived that President Jimmy Carter (1924–; President 1977–1981) did not handle the hostage crisis well. His response to the Afghan invasion—keeping American athletes out of the 1980 Olympics in the Soviet capital of Moscow— seemed weak at best. These events helped lead to the election of Ronald Reagan (1911–; President 1981–1989).

While the Soviets fought the mujahideen in Afghanistan during the 1980s, Iran fought an even bigger war against Iraq (ee-RAHK) to the west. In fact, the Iran-Iraq War (1980–1988), which pitted the nation that had once been Persia against what had once been Babylonia, was the largest con-

President Jimmy Carter signs the Mideast Peace Treaty, Washington, DC, 1979. *UPI/Corbis-Bettmann. Reproduced by permission*

flict since World War II (1939–1945). It claimed more than 1.5 million lives and resulted in a *stalemate*—that is, a tie.

The unhappy history of the region continued even after the death of the Ayatollah and the withdrawal of Soviet troops from Afghanistan, both in 1989. Many of the mujahideen proved to be as ruthless as the Communists they replaced, and they continued to fight amongst themselves. Iran remained a fundamentalist Islamic republic, though its leaders did begin relaxing some aspects of its system.

A Zoroastrian postscript

As for Zoroastrianism, once the religion of millions, by the late twentieth century its believers numbered in the thousands. The majority of them lived in India, where they were called "Parsis" in recognition of their Persian origins. In the Indian city of Bombay, they practiced unusual death rituals: instead of burying their dead or *cremating* (KREE-mait-ing;

Shiite Fundamentalism

Even though it begins with the letters "F-U-N," there is very little about fundamentalism that is fun. Religious fundamentalists are people who demand a return to the basic traditions of their religions, which tend to be rather harsh.

The Islamic religion forbids believers to eat pork or drink alcohol, but Islamic fundamentalists go many steps beyond rules such as these. Under fundamentalist law, women are supposed to wear veils and live as virtual slaves to their husbands, who have all power over them. Men may not wear neckties or shave. Movies, perfume, dancing, Western-style clothing, artwork that depicts human beings, and rock music—in fact, almost anything that does not directly relate to Islam—is forbidden.

Most Muslims around the world observe the prohibition against eating pork, but often in nations that are more modern, adults of legal drinking age are able to purchase alcohol. More important,

women do not have to wear veils, and some are even able to pursue careers and compete with men. At night, people dance in clubs, and teenagers are free to listen to their favorite rock groups.

The majority of Muslims belong to the Sunni (SOON-ee) sect, with which the smaller Shiite group differs over a number of issues. There are Sunni fundamentalists, as in Afghanistan, and there are also more liberal Sunnis, as in Egypt. There are also relatively liberal Shiites, but the Shiites who have attracted the most attention are the fundamentalists who took over Iran in 1979.

Under their control, Iran is a *theocracy* (thee-AHK-ruh-see), a government controlled by religious leaders. In Iran, a person who refuses to abide by Islamic law can be put to death. It is *ironic* that in the twentieth-century Iran, which in the early days of the Persian Empire was noted for its religious *tolerance,* would become one of the most religiously intolerant nations on earth.

burning) them, they placed dead bodies at the top of high platforms, which they called "towers of silence." Vultures flew down to the towers and picked the bodies clean, a site often witnessed by visitors passing through Bombay on trains.

At the end of 1991, Zoroastrianism briefly entered headlines with the death of singer Freddie Mercury (1946–1991). Mercury, born Farookh Bulsara (fah-ROOK bool-SAHR-uh), came from a Zoroastrian family who had fled Iran because of religious persecution. After moving to England, he helped form a rock group, Queen, that sold millions of albums with hits such as "Bohemian Rhapsody" (1975) and "We Will Rock You/We Are the Champions" (1978). When Mercury died of AIDS, his family held a Zoroastrian funeral service; unlike the Parsis of India, however, they had his body cremated.

For More Information

Books

Burrell, Roy. *Oxford First Ancient History.* New York: Oxford University Press, 1991, pp. 80-81.

Dijkstra, Henk. *History of the Ancient & Medieval World,* Volume 3: *Ancient Cultures.* New York: Marshall Cavendish, 1996, pp. 361-78.

Dué, Andrea, ed. *The Atlas of Human History: Cradles of Civilization: Ancient Egypt and Early Middle Eastern Civilizations.* Text by Renzo Rossi. New York: Macmillan Library Reference USA, 1996, pp. 52-55.

Dué, Andrea, ed. *The Atlas of Human History: Civilizations of Asia: India, China and the Peoples of Southeast Asia and the Indian Ocean.* Text by Renzo Rossi and Martina Veutro. New York: Macmillan Library Reference USA, 1996, pp. 12-15.

Hartz, Paula. *Zoroastrianism.* New York: Facts on File, 1999.

Mannetti, Lisa. *Iran and Iraq: Nations at War.* New York: F. Watts, 1986.

Martell, Hazel Mary. *The Kingfisher Book of the Ancient World.* New York: Kingfisher, 1995, pp. 94-97.

Neurath, Marie. *They Lived Like This in Ancient Persia.* Illustrations by John Ellis. New York: F. Watts, 1970.

Tubb, Jonathan N. *Bible Lands.* New York: Knopf, 1991, pp. 52-53.

Web Sites

Avesta-Zoroastrian Archives. http://www.avesta.org/avesta.html (April 13, 1999).

Cyrus the Great. http://www.oznet.net/cyrus/ (April 13, 1999).

"Historical Notes" (on Persia). http://www.anglia.ac.uk/~trochford/glossary/history.html (April 13, 1999).

"Images of Ancient Iran." http://tehran.stanford.edu/Images/Ancient/an5.html (April 13, 1999).

"Pictures from Ancient Iran." http://www.abadan.com/iranancient.html (April 13, 1999).

The Saga of the Aryans Home Page. http://www.ozemail.com/au/~zarathus/index.html (April 13, 1999).

India

Asia is a continent, the world's largest; but India is commonly called a subcontinent because of its size, its varied terrain, and the high mountains that separate it from the Asian landmass. An area of more than 1.7 million square miles (4.4 million square kilometers), it contains the modern nations of India, Pakistan, and Bangladesh. The highest mountain ranges in the world form its northern border: the Himalayas, which separate India from Nepal and other mountain kingdoms, as well as Tibet in China, to the northeast; the Karakorams, at the place where India and Pakistan meet in the north; and the Hindu Kush, which form the border between Pakistan and Afghanistan in the northwest. South of the mountains is a huge strip of fertile land created by the flood plains of the Indus River in the west and the Ganges River in the east. The overwhelming majority of the subcontinent's people live in these river valleys, because much of India—in particular the Thar Desert, which reaches between the river valleys and the vast Deccan *Plateau* in central and south India—is extremely dry and hot. (The rest of India, except for its mountain regions, is extremely humid and hot.) The subcontinent juts out into

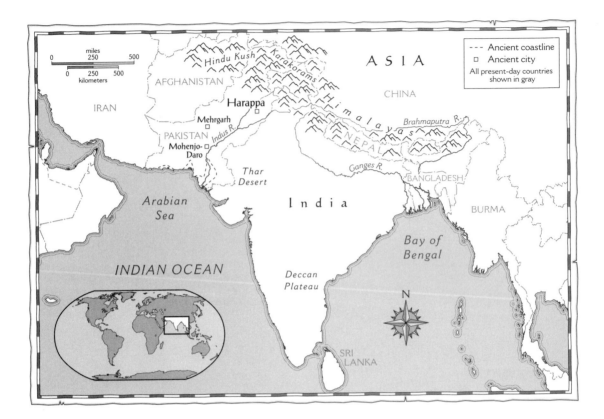

Map of India.
XNR Productions.
The Gale Group.

the Indian Ocean, with the Arabian Sea to the west and the Bay of Bengal to the east. Off the coast is the island nation of Sri Lanka.

Why India is important

Though the Indian subcontinent is less than half the size of the United States, it contains about five times as many people, or one-fifth of the world's population. From India came two of the world's most prominent religions, Hinduism and Buddhism, which respectively claim the third- and fourth-largest numbers of believers after Christianity and Islam. In ancient times, the peoples of the Indus Valley civilization created a culture equal to, and in some ways more advanced than, those of Egypt and Mesopotamia. Geographically, theirs was the largest civilization of their time, and their cities the most impressive—not least because they possessed the world's first *drainage system.* The Indo-Europeans who conquered the Indus Valley, cousins of the peoples who established the cultures of Europe [see sidebar, "The Decline of the Indus Valley Civilization"], developed a highly complex civilization with an enormous literary and religious legacy. Under the later empires of ancient India, mathematicians developed the number system in use throughout the world today, and scientists made discoveries seldom equaled by Europeans before the *Renaissance.*

The Indus Valley civilization (c. 2500 B.C.–c. 1500 B.C.)

As early as 6000 B.C., villages began appearing in the valley formed by the Indus (IN-dus) River. The town of Mehrgarh (mare-GAR), for instance, was a small settlement at the foot of the mountains separating the subcontinent from what is now Iran and Afghanistan. It appears that the people of Mehrgarh *domesticated* (tamed) sheep, goats, and cattle; grew various grains; used stone tools; and may have engaged in *trade* (exchange of goods) with peoples in surrounding areas.

Eventually these villagers moved southward, into the flood plains created by the Indus, where the soil was better for farming. This better physical environment made possible the establishment of walled cities containing thousands of people. Technology advanced: from making tools of stone, the craftsmen of the Indus Valley began creating knives, axes, and arrows from copper. They also produced pottery and small figures of male and female *deities.*

As to exactly who the people or peoples of the Indus Valley were—that is, their place of origin and their *ethnicity* (eth-NIS-i-tee)—historians know little. The Indo-Europeans who later invaded the area described them primarily by the ways in which they differed from themselves. Whereas the Indo-Europeans were Caucasians ("white," in everyday terms), they referred to the inhabitants of the Indus Valley as "people with a black skin." It is also apparent that the Indus Valley peoples had flatter noses than those of the Indo-Europeans, who called them "noseless."

These terms suggest that the peoples of the Indus Valley may have shared some racial characteristics with the peo-

Words to Know: India

Ascetic: A person who renounces all earthly pleasures as part of their search for spiritual truth.

Caste system: A system of ranking people into very specific social groups, which prevailed in India from ancient times to the modern day.

Charioteer: Someone who drives a chariot, a horse-drawn wagon.

Citadel: A fortress.

Civil servant: Someone who works for the government.

Commentary: A written work that helps to explain another work.

Craftsman: A skilled worker who produces items according to his specialty.

Cremation: The burning, as opposed to the burying, of a dead body.

Deforestation: Cutting down trees and other plant life, which often has disastrous environmental consequences.

Domesticate: To tame a wild animal.

Drainage system: The use of pipes and sewers to transport waste water from a high-population area to a place where it can be disposed of safely.

Economy: The whole system of production, distribution, and consumption of goods and services in a country.

Enlightenment: In Eastern religions, a state of being at one with God, the universe, or some other form of higher truth.

Epic: A long poem that recounts the adventures of a legendary hero.

Fasting: Deliberately going without food, often but not always for religious reasons.

Godhead: The divine nature or essence of God.

Granaries: Warehouses for storing grain.

Grid: A network of evenly spaced lines that intersect one another at right angles, as horizontal and vertical lines do.

Immunization: Taking measures to protect people from getting a specific illness, often by injecting them with a small dose of the virus that causes the illness.

Indo-European languages: The languages of Europe, India, Iran, and surrounding areas, all of which share common roots.

Industrial Revolution: A period of rapid development, beginning in about A.D. 1750, which transformed the economies of the West from agriculture-based to manufacturing-based systems.

Irrigation: A method of keeping crops watered, often by redirecting water supplies.

Islam: A faith that arose in Arabia in the A.D. 600s, led by the prophet Muhammad (A.D. 570?–632).

Linguist: A scholar who studies languages.

Literary: Referring to or involving literature.

Mantra: A chant used by participants in Eastern meditation, thought to aid the worshiper in concentrating on the Godhead.

Mass-production: A manufacturing system in which goods are produced in large quantities, rather than one at a time.

Meditation: In Eastern religion, the focusing of one's thoughts on the Godhead, which usually takes place in an atmosphere of stillness and quiet.

Metropolis: A very large, important city.

Middle Ages: The period from the fall of the Roman Empire to the beginning of the Renaissance, roughly A.D. 500 to 1500.

Middle class: A group in between the rich and the poor, or between the rich and the working class.

Migration: Movement by a large group of people from one place to another.

Missionaries: People who travel to other lands with the aim of converting others to their religion.

Pantheon: All the recognized gods in a religion.

Pyre: A bonfire on which a body is cremated.

Racist: A person who believes that race is the primary factor that determines peoples' abilities and that one race is superior to others.

Raja: An Indian noble or prince of lesser rank than a king or an emperor.

Reincarnation: The idea that people are reborn on earth, and live and die, again and again.

Renaissance: A period of renewed interest in learning and the arts that began in Europe in the 1300s and continued to the 1700s.

Ritual: A type of religious ceremony that is governed by very specific rules.

Seal: An emblem or a symbol that takes the place of a name or signature, which is often pressed into wax or hot clay to make a permanent mark.

Shrine: A holy place for believers of a religion.

Soma: An intoxicating drink used in Vedic and Zoroastrian religious rituals.

Stupa: A dome-shaped Buddhist temple.

Sultan: A type of king in the Muslim world.

Trade: The exchange of goods for units of value (money, gold, or other goods) between two individuals or two countries.

Trinity: A group of three gods, usually the highest in a religion.

Urban planning/city planning: Careful design of cities to handle problems such as overcrowding, traffic, and waste disposal.

Vegetarian: Someone who does not eat meat or—in some cases—products such as eggs and cheese that come from animals.

ple who lived south of the Sahara Desert in Africa, however, there is no clear evidence that they came from that part of the world. What is clear is that the Indo-Europeans looked down on the peoples they conquered. Yet the Indus Valley civilization was one of the most advanced in all of human history.

The establishment of great cities

The Indus Valley civilization truly came into its own in about 2500 B.C., when its people established two great cities at Harappa (huh-RAH-puh) and Mohenjo-Daro (moh-HIN-joh DAHR-oh), which lay about 400 miles south of Harappa along the Indus. These two cities, discovered by British archaeologists in the 1920s, represented a triumph of *urban planning.* The cities established by the Egyptians and the Sumerians at around the same time seem to have sprung up without any clear plan. In Harappa and Mohenjo-Daro, by contrast, the wide, straight streets formed a *grid,* intersecting one another at right angles as though they had been carefully laid out—as they obviously were.

The center of Harappa was a great *citadel,* or fortress. Outside the citadel were neatly arranged areas where workers lived. Each city also included enormous public buildings not unlike the city hall or the post office in a great urban center of today. There were temples and *granaries,* warehouses for storing grain. Little booths on each street may have provided a station for a night watchman or a policeman. Mohenjo-Daro had an enormous public bath and another great building for public meetings.

Equally impressive were the private dwellings. Houses had two or three stories and were built around an inner courtyard. Windows, and possibly also wooden balconies, opened onto this courtyard, whereas the walls of the house facing the street were windowless to keep out noise and heat. This design continues to be used in many parts of the Indian subcontinent and neighboring countries today. But the most remarkable aspect of homes in the Indus Valley—indeed, one of the greatest triumphs of their civilization—could be found in the humblest part of the home: the bathroom.

Whenever large numbers of people come together in cities, there is always a great potential for health hazards.

Human beings create waste: not only the garbage from their homes, which must be disposed of properly so that people do not get sick from the bacteria in rotting food, but also the waste from their bodies. In Europe during the Middle Ages (A.D. 500–1500), when toilets were crude at best, people simply dumped their waste into the streets. Germs spread, and with them diseases that killed millions and millions of people. But in India thousands of years earlier, brilliant engineers developed indoor toilets and a system of clay pipes to carry the waste into public sewers.

By ancient standards, Harappa and Mohenjo-Daro were huge: each was about three miles around. Based on the size of the granaries at Harappa, it appears that as many as 40,000 people lived in the city. Though a medium-sized town by modern standards, in ancient times, such a great number qualified Harappa as a *metropolis* (meh-TRAHP-uh-lis)—that is, a major urban center on the order of modern-day New York City, New York, or Los Angeles, California.

Modern-day New York City is an example of a metropolis. *Archive Photos. Reproduced by permission.*

There were many other such sites throughout an area of about half a million square miles in the Indus Valley, making the Harappan culture (as it is sometimes called) the most widespread of all civilizations at the time. Between the cities were enormous agricultural areas, where farmers grew wheat, barley, rice, and a variety of fruits and vegetables. They also raised sheep, cattle, and pigs, and evidence suggests that they domesticated animals ranging from the horse to the house cat to the elephant.

But the Harappan *economy* was not solely based on agriculture. Craftsmen produced pottery, cloth, jewelry of silver and gold, and items made of bronze. It also appears that the peoples of the Indus Valley *imported* goods from the Sumerians to the west. Not only did they possess carts drawn by bulls but they also used boats to transport items such as gold, silver, and copper. Imported items included gold and silver, as well as various minerals used in making beads. Beads have been an important part of fashion in India—where people wear them all over their bodies, including on nose rings—ever since. As a further mark of the Harappans' advanced system, evidence uncovered by archaeologists suggests that some of the pottery from the Indus Valley may even have been *mass-produced* (produced in quantity rather than one at a time), which would indicate an extremely high level of development.

Given the impressive achievements of their culture, it is not surprising to learn that the Harappans also possessed a highly developed form of writing. The written and spoken language of the Harappans is often described as Dravidian (drah-VID-ee-uhn), which is actually the name for a family of languages. They used a form of writing that involved about 400 different symbols. Though archaeologists have found a number of examples, most of these are *seals* and therefore do not use many words. Partly for this reason, no one has ever been able to translate the writings of the Harappans.

The decline of the Indus Valley civilization

Historians know little about the religion of the Indus Valley, though it appears that the Harappans used fire in their religious *rituals* (religious ceremonies)—an idea that would later be absorbed into Zoroastrianism. Even less is known

Mass production: How many pins can one worker produce?

Archaeological evidence from the Indus Valley suggests that some of that civilization's pottery was mass-produced. If this is so, it would mean that manufacturing methods in Harappa were several thousand years ahead of their time. In most ancient societies, craftsmen produced goods by slow and painstaking processes, performing all the operations involved in making the product. The same worker might shape a clay pot, bake it, paint the finished product, and perform all the other necessary operations. This was the way for thousands of years, until the *Industrial Revolution* in England in the mid-1700s brought about mass production. The Industrial Revolution transformed the economic systems of Europe and North America, which had formerly been centered around agriculture, to systems based on manufacturing.

In 1776, the British economist Adam Smith (1723–1790) offered an example of the difference between old production methods and mass production. Visiting an old factory that produced straight pins, Smith found that there were eighteen separate operations or jobs involved in manufacturing a pin. By the old preindustrial methods, a single worker would perform all the operations and could produce as many as twenty pins a day. But then Smith visited a new-style factory, which employed ten people. Instead of performing all eighteen operations, each worker performed one or two. When they had completed their job, they passed the pin on to the next worker, who performed another operation on it, and so on.

One might think that ten people would produce about ten times as many pins as the single worker did, but that was not so. Using mass-production methods, the workers in the second factory produced more than 2,400 times as many pins as a single worker in the old factory—well over 4,800 pins per worker.

about the political organization of the area, but it is safe to guess that the Harappans lived under a powerful government, just as the Egyptians of the Old Kingdom did. The Egyptian pyramids and the great cities of the Indus Valley both seem to suggest a highly organized society, something that does not simply happen by itself.

Without a strong ruler or a belief system to unite them (a religion, for instance, or in America, love of liberty), people tend to be disorganized, like the Israelites in the time of the judges. It is clear that the Harappans had strong leadership. It is just as clear that at some point, the power of their leaders began to fade. Between 1900 and 1700 B.C., the Indus Valley civilization underwent a long period of decline and decay. Again like Egypt, this fact is strikingly obvious in the Harappans' architecture. Just as Egyptian pyramids of the Fifth Dynasty proved to be far less enduring than the ones of the Fourth Dynasty, later Harappan structures were poorly built, often constructed with used bricks.

A number of outside factors contributed to the decline of the Indus Valley civilization. It appears that the Harappans faced a series of environmental problems, including flooding and *deforestation* (dee-fohr-es-TAY-shun) caused by poor farming methods. Another environmental factor may have been an increase in the salt content of the water they used to *irrigate* their fields. Furthermore, it is quite possible that disease spread among the inhabitants of the great Indus Valley cities, a situation that may have resulted from the breakdown of their plumbing and sewer systems. Whatever the case, by about 1700 B.C., the cities of Harappa and Mohenjo-Daro were virtually deserted. The land was ripe for new conquerors.

The Indo-Europeans (c. 1500–c. 500 B.C.)

In modern times, it may not seem as though the peoples of India or Iran have much in common with the peoples of Europe or with the descendants of European peoples who live in the Americas. But in fact these groups are all related by race and language. Thus Asian Indians, though their coloring tends to be much darker than that of most Europeans, have facial features similar to those of their Western cousins.

More important, the languages of the Indian subcontinent, Europe, Iran, and surrounding areas are all part of the same Indo-European "family of languages." Within this family, certain languages are more closely related than others— much as brothers and sisters are closer to one another than they are to cousins—but all are united by a common Indo-European thread. For instance, the name of the Indo-Europeans' goddess of fire, Agni (AG-nee) is related to the Latin word *ignis* (IG-nis), which also means "fire"; these words are in turn reflected in the English word *ignite*.

In studying most ancient groups, archaeologists are able to uncover ruins that provide a wealth of knowledge. The Indo-Europeans, however, were nomads and therefore left behind little physical evidence of their migration to India. Thus the real detective work concerning the Indo-Europeans has fallen to *linguists,* scholars who study language.

One can "dig" into a language just as archaeologists dig into a site. Just as there are deeper and deeper layers beneath the surface of the earth, so there are "layers" within a language. In English, for instance, there is a thick layer of Latin on top of an even thicker layer of German. At perhaps the deepest layer of all is the Indo-European root that unites English with the ancient languages of India, particularly Sanskrit [SAN-skrit].

The coming of the Indo-Europeans

Only in the A.D. 1800s did linguists such as the Grimm brothers of Germany (also famous for their fairy tales) become aware of the link between the various languages of the Indo-European family. This discovery greatly increased historians' understanding of the migrations that occurred in the ancient world. From what they were able to uncover, it appears that in about 3000 B.C., a group of people began to spread out from what is now eastern Europe.

Because they ultimately conquered regions spanning from Europe to India, this group came to be known as "Indo-Europeans." Some Indo-Europeans moved westward into Europe, whereas others spread into what is now Afghanistan. The latter tribes were called *Aryans* (AIR-ee-uhnz). It is important to stress that all Aryans were Indo-Europeans, but not all Indo-Europeans were Aryans. Even more significantly, both terms describe linguistic groups, not "races." This must be emphasized because in the twentieth century, Adolf Hitler and other *racists* would claim that the Aryans were a "superior" race that settled in Europe [see sidebar, "Indo-Europeans and Aryans"].

Between 2000 and 1500 B.C., the Aryans split into two groups. Some moved westward into what is now Iran, while others ventured eastward into India. To do so, the invaders had to cross the high mountains of the Hindu Kush (HIN-doo

Indo-Europeans and Aryans

Lies usually involve at least a little truth; otherwise people would not believe them. So it was with the lies promoted by Adolf Hitler (1889–1945)—leader of the Nazi Party and dictator of Germany from 1933 to 1945—concerning the Aryans. It is true that there was a group called the Aryans, a term for the Indo-European tribes that invaded Iran and India in about 1500 B.C., and it is also true that they were historically linked with the peoples who later settled Europe. But the Aryans never moved to Europe. More important, they were never what Hitler said they were: a race of blond-haired, blue-eyed people that included the Germans and other western Europeans.

The Aryans, Hitler taught, were racially superior to the dark-eyed, dark-haired Jews, and therefore it was his job as an Aryan to wipe them off the face of the earth—as he tried to do during World War II (1939–1945), when the Nazis killed millions of Jews. In fact Hitler and many other Nazi leaders had dark hair and dark eyes; also, the word "Jew" describes a religion, not a race. It is true that the majority of Jews are descendants of the Semitic-speaking peoples who inhabited Palestine in ancient times, but so are Arabs—and Nazi Germany had friendly relations with various Arab groups, simply because they also were in conflict with the "Jews" over control of Palestine.

In addition, Hitler, who claimed that white "Aryans" were superior to the darker-skinned peoples of the world, nonetheless allied his country with the non-Caucasian Japanese. Of course, most people from India, though classified racially as Caucasians, are not white-skinned either. But in part because they considered the Indians to be their Aryan "brothers," the Nazis made a minor effort to encourage them to join Germany in making war against Britain.

If all this seems complicated, it is. Lies usually are. The truth, on the other hand, is simple: there is and was no such thing as an Aryan "race." But this did not stop the Nazis from taking as their emblem the *swastika* (SWAHS-ti-kuh), an ancient Aryan symbol. In Sanskrit, the word swastika means "well-being," and Hindus considered it a sign of good luck. Thanks to the Nazis, however, the swastika came to be a symbol of evil.

KÜSH) that separate the Indian subcontinent from Afghanistan, a difficult journey. Once they went down on the other side, however, they discovered a lush river valley containing dark-skinned groups of people, the descendants of the Harappan civilization.

Eventually the Indo-Europeans spread across the two great river valleys of India, some moving eastward into the valley of the Ganges (GAN-jeez), others settling in the Indus Valley. Because a number of rivers fed into the Indus, the latter area came to be known as Punjab (POON-jahb), an Indo-Aryan term meaning "five rivers."

The caste system

As everyone learns in school, when Christopher Columbus arrived in the New World, he thought he had reached India, and therefore called the Native Americans "Indians." It was a name that stuck, and it has created confusion ever since; thus people often say "Asian Indian" when referring to the true Indians of India. In fact the Europeans who invaded North and South America in about A.D. 1500 dealt with the natives using methods similar to those of the Indo-Europeans who invaded India in about 1500 B.C. In both situations, a group with greater military strength subdued the natives, killing off many and treating the rest as second-class citizens.

The *Rig Vega* (REEG VAY-dah) describes battles between the Indo-Europeans and the natives of India, but for the most part the invaders used the *caste system* to control them. The word "caste" (KAST) is similar in meaning to *class,* a term for various levels in society—for instance, rich, poor, and middle class. But caste has much more far-reaching implications.

In America, for instance, a poor person who works hard has a strong chance of becoming wealthy and thus changing his or her class; not so in the caste system, which the Aryans imposed, and which the Indian government did not outlaw until the twentieth century. A person was born into a caste and could never hope to change his or her status. Rules of caste dictated all kinds of social situations and even came to have a religious significance as well.

At the time they invaded India, the Aryans had a more or less typical class system, which, though it kept the poor people down, was still not as rigid as the caste system. The caste system came into being after the invasion and probably resulted from the Indo-Europeans' fear of the people they had conquered. The native Indians greatly outnumbered them; therefore, in order to keep themselves from being swallowed by the larger population, the Aryans created a system to prevent intermarriage between natives and themselves.

At the time of the invasion, warriors occupied the upper classes of Aryan society. In the caste system, priests outranked them—an interesting change, given the later religious significance of castes. Thus the top caste became the *Brahmans* (BRAH-muhnz), priests whose name was taken from the Sanskrit word for God. Next, but close in rank to the Brahmans, came the warriors, or *Kshatriyas* (K'SHAH-tree-ahz). Well below the Kshatriyas were the landowners and tradespeople, known as *Vaisyas* (vah-EES-yahz). Far below the Vaisyas were the *Shudras* (SHOO-drahz), who were servants.

But there was an even lower rank than the Shudras, one so low it was not even part of the caste system: the Untouchables. The Untouchables did jobs that nobody else wanted to do, such as hauling waste. The Indo-Europeans classified the native peoples they had conquered as Untouchables; no wonder, then, that many of the Harappans' descendants escaped Indo-European rule. The ones who fled came to be known as Dravidians. The Dravidians ultimately moved to south India and the island of Ceylon (seh-LAHN), which in modern times is the nation of Sri Lanka (SHREE LAHNG-kah). Though they initially adopted the religion brought by the Indo-Europeans, as Untouchables they had little reason to embrace Hinduism; therefore in time they accepted a new faith, one that rejected the caste system.

The literature of the Indo-Europeans

Indo-European culture produced a vast body of literature, classified as the Vedas (VAY-dahz) and the Epics. The word *Veda* means "sacred love." An *epic* is a long poem that recounts the adventures of heroic figures. So important were these two collections of works that they gave their names to two phases in the ancient history of India: the Vedic Age (c. 1500–c. 1000 B.C.) and the Epic Age (c. 1000–c. 500 B.C.) Like much ancient literature, these began as oral works and were only written down much later.

Most important of the Vedas was the *Rig-Veda*. The word *rig* in Sanskrit means "hymn." The *Rig-Veda* is a collection of some 1,000 hymns or sacred songs divided into ten books. Together, they form a long celebration, praising the gods for delivering the land of the Indus Valley to the conquerors. This concept is similar to parts of the Old Testament, in which the Israelites praised God for delivering them into the Promised Land. The *Rig-Veda* celebrates the Sun, the Earth, the joys of life—and *soma* (SOH-muh). Soma was a type of drink, a cross between alcohol and a drug, which the Indo-Europeans drank in religious ceremonies.

The *Sama-Veda* (SAH-mah) consists of chants for use in various types of religious rituals. The *Yajur-Veda* (YAH-zhoor) includes hymns to be sung with the offering of *sacrifices*. Finally, there is the *Atharva-Veda* (ah-THAHR-vah), which provides a set of magical spells to help in conceiving children, living a longer life, destroying enemies, and warding off evil spirits.

Just as the Jews later wrote various *commentaries,* such as the Talmud, to provide better understanding of their scriptures, so were several commentaries attached to the Vedas. The *Brahmanas* (brah-MAHN-ahz) offer an explanation of various details contained in the Vedas. The *Aranyakas* (ah-rahn-YAH-kahz), written by a group of priests who retreated to the wilderness, give still more details. Finally, there are the *Upanishads* (oo-PAHN-i-shahdz), whose name is related to a term for "sitting down before a teacher." The *Upanishads* are written in the form of discussions between teachers, or *gurus* (GOO-rooz), and their students.

A guru is a spiritual guide in Hinduism. Photograph by Spiros Mantzarlis. *Reuters/Archive Photos. Reproduced by permission.*

Like the Vedas, the Epics were written as poems, but these tell a story as well. The *Mahabharata* (mah-HAH-bah-rah-tah; the word *Bharat* is Sanskrit for "India") consists of more than 200,000 lines, making it the longest epic poem in human history. It is more than ten times as long as the Greeks' *Iliad* and *Odyssey* combined. Composed some time between 300 B.C. and A.D. 300, it tells of a long conflict between two families, the Pandavas (pahn-DAH-vahz), who symbolize good, and the

Indra, Hindu god of fire and light. *Archive Photos. Reproduced by permission.*

Kauravas (koh-RAH-vahz), who symbolize evil. Its central figure is the prince Krishna (KREEZH-nah), a god in human form; and its most important part is the *Bhagavad-Gita* (BAH-guhvahd GEE-tah). In the latter, Krishna, disguised as a *charioteer,* carries on a long discussion of life, death, and suffering with the prince Arjuna (ahr-ZHOON-ah) just before they go into battle.

The *Mahabharata* abounds in such religious teachings, whereas the *Ramayana* (rah-mah-YAH-nah), a much shorter work, consists of a simple, straightforward story. It is the tale of how King Rama (RAH-mah), with the help of his monkey Hanuman (hah-NOO-mahn), rescues his wife Sita (SEE-tah) from the clutches of the demon Ravana (rah-VAH-nah.) (The 1995 film *The Little Princess* begins with the heroine recounting the story of the *Ramayana,* complete with a dramatization of the tale's plot.) Both the *Ramayana* and the *Mahabharata,* as well as a collection of folk tales called the *Puranas* (poo-RAH-nahz), have continued to be popular.

The religions of India

The literature of the Aryans is full of religious importance. In fact, religion was a central fact of the ancient Indians' lives. The faith that the Aryans brought with them to the Indian subcontinent is called Vedism (VAY-dizm) to distinguish it from Hinduism (HIN-doo-izm), which developed from it in about 300 B.C. In fact, however, the two religions are closely linked. Likewise Buddhism (BÜ-dizm) developed out of Hinduism, and today the faiths stand side by side, much like Judaism and Christianity.

Vedic gods included Agni (AG-nee), the god of fire; Soma, who ruled over the intoxicating drink of the same name; and Indra (IN-drah), a king of the gods. The *Rig-Veda* refers to three families of gods, with eleven deities in each family. Some of these gods survived in the later Hindu religion, whereas others were transformed. The Hindus developed many other gods as well.

Though the Vedic and Hindu religions worshiped many gods, they retained a belief in a single, supreme figure: not so much a deity as a spirit or an idea that they called Brahman. All the other gods are part of Brahman, but separate as well. At the center of the Hindu *pantheon* (PAN-thee-ahn), or group of gods, is the *trinity,* an inner circle of three gods: Brahma, the creator of life; Vishnu (VEEZH-noo), the preserver of life; and Shiva (SHEE-vah), the destroyer of life. Many other gods are related to these in some way: thus Krishna is considered to be Vishnu in another form, and Kali (KAH-lee), the goddess of destruction, is a wife to Shiva.

The system of gods in the Hindu religion is exceedingly complicated. Although one can learn much about Hinduism from studying about them, to do so is a bit like trying to understand a tree simply by looking at its flowers. At the heart of Hinduism and other Eastern religions are certain core ideas that are at least as important as the gods themselves if one is to understand the religion embraced by the ancient Indians—and by the Indians of today.

Central beliefs of Hinduism

Hundreds of millions of people in present-day India and elsewhere continue to uphold the basic beliefs of Hinduism, handed down by the Indo-Europeans more than 3,000 years ago. During the *Middle Ages,* various Hindu schools of thought evolved, and within the Hindu religion, there are many varieties of belief. Nonetheless, the basic system of belief has remained, making Hinduism—a faith with no specific founder—the world's oldest religion.

One often hears people speak of Eastern and Western religions, though in fact the so-called Western religions—most notably Judaism, Christianity, and Islam—came from the Middle East. Western religions are sometimes called "revealed religions," meaning that in each case, the deity has revealed his truths directly to humankind through a sacred book. Western

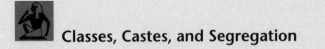

Classes, Castes, and Segregation

All societies have classes, and Aryan society at the time of the Indo-Europeans' arrival in India was no exception. There were warriors and nobles, the top rung of the social ladder; then came the priests; and below them were the common people.

In virtually every civilization on earth during ancient times and the Middle Ages, there were these same three groups: an upper class of royalty, nobility, knights, and *aristocracy* (air-uh-STAHK-ruh-see; the very rich); a class of priests, scribes, scholars, and perhaps scientists just below them; and far below these two classes, the great mass of people, who did all the physical work. Sometimes there might be a fourth group, beneath the priests and scholars and above the masses, composed of craftsmen or tradesmen.

This system prevailed until the great social and economic changes that followed the *Renaissance* (RIN-uh-sahnts) and later the Industrial Revolution. These events helped create new classes and particularly brought about the rise of the *middle class* and working class from the "fourth group" composed of craftsmen or tradesmen. But out of the Industrial Revolution also came *Marxism*, named after the philosopher Karl Marx (1818–1883), who proposed a political system that would eliminate all classes.

During the twentieth century, the Soviet Union and other Marxist (or Communist) countries supposedly created classless societies, but in fact their social systems were as rigid as any since the Middle Ages. There were still kings and nobles, only now they were Communist Party leaders. Likewise Communist society, despite its official atheism (Godlessness), still had priests of a sort, only now they were writers, educators, and other intellectuals. Of course there were still the masses of people, still doing all the physical work.

religions place a high emphasis on the individual person, who must work out a personal relationship with God.

Eastern religions such as Hinduism, on the other hand, are not nearly so concerned with the individual. Instead, Hinduism views all living creatures as part of a vast circle of life. To a certain extent, Hindus believe that people cannot do much to affect their destiny. Nor is there an idea of Heaven and Hell, as in Christianity and Islam. In Hinduism, a person does not die once, but many times. Nor is he or she born once; rather,

A truly classless society, of course, is probably impossible, but the United States (a nation with an economic system almost opposite of Communism) has come closer to it than any society on earth. Even so, the class system is quite strong in America. People at the bottom levels of society are often made to believe that they can never do anything to improve their situation. Likewise people at the absolute top of society can seemingly do no wrong. If one looks closely, one might see the same old classes, with politicians and corporate executives in place of kings and nobles; athletes, movie stars, and members of the media in place of priests; and below these two ranks, the common people—much better off than in ancient times, but still ruled by the two other groups.

America's wealthiest, most powerful families, many of whom live in New York and New England, are sometimes called "Brahmans," the name of the highest caste in India. It is interesting that such a nickname came about, because most of America's Brahmans (like most Americans in general) would say that all people are created equal. The Indian caste system, on the other hand, was based on the idea that people are created unequal. A Brahman could not change his luck, which was good; but neither could an Untouchable, a fact that condemned millions and millions of people to lives of misery.

In contrast to a class system, the caste system was more like the official policy of racial segregation that existed in the southern United States up until the 1960s, and in South Africa until the early 1990s. The end of segregation in the American South came about in large part through the efforts of the Rev. Martin Luther King, Jr. (1929–1968), a great admirer of the Indian leader Mohandas K. Gandhi (1869–1948). Thanks to Gandhi's efforts, the caste system in India was officially outlawed in 1947.

Hindus believe that a person is *reincarnated* (ree-in-KAHR-nay-ted) thousands of times.

In the present life, a person may be rich and beautiful, but in the next life, they may find themselves in a lower caste. They may come back as an Untouchable or even as an animal. On the other hand, a member of a lower caste may be reincarnated as a member of a higher one. Because they believe that people can come back to life as animals, Hindus have a deep respect for animal life. For this reason, most of them are *vege-*

tarians (people who do not eat meat). Animals are given positions of honor in Hindu life. Thus in modern Indian cities, one may see cows wandering around freely. Cars stop regularly to let them cross busy streets. In some places, one may even see *shrines,* or holy places, dedicated to animals.

Karma and reincarnation

The question of whether one reincarnates to a higher or lower level revolves around *karma* (KAHR-mah). Karma is a bit like the Western idea of destiny, but it is much harder to change one's karma. Nonetheless, good actions generate good karma, increasing the possibility of a higher reincarnation, whereas bad actions generate bad karma. For this reason, Hindus, like people of many other religions, believe that it is good to give up a life of pleasure and worldly possessions in order to seek greater personal wisdom, or *enlightenment.*

Hindus who are most dedicated to enlightenment become gurus or holy ones who practice *fasting* (not eating) and *meditation* (contemplative thinking) in an attempt to empty the mind of all thoughts and desires. As part of their meditation, they may use *mantras* (MAHN-truhz), chants that are thought to aid the worshiper in releasing thoughts of self and concentrating on the Brahman. A simple and well-known mantra is the single word *Om* (AUM). Through meditation and right living, it is believed, the believer can become one with the Brahman, also called the "Godhead."

These are some of the basic ideas of Hinduism, but it should be emphasized that the religion of India is as vast and varied as the land itself. In fact, Hinduism and India are very closely tied: hence the words *Indus, India, Hindu,* and *Hindi,* the name for one of the most important of the many languages spoken on the subcontinent, share common roots.

Just as it is impossible to study the history of the Israelites without studying their scriptures, so the Vedas and other great writings of ancient Indian civilization can be understood only by referring to the Vedic and Hindu religions. Hinduism in turn greatly influenced the visual arts; for example, India is famous for statues of gods with many arms. Through the caste system, Hinduism has had far-reaching social implications and has greatly affected the entire fabric of life in India.

Buddhism

Around the end of the Epic Age, a new religion sprang up in the northeastern part of the Indian subcontinent. Buddhism shared many of Hinduism's beliefs, but it focused on ending the cycle of reincarnation and achieving *Nirvana* (nuhr-VAH-nah), a term that suggests the idea of blowing out a fire. The "fire" in this case was personal desire; by subduing all thoughts of self, Buddhists believe that an individual can become one with the Godhead.

Also unlike Hinduism, Buddhism had a definite founder, a young prince born c. 563 B.C. in northern India between the Ganges and the Himalayas. His name was Siddartha Gautama (sid-AHR-tah GOW-tuh-muh), but he is known to history simply as "the Buddha," a term that means "The Enlightened One." Raised in incredible luxury, the prince was never allowed to learn that suffering existed; but at the age of 29, his curiosity led him to sneak out from the palace of his father. Beyond its walls, he discovered a world of horrible disease and misery—the reality of life in ancient India and most other parts of the world.

The young Siddartha was so moved by what he had seen that he decided to embark on a journey to discover the reason for suffering and the path to the enlightenment that would end such suffering. For many years, he studied with various holy men and *ascetics* (uh-SET-ikz). An ascetic is someone who renounces all earthly pleasures, even such basic ones as food and shelter, as part of the search for spiritual truth. Eventually, however, Siddartha decided that punishing the body was not the best way to enrich the spirit, and he broke with the ascetics. He spent many more years seeking truth and eventually became enlightened—that is, he understood the reasons for suffering, and the way to escape it. From then on, he was known as the Buddha.

For the remainder of his life (he died in about 483 B.C.), the Buddha taught his belief system, which he called the "Middle Way." It involved accepting "Four Noble Truths": that pain is a part of human life; that desire leads only to suffering and ultimately destruction; that only by giving up one's desires can one achieve Nirvana and end the cycle of reincarnation; and that one must follow a set of principles he called "the Eightfold Path" [see sidebar, "The Eightfold Path of Buddhism"] in order to achieve Nirvana.

The eightfold path of Buddhism

The Buddha (c. 563–c. 483 B.C.) taught that only by following the "Eightfold Path" could one reach the state of Nirvana and thus be freed from the endless cycles of reincarnation. The eight aspects of this path are:

1. Facing the realities of life, including the facts of suffering and death.

2. Holding right and good intentions.

3. Having right speech, which means avoiding gossip and lies.

4. Being honest and not breaking earthly laws.

5. Living a righteous life.

6. Opposing evil.

7. Maintaining a sober mind, free of false beliefs.

8. Engaging in "right concentration" through regular meditation.

Though Buddhism clearly shared many ideas with Hinduism—and in fact many Hindus believe that Buddha was the god Vishnu in human form—the differences between the two faiths are at least as important. Most notable, of course, is the Buddhist belief that one can escape the Hindus' endless cycle of reincarnation. Another important difference is the Buddhists' rejection of the Hindu gods and the rituals associated with them. (In fact, the concept of a "god" as such is not an important aspect of Buddhism.)

From a social standpoint, however, by far the most significant change presented by the Buddhists was their refusal to accept the caste system. Among the Buddha's earliest followers were a barber, who of course was a member of a lower caste, and a king, who like Siddartha himself was a Kshatriya. Buddhists did not care about the social distinctions that were an important part of Hinduism. For that reason, their religion spread quickly among the lower castes.

Other religions of the Indian subcontinent

It appears that Zoroastrianism had some influence in India. For instance, *soma* was a part of early Zoroastrian rituals, as it was in the Vedic religions. Zoroastrianism spread to India along with the Persian Empire and declined after that empire fell.

After ancient times, other religions would come to India, most notably Islam. The latter would become the dominant faith in the extreme western and eastern ends of the subcontinent. These areas are now known as Pakistan (PAH-kee-stahn, site of the Indus Valley civilization) and Bangladesh (BAHNG-lah-desh). Another important faith was Sikhism (SEEKizuhm), which like Buddhism developed out of Hinduism. Sikhism took hold in northwestern India during the A.D. 1400s.

But during ancient times, when the arrival of those faiths still lay far in the future, the only significant religion other than the Vedic/Hindu faith and Buddhism was Jainism (JYN-izm). The founder of the Jain faith was Vardhamana Mahavira (vard-hah-MAH-nah mah-hah-VEER-ah; 599–527 B.C.). Like Buddhism, Jainism originated in the eastern part of India. In fact, there are numerous similarities between the two religions and their founders, who lived at about the same time. Like Siddartha, Mahavira was born a Kshatriya, but he left his home around the age of thirty to embark on a life of meditation and study. After twelve years, he reached a state of enlightenment, becoming known as *Jina* (JEE-nah), or "Conqueror."

Though completely separate from Buddhism, the principles of Jainism are remarkably similar, involving a quest to be freed from the cycles of reincarnation. On the other hand, Jains, as believers in this faith are called, place a great emphasis on ascetic practices, which the Buddha opposed in favor of his "Middle Way." Jainism gained far fewer converts than Hinduism or Buddhism. In modern India the religion claims only about 3.5 million believers. Nonetheless, the Jains' belief in *ahimsa* (ah-HEEM-sah), or nonviolence, would have a great impact on the Mahatma Gandhi, India's greatest modern leader.

A period of upheaval (c. 500–324 B.C.)

By the end of the Epic Age, in the 500s B.C., there was no longer such a thing as one Indo-European civilization in India. Instead, the Indo-Europeans had split into more than a dozen different kingdoms, the most important of which was Magadha (MAH-guh-duh), in eastern India. While Siddartha was on his quest for enlightenment, he spent most of his time in Magadha, a highly organized state formed in the 600s B.C.

Magadha would later come to prominence as the center of the Mauryan Empire. In between the end of the Epic Age (which, it should be stressed, was not a clearly defined period of time) and the rise of the Mauryan Empire, there were roughly two centuries of upheaval, or unrest. During this time, various princes, or *rajas* (RAH-zhahz), within India fought for control. The beginning and end of the era were marked by invasions from the west.

The first invading force came from Persia, when Darius I marched against India in 521 B.C. Three years later, the Persians had conquered the entire Punjab region. They managed to hold on to it for many years, but as their empire declined, local rajas reclaimed power in the region.

The second invasion occurred in 326 B.C., when 250,000 soldiers under Alexander the Great crossed the Indus. They moved eastward, deep into the Punjab, and Alexander might have kept going, but his troops were ready to go home. They reached the Beas (BEE-ahs) River in July of 326 B.C., then turned back toward Greece. After the Greeks left, it appeared that they had made almost no lasting cultural impact on India, but the Greek influence would resurface more than a century later. In the meantime, India saw the rise of a new conqueror inspired by the conquests of Alexander the Great.

The Mauryan Empire (324–184 B.C.)

In 324 B.C., a new king named Chandragupta Maurya (kahn-drah-GOOP-tah MOHR-yah; r. 324–301 B.C.) took the throne of Magadha and established a new dynasty. In his capital of Pataliputra (pah-tuh-lee-POO-trah), northwest of modern-day Calcutta (KAL-kuh-tuh) on the Ganges River, he raised an army of 700,000 soldiers and 10,000 chariots, along with a force unique to the India: 9,000 elephants. Taking advantage of the power vacuum left by Alexander's departure, Chandragupta created an empire that would grow to include virtually all of the Indian subcontinent, except for the Dravidian stronghold in the south.

Legend has it that Chandragupta had a brilliant advisor, a Brahman named Kautilya (kow-TEEL-yah), who authored a book called the *Arthashastra* (ahr-thah-SHAHS-trah). The latter provided advice to rulers on how to govern. Although the book certainly existed, historians do not believe that Kautilya wrote the entire work. Nonetheless, the *Arthashastra* has aided scholars of India in understanding the organization of the Mauryan Empire. So have the writings of

Megasthenes (meh-GAS-theh-neez), a Greek who spent time in the court of Chandragupta.

The Mauryan Empire was a splendid one, and Pataliputra was said to be the greatest city of that time. Its size—8 miles (12.9 kilometers) long and 1.5 miles (2.4 kilometers) wide—shows the extent to which cities had grown since the time of the Indus Valley civilization. Around the city stood some 570 guard towers, and beyond them a *moat* 900 feet (274.3 meters) wide and 30 feet (9.1 meters) deep. Equally impressive was the level of organization in Chandragupta's government. There was an extensive network of *civil servants,* including spies who reported to the emperor on any opposition to his rule.

Late in his reign, Chandragupta went up against Seleucus, who had taken control of Persia after Alexander's death. By defeating the Seleucids, he secured his control over the western part of the subcontinent. But Chandragupta feared that one of his subjects would assassinate him. When a famine spread throughout the land, he decided to step down from the throne in 301 B.C. He became a Jain, adopting a lifestyle of fasting and later dying of starvation.

Just as Cyrus I of Persia was followed by the much less remarkable Cambyses, the next ruler, Chandragupta's son Bindusara (bin-doo-SAHR-ah), was a minor figure. Bindusara died in about 270 B.C., and as with the Persians, a power struggle ensued. Some time in the 260s B.C., a unifying leader comparable to Persia's Darius I took the throne; but whereas Darius came from outside the royal family, Asoka (ah-SHOH-kah; c. 302-c. 202 B.C.) was the son of Bindusara and the grandson of Chandragupta.

In the beginning of his reign, Asoka behaved like a typical conqueror of ancient times. He fought many wars and spread his empire throughout the subcontinent in a series of victories that left many of his enemies dead. In the eighth year of his reign, however, after a particularly bloody battle, Asoka became disgusted when he realized how many lives he had destroyed. This led him to renounce warfare and convert to Buddhism.

With Asoka's religious conversion, the entire character of the Mauryan Empire changed. He devoted himself to making life better for his subjects, and he commanded that his

Line of eight stupas on top of rocky hillside in the Indus Valley. *Corbis/Nevada Weir. Reproduced by permission.*

principles of government be carved onto large rocks that can still be viewed today. One such inscription reads: "There is no better work than promoting the welfare of the whole world. Whatever may be my great deeds, I have done them to discharge my debt to all beings." These were remarkable words, particularly from an ancient monarch. Asoka reinforced them with deeds. He appointed officials he called "inspectors of morality" to ensure that people were being treated well. He instituted a number of public works projects such as the planting of trees to provide travelers with shady places to rest.

Asoka set out once again to conquer the world, only this time with faith and not the sword. He sent *missionaries* to bring the Buddhist message to far-flung places, including Egypt and Greece. Though Buddhism never took hold in those countries, it did spread to Ceylon, where it replaced Hinduism as the dominant religion. Both in Ceylon and in India, Buddhists built huge domed temples of stone called *stupas* (STOO-pahz).

The ten avatars of the Hindu god Vishnu. **Illustration.** *Archive Photos. Reproduced by permission.*

After Asoka's death in about 232 B.C., however, Buddhism in India began to decline. So did the Mauryan Empire. During his lifetime, a number of would-be emperors had vied for the throne, and their rivalries helped send the empire into a state of disarray. To rule such a vast state required a strong ruler such as Chandragupta or Asoka, but none appeared. By 186 B.C., the Mauryan Empire had ceased to exist.

More upheaval (184 B.C.–A.D. 320)

For the next five centuries, a number of forces competed for control of India. A dynasty called the Sungas (SOONG-ahz) took over the Mauryan Empire. They were weak rulers, and they faced a series of threats from the west.

In about 200 B.C., a new force had arisen in Bactria (BAK-tree-uh), which is now part of Iran and Afghanistan. This group revolted against the weakened Seleucids. Because they were heavily influenced by the Greek legacy of Alexander, the

Westerners' Lingering Fascination with India

For as long as India has existed, Westerners have remained fascinated with it—both with the real India, and with the India they have imagined. When Alexander the Great arrived in 326 B.C., he and his troops expected to find all sorts of strange things: giant ants that could dig for gold, wool that grew on trees, and men with feet so big they could lie on their backs and use them to shade themselves from the sun.

The great Italian traveler Marco Polo (1254–1324) became one of a few Westerners to glimpse the splendors of India during the Middle Ages. As the Western desire for learning grew in the period after A.D. 1500, more travelers came. The British were particularly fascinated with India. In the 1800s British authors would write numerous stories set on the subcontinent.

Perhaps the most famous of these British writers was Rudyard Kipling (1865–1936), who celebrated India in works such as *The Jungle Book* (1894) and

Kim (1901). In spite of his fascination with India and Indians, Kipling clearly believed that the British were superior to the Indians, an idea reflected in works such as the 1892 poem "Gunga-Din," the story of a brave Hindu water-carrier who dies while serving his British masters. Many of Kipling's writings were for children, as were those of Frances Hodgson Burnett (1849–1924), who included Indian scenes in works such as *The Little Princess* (1905).

During the nineteenth century, Westerners tended to view India as the land of mystics and snake charmers, of swamis (holy men) who could lie on beds of nails or walk over hot coals. Thus they viewed Indian religion as something like a carnival sideshow. Beginning as early as the 1890s, however, Westerners began to take a more serious interest in the belief systems of the East. This movement culminated during the 1960s, thanks in large part to the Beatles' George Harrison

adjective "Greco" (GREH-koh) is often attached to their kingdom. During the 100s B.C., the Greco-Bactrians advanced deep into the subcontinent, at one point even reaching Pataliputra. The Sungas fought them back, but much of what is now Pakistan and Afghanistan came under Greco-Bactrian control.

Eventually the Greco-Bactrians were overtaken by the Sakas (SAH-kahz), who descended from the Scythians. The Sakas occupied much of the Punjab in the 100s B.C. Meanwhile, the Sunga dynasty gave way to the Kanvas (KAHN-vahz), who were

(1943–). Led by Harrison, the Beatles tried transcendental meditation (TM), a Hindu *cult*. Although Harrison and the other members of the group soon lost interest in TM, Harrison later converted to Hinduism.

Harrison's interest in Indian religion sprang from his fascination with Indian music, which is played on instruments such as the sitar (SIH-tar). The sitar is a stringed instrument like the guitar, though much more difficult to play. This did not stop Western rock stars from experimenting with it on songs such as the Beatles' "Norwegian Wood" (1965). Harrison also introduced Western audiences to the exotic, dreamy sounds of traditional Indian music as played by Ravi Shankar (RAH-vee SHAHNG-kahr, 1920–). Indian music had a great influence on Western rock during the late 1960s. For a brief time the Nehru jacket worn by Indian Prime Minister Jawarharlal Nehru became a popular fashion item among Western youth.

More important was the spread of Indian religious ideas in the West. Interest in Hinduism and Buddhism grew during the 1970s, but so did Eastern cults such as TM or Hare Krishna (HAHR-ee KREEZH-nah). Often Hare Krishnas, a group distinguished by their long robes and shaved heads, could be seen at airports in America and Europe, selling copies of the *Bhagavad-Gita*. But the influence of Eastern ideas has extended far beyond the reach of such cults. By the latter part of the twentieth century, words such as *karma* and *yoga* (the Indian practice of meditation) were a part of the English language.

Western movies about India include the Academy Award-winning film *Gandhi* (1982), which portrays the life of modern India's most prominent leader; *Lives of a Bengal Lancer* (1935); *Gunga Din* (1939); *Kim* (1950); Disney's *Jungle Book* (1967); and *City of Joy* (1992).

even weaker. After the short rule of the Kanvas ended, much of India came under the control of various small-scale rajas. As for the Sakas, who modeled themselves on the Greeks—for instance, their coins contained Greek inscriptions—they managed to hold on to the Punjab until the late A.D. 300s.

Kanishka takes the throne

Outside the Indian subcontinent, a new and far more threatening force was gathering its power. Driven out by the unification of China in 221 B.C., a number of nomadic tribes from Central Asia had moved westward. One of these was the Yüeh-Chih (you-WAY CHEE), who arrived in Bactria in 165 B.C. The strongest of the five Yüeh-Chih tribes came to be called the Kushans. Eventually they invaded the Punjab. Between about 100 B.C. and the time their greatest ruler, Kanishka (kah-NEESH-kah), took the throne in about A.D. 78, the Kushans subdued an enormous area that stretched from the Ganges deep into Central Asia.

Kanishka was a Buddhist, and by uniting such a large area of territory, he was able to spread the religion northward into China, where it came to have much greater importance than in India. This would prove to be the greatest legacy of the Kushans, who in spite of their sizeable empire declined rapidly after the time of Kanishka.

In the aftermath, the western part of the Indian subcontinent came under the domination of the Sassanians from Persia, as well as the Sakas, whose power still lingered. By then, however, a new force was arising from the west: Rome. The Romans engaged in extensive trade with India, whose wealth—in the form of jewels, ivory, spices, and other goods—was well-known in Europe.

Up to this point, the principal kingdoms of the Indian subcontinent had been based either in the Punjab and Indus Valley to the west or on the Gangetic (gan-JET-ik) Plain surrounding the Ganges to the east. But some time after 100 B.C., new kingdoms appeared on the Deccan Plateau to the south. Most important of these was the Satavahana (sah-tah-vah-HAH-nah) kingdom, which ruled the western Deccan until the A.D. 200s. There were also several important Tamil dynasties who controlled areas to the east and south.

The Gupta Empire (A.D. c. 320– c. 540)

For many centuries, the Kushans and various other small principalities controlled the Gangetic Plain, but in about A.D. 320, a great ruler like Chandragupta arose to build a new empire based in Magadha. His name was also Chandra Gupta (r. A.D. 320–335), but the two parts of his name were separated, just like a modern person's: Chandra—sometimes shown as

Candra—was his personal name, and Gupta the name of his family, a title which attached to the dynasty he founded.

As for whether or not Chandra Gupta was actually descended from Chandragupta, historians are unclear on this point. What is clear is that Chandra Gupta built a great new empire that would usher in what is known as the "Golden Age" of ancient India. He extended his rule throughout the Gangetic Plain, and his son Samudra Gupta (sah-MOOD-rah; r. c. A.D. 335–376) broadened the reaches of the empire to include much of the subcontinent. In the south, Samudra defeated the Pallavas (pah-LAH-vuhz), a minor dynasty, and conquered the Punjab to the west with much bloodshed. By the time he died, the only other major force in northern India was the Sakas.

Chandra Gupta II (r. A.D. c. 380–c. 415) proved to be the greatest of the Gupta rulers. He dealt with the Sakas and spread his control over the areas of central India that had been ruled by a dynasty called the Vakatakas (vah-kuh-TAH-kuhz). His empire never reached the dimensions of Asoka's because his authority over the Punjab and the Deccan was much less firm than that of the earlier conqueror; nevertheless, the Gupta Empire proved to be the greatest since that of the Mauryans.

The Golden Age

The Guptas established peace and prosperity throughout the lands under their rule. This political stability resulted in a golden age comparable to that of Greece. The centuries of Gupta rule saw great advancements in the arts and sciences, and they established a distinctly Hindu culture. As for Buddhism, its heyday in India was over, and from then on, its influence would be strongest outside the country of its birth.

Nonetheless, one of the outstanding examples of painting from the Golden Age of Gupta India can be found in the Buddhist temples of Ajanta (ah-ZHAN-tah) in central India. The temples themselves, carved from solid rock, are a work of art. Their walls contain numerous scenes from the life of the Buddha. Like much art from the Gupta era, these paintings are highly realistic in their portrayal of human figures. Even the chemical makeup of the paints themselves shows great technological advancement.

Prince Gautama and female figure, cave painting at Ajanta, India. *Corbis/Charles & Josette Lenars. Reproduced by permission.*

Making something stick to a surface is not always easy, as anyone who has ever tried to tape a piece of paper on a concrete block wall knows. The Buddhists of Ajanta, in order to make their paints adhere to the rock walls of the caves, used a mixture of clay, straw, hair, and even cow dung. They covered this with white plaster, and then while the surface was still wet, painted scenes on them. Italian artists of the Renaissance, such as Michelangelo (1475–1564), would use similar methods some twelve centuries later.

The Gupta age was also rich in sculpture, most of it with religious themes. These included statues of Hindu gods such as Shiva as well as figures of the Buddha. Even the coins issued by the Gupta Empire showed impressive-looking deities such as the Hindu god of war, Kartikeya (kar-tee-KIE-yah), shown with six heads and ten arms. As for the architecture of the Guptas, many of its notable examples could be found in the many Hindu temples built during this time.

The Guptas also built schools, where children were educated in the rich literary history of their people. Students began school at the age of nine, but where they went from there depended on their caste. By then, the original four castes had developed into thousands of groups. Children of the lower castes learned practical trades such as woodworking and textilemaking. The children of the higher castes, by contrast, studied the *Upanishads,* the *Ramayana,* and the *Mahabharata* [see sidebar, "Classes, Castes, and Segregation"]. When they finished their secondary education, they might go on to one of the universities established under the Guptas' reign, where they could study subjects ranging from agriculture to philosophy.

As advanced as Gupta arts and education were, however, the most outstanding features of the civilization were its achievements in the sciences, including medicine and astronomy, and in mathematics. In medicine, Indian surgeons set broken bones and even performed plastic surgery, a type of operation to change a person's physical appearance. Still more remarkable were the Indian doctors' discoveries regarding what modern people would call germs and viruses. It appears that they understood the importance of maintaining a clean, sterile environment for performing surgery—something Western doctors would not figure out until the 1800s.

Research by Indian scientists and physicians in the area of *immunization* also proved to be about 1,500 years ahead of its time. To protect someone against a disease by injecting them with the thing that causes that disease might seem completely backward, but as modern scientists know, that is precisely the way to protect people against smallpox and similar viral infections. Smallpox was a major problem at the time of the Guptas, and doctors figured out that by injecting patients with a diluted form of the cowpox virus, they could protect them from the horrible illness.

In the realm of astronomy, the Indians figured out that planets and moons are not sources of light (as many Westerners continued to believe for centuries) but rather reflect the light of the Sun. They were also aware that Earth is round and that it revolves. Indian mathematicians developed the system of ten numerals used today. These were later adopted by the Arabs, and thus came to be known (incorrectly) as "Arabic numerals." They also used a decimal system, understood diffi-

Indian Mathematical Discoveries

Among the discoveries of Indian mathematicians of the Gupta Empire was the system of ten numerals. Other mathematical ideas that the Gupta mathematicians appeared to understand, though they did not necessarily discover them, included the decimal system, negative numbers, imaginary numbers, and algebra.

Ten numerals: It is possible to develop a mathematical system based on just four numerals, or seven, or any other amount; but by far the most practical method is a system based on ten numerals, from 0 to 9. Virtually all types of mathematics in use today involve a "base-10" system of numerals.

Decimal system: In a decimal number, each place after the decimal point can be thought of as a separate fraction, with the denominator (the number on the bottom) a multiple of 10. In the decimal number 0.534, for instance, the first number to the right of the decimal point is equal to 5/10; the second equals 3/100; and the third is the same as 4/1000. As one moves farther away from the decimal point, the denominator grows larger by a factor of 10—and thus the value of the fraction grows smaller. If a number is in the fifth position to the right, for instance, one

can know that the denominator is 10 to the fifth power.

Negative numbers: A negative number is simply a number below 0. These numbers are "real," as anyone who has ever had an overdrawn checkbook knows. If a person has $100 in his account, and he writes a check for $120, that means he has -$20 in his account. To get back to $0, he will have to deposit $20.

Imaginary numbers: An imaginary number is the square root of a negative number. Any number can be squared, or multiplied by itself: thus 2 squared is 4. But what about the square root of -4? Obviously it cannot be 2; nor can it be -2, because multiplying a negative number by itself creates a positive number. Thus it is an imaginary number. As strange as such a concept sounds, it can be useful for solving complex equations.

Algebra: Algebra is a type of mathematics that makes it possible to find the value for a previously unknown number, which is called a variable. A simple algebraic equation would be "8 = 2x." The term *2x* means 2 multiplied by the variable x. Obviously, if x can be multiplied by 2 to equal 8, then 8 can be divided by 2 to find x. Once this is done, the value of x (4) can be found easily.

cult concepts such as negative numbers and imaginary numbers, and used basic concepts of algebra.

Decline of the Guptas

Kumara Gupta (koo-MAHR-ah; r. A.D. c. 414–454), who succeeded Chandra Gupta II, presided over an empire that was still strong, but he faced a powerful threat from the north. The Indians called these invaders Hunas (HOO-nuhz), but Western writers refer to them as "White Huns." Like their cousins the Huns, who were helping to bring down the Roman Empire at about the same time, the Hunas had been displaced from northern China by the Chinese. Now they were looking for new lands to conquer.

The Hunas attacked the Gupta Empire in about A.D. 450. Kumara died in the middle of this war, and though his son Skanda Gupta (SKAHN-dah; r. c. A.D. 454–467) drove them out, the Huns had weakened Gupta rule. After a period of power struggles, Budha Gupta took the throne in A.D. 475 and reigned for twenty years, during which time many princes and rajas competed for power. The Hunas, who turned their attention to Sassanian Persia for a time, returned in about A.D. 500. Within less than half a century, they had effectively destroyed Gupta rule.

India from the Middle Ages to modern times

For nearly 500 years, India remained in a state of disarray that made it ripe for conquest from outside. This came in about A.D. 1000, when the Muslim Turks swept in. For almost 400 years, they would control a wide swath of Indian territory from the Arabian Sea to the Bay of Bengal, an area that included the river valleys of the Indus and the Ganges. This kingdom was called the Delhi Sultanate (DEL-ee SUL-tun-et), a name that referred to the city of Delhi, where the *sultan* ruled.

In 1398, a Central Asian conqueror named Timur (TEE-moor) attacked the Delhi Sultanate. In 1526, a descendant of his named Babur (bah-BOOR) established the Mogul (MOH-guhl) Empire. The Moguls would rule for many years. Among their kings was Shah Jahan (SHAH jah-HAHN), who built the

Taj Mahal, photograph.
Archive photos. Reproduced by permission.

famous Taj Mahal (TAHZH muh-HAHL) as a tomb for his beloved bride. By the late 1600s, the Hindu Marathas (muh-RAH-thuhz) were challenging the Muslim Moguls. Fighting between the two groups opened the way for Great Britain to conquer India.

The British began to acquire Indian territory beginning in 1765, and over the next 122 years, they fought numerous wars to extend their control. By 1887, the entire subcontinent belonged either to Britain or to local rulers subject to the British Crown. Though the British were not always kind to their Indian subjects, they also instituted a number of reforms, most notably in 1829, when they outlawed the Hindu custom of *suttee* (SUH-tee). After death, a Hindu was *cremated* on a funeral *pyre*. By the rules of suttee, a man's widow was expected to burn herself to death on the pyre.

British power weakened with the heavy losses it suffered in World War I (1914–1918). The period leading up to

World War II (1939–1945) saw the rise of an independence movement led by Mohandas Gandhi (moh-HAHN-dus GAHN-dee; 1869–1948). Gandhi was sometimes called the Mahatma (mah-HAHT-muh), which means "great soul." He was both a powerful political and religious leader, and his movement gathered enormous strength. In 1947, Britain granted independence to India.

Fighting quickly broke out between Hindus and Muslims, and Gandhi himself was *assassinated*. The conflict led to the establishment of Pakistan as a separate state with a Muslim majority. The country was divided into two parts separated by more than 1,000 miles (1,609 kilometers) of Indian territory. India fought wars with China and later Pakistan, and a bloody 1971 clash with Pakistan resulted in the establishment of Bangladesh (formerly East Pakistan) as an independent nation.

Indira Gandhi, photograph.
AP/Wide World Photos.
Reproduced by permission.

For the better part of fifty years, India was led by a single family. First came Jawarharlal Nehru (yah-wahr-hahr-LAHL NAY-roo; 1889–1964), a follower of Gandhi, who served as prime minister from 1947 to 1964. His daughter Indira Gandhi (in-DEER-uh; 1917–1984; no relation to Mohandas Gandhi) was an outspoken figure who led the nation from 1966 to 1977, and again from 1980 until her assassination in 1984. Indira Gandhi's son Rajiv (rah-ZHEEV; 1944–1991) took her place as prime minister until he was voted out in 1989. Two years later, during an election campaign, he too was assassinated.

Political unrest has been far from the only problem that has plagued modern India. There are fifteen major languages in the country, and hundreds of ethnic groups live in uneasy relations with one another. Although the caste system was abolished in 1947, poverty is still widespread. In 1999 the average Indian earned $1,600 a year, compared with $28,600 for the average American. Nonetheless, the country has made massive efforts at reform and has done so while maintaining

Hindu traditions that date back thousands of years. Western peoples, while possessing far greater material wealth than most Indians, have remained fascinated with the varied and exotic culture of India.

For More Information

Books

Breuilly, Elizabeth; Joanne O'Brien; Martin Palmer. *Religions of the World: The Illustrated Guide to Origins, Beliefs, Traditions & Festivals.* New York: Facts on File, 1997, pp. 85-125, 138-49.

Dijkstra, Henk. *History of the Ancient & Medieval World,* Volume 3: *Ancient Cultures.* New York: Marshall Cavendish, 1996, pp. 379-90.

Dué, Andrea, ed. *The Atlas of Human History: Civilizations of Asia: India, China and the Peoples of Southeast Asia and the Indian Ocean.* Text by Renzo Rossi and Martina Veutro. New York: Macmillan Library Reference USA, 1996, pp. 16-23.

Ganeri, Anita. *Exploration into India.* New York: New Discovery Books, 1994.

Ganeri, Anita. *Religions Explained: A Beginner's Guide to World Faiths.* Marcus Braybrooke, consultant. New York: Henry Holt and Company, 1997, pp. 34-49.

Kalman, Bobbie. *India: The Culture.* New York: Crabtree Publishing Company, 1990.

Kalman, Bobbie. *India: The Land.* New York: Crabtree Publishing Company, 1990.

Kalman, Bobbie. *India: The People.* New York: Crabtree Publishing Company, 1990.

Martell, Hazel Mary. *The Kingfisher Book of the Ancient World.* New York: Kingfisher, 1995, pp. 52-61.

Odijk, Pamela. *The Indians.* South Melbourne, Australia: Macmillan, 1989.

Sarin, Amita Vohra. *India: An Ancient Land, a New Nation.* Minneapolis, MN: Dillon Press, 1984.

Stewart, Melissa. *Science in Ancient India.* New York: F. Watts, 1999.

Suthren-Hirst, Jacqueline. *The Story of the Hindus.* New York: Cambridge University Press, 1989.

Web Sites

Essence of India—Arts & Culture—Indian History. http://www.cyberindian.com/india/history.htm (April 22, 1999).

Exploring Ancient World Cultures: India. http://eawc.evansville.edu/inpage.htm (April 22, 1999).

Harappa Doorways. http://www.harappa.com/welcome04.html (April 22, 1999).

The History of Punjab. http://bucrf15.bu.edu/~rajwi/punjab/history.html (April 22, 1999).

Jainism. http://www.angelfire.com/jainism/ (April 22, 1999).

NM's Creative Impulse: India. http://history.evansville.net/india.html (April 22, 1999).

Where to Learn More

The following list of resources focuses on material appropriate for middle school or high school students. The list is divided into two sections: Books, and Web Sites. Please note that the web site addresses were verified prior to publication, but are subject to change.

Books:

Barber, Richard W. *A Companion to World Mythology.* Illustrated by Pauline Baynes. New York: Delacorte Press, 1979.

Bardi, Piero. *The Atlas of the Classical World: Ancient Greece and Ancient Rome.* Illustrations by Matteo Chesi, et al. New York: Peter Bedrick Books, 1997.

Bowra, C. M. *Classical Greece.* New York: Time-Life Books, 1965.

Breuilly, Elizabeth; Joanne O'Brien; Martin Palmer. *Religions of the World: The Illustrated Guide to Origins, Beliefs, Traditions & Festivals.* New York: Facts on File, 1997.

Brumbaugh, Robert S. *The Philosophers of Greece.* Albany, NY: State University of New York Press, 1981.

Burrell, Roy. *Oxford First Ancient History.* New York: Oxford University Press, 1991.

Davidson, Basil, and the Editors of Time-Life Books. *African Kingdoms.* Alexandria, VA: Time-Life Books, 1978.

Dijkstra, Henk. *History of the Ancient & Medieval World*, Volume 2: *Egypt and Mesopotamia*. New York: Marshall Cavendish, 1996.

Dijkstra, Henk. *History of the Ancient & Medieval World*, Volume 3: *Ancient Cultures*. New York: Marshall Cavendish, 1996.

Dijkstra, Henk, editor. *History of the Ancient & Medieval World*, Volume 11: *Empires of the Ancient World*. New York: Marshall Cavendish, 1996.

Dué, Andrea, editor. *The Atlas of Human History: Civilizations of Asia: India, China and the Peoples of Southeast Asia and the Indian Ocean*. Text by Renzo Rossi and Martina Veutro. New York: Macmillan Library Reference USA, 1996.

Dué, Andrea, editor. *The Atlas of Human History: Civilizations of the Americas: Native American Cultures of North, Central and South America*. Text by Renzo Rossi and Martina Veutro. New York: Macmillan Library Reference USA, 1996.

Dué, Andrea, editor. *The Atlas of Human History: Cradles of Civilization: Ancient Egypt and Early Middle Eastern Civilizations*. Text by Renzo Rossi. New York: Macmillan Library Reference USA, 1996.

Ganeri, Anita. *Religions Explained: A Beginner's Guide to World Faiths*. Marcus Braybrooke, Consultant. New York: Henry Holt and Company, 1997.

Harker, Ronald. *Digging Up the Bible Lands*. Drawings by Martin Simmons. New York: Henry Z. Walck, 1972.

Hunter, Erica C. D. *First Civilizations*. New York: Facts on File, 1994.

Langley, Myrtle. *Religion*. New York: Knopf, 1996.

Leonard, Jonathan Norton. *Ancient America*. Alexandria, VA: Time-Life Books, 1967.

Martell, Hazel Mary. *The Kingfisher Book of the Ancient World*. New York: Kingfisher, 1995.

Percival, Yonit and Alastair. *The Ancient Far East*. Vero Beach, FL: Rourke Enterprises, 1988.

Putnam, James. *Pyramid*. New York: Knopf, 1994.

Smith, F. LaGard, editor. *The Narrated Bible*. Eugene, OR: Harvest House, 1984.

Swisher, Clarice. *The Ancient Near East*. San Diego, CA: Lucent Books, 1995.

Tubb, Jonathan N. *Bible Lands*. New York: Knopf, 1991.

Whitehouse, Ruth and John Wilkins. *The Making of Civilization: History Discovered through Archaeology*. New York: Knopf, 1986.

Web Sites

Archaelogy's Dig. http://www.dig. archaeology.org/ (accessed on June 16, 1999).

"Bulfinch's Mythology." http:// www.webcom.com/shownet/ medea/bulfinch/welcome. html (accessed on June 21, 1999).

Exploring Ancient World Cultures. http://eawc.evansville.edu (accessed on February 14, 1999).

Mr. Donn's Ancient History Page. http://members.aol.com/ donnandlee/index.html (accessed on February 25, 1999).

Resource Pages for Biblical Studies. http://www.hivolda.no/asf/ kkf/rel-stud.html (accessed on June 28, 1999).

Roman Sites-Gateway to 1,849 Websites on Ancient Rome. http://www.ukans.edu/ history/index/europe/ ancient_rome/E/Roman/ RomanSites*/home.html (accessed on June 28, 1999).

Index

Bold type indicates main entries and their page numbers.

Italic numerals indicate volume numbers.

Illustrations are marked by (ill.).

Q

Quetzalcóatl *2:* 273 (ill.)

R

Ra *1:* 7, 14
Ramses the Great (See Ramses II)
Ramses II *1:* 38, 142 (ill.)
Reincarnation *1:* 195
Rig Vega 1: 189
Roman alphabet *2:* 374
Roman numerals *2:* 394
Rome *2:* **373-420**
Rosetta Stone *1:* 42 (ill.)
"Royal Road" *1:* 165
Rubicon River *2:* 401
Rule of law 2: 382

S

Sadat, Anwar *1:* 44
Sahara *1:* 2; *2:* 286, 287
Saharan rock art *2:* 287
Sama-Veda 1: 191
Samnites *2:* 385
San Lorenzo *2:* 268
Sarah *1:* 90-91
Sarai (See Sarah)
Sarcophagus 1: 22, 32 (ill.)
Sargon *1:* 58
Sargon II *1:* 74
Sassanians *1:* 170
Saul *1:* 99-100
Saul of Tarsus (See Paul)
Savanna *2:* 286 (ill.)
Schliemann, Heinrich *2:* 316, 319
Scipio the Younger *2:* 390
Scythians *1:* 147
Sea Peoples *1:* 142
Second Intermediate Period of Egypt *1:* 29
Second Triumvirate *2:* 402
Selassie, Haile *2:* 302 (ill.)
Sennacherib *1:* 125
Set *1:* 6, 15
"Shah of Iran" *1:* 172
Shamash-shum-ukin *1:* 75
Shamshi-Adad I *1:* 71
Shang Dynasty *2:* 222
Shiite Fundamentalism *1:* 171, 175
Shu *1:* 14

Shudras *1:* 190
Silt *1:* 3
Sinai Peninsula *1:* 2
Sixth Cataract *1:* 3
Slavery *2:* 301
Socrates *2:* 234 (ill.), 357
Socratic Method *2:* 357
Sophocles *2:* 360
Sparta *2:* 335, 353
Spartacus *2:* 398, 399 (ill.)
Sphinx *1:* 11 (ill.), 19, 37
"Spring and Autumn Period" *2:* 230
Stairs of the Jaguars *2:* 275
Stalin, Joseph *1:* 151 (ill.)
Stargate 1: 45
Step Pyramid of King Zoser *1:* 14, 17 (ill.)
Stoics *2:* 371
The Story of Sinuhe 1: 26
Stupas *1:* 202 (ill.)
Suez Canal *1:* 44
Sulla, Lucius Cornelius *2:* 397 (ill.)
Sumer *1:* 50
Sumerians *1:* 51
Sun Yat-sen *2:* 250
Syria *1:* 126, 131

T

Taharqa *2:* 291 (ill.)
Tai-ping Rebellion *2:* 249
Taj Mahal *1:* 212 (ill.)
Taoism *2:* 235
Tao te Ching 2: 235
Tefnut *1:* 14
Temple of Artemis at Ephesus *2:* 361
Ten Commandments *1:* 45, 97-98
"Ten Lost Tribes of Israel" *1:* 74
Ten Plagues of Egypt *1:* 96
Teotihuacán *2:* 269, 272
The Testament of Amenemhet 1: 27
Thales *2:* 341
Thebes *2:* 321, 334
Theogony 2: 322
Thermopylae, Battle of *2:* 333, 345
Thucydides *2:* 356
Thutmose III *1:* 33-34
Tianamen Square *2:* 254 (ill.)
Tiglath-Pileser I *1:* 72, 125
Tlachli 2: 274
Toltecs *2:* 273